Interrogating Pedagogies

Archaeology in higher education

Lampeter Workshop in Archaeology 3

Edited by

Paul Rainbird
Yannis Hamilakis

BAR International Series 948
2001

Published in 2016 by
BAR Publishing, Oxford

BAR International Series 948

Interrogating Pedagogies

ISBN 978 1 84171 240 6

BAR Publishing is the trading name of British Archaeological Reports (Oxford) Ltd.
British Archaeological Reports was first incorporated in 1974 to publish the BAR
Series, International and British. In 1992 Hadrian Books Ltd became part of the BAR
group. This volume was originally published by Archaeopress in conjunction with
British Archaeological Reports (Oxford) Ltd / Hadrian Books Ltd, the Series principal
publisher, in 2001. This present volume is published by BAR Publishing, 2016.

Printed in England

BAR

PUBLISHING

BAR titles are available from:

BAR Publishing
122 Banbury Rd, Oxford, OX2 7BP, UK
EMAIL   info@barpublishing.com
PHONE   +44 (0)1865 310431
FAX   +44 (0)1865 316916
www.barpublishing.com

Contents

Interrogating pedagogies: archaeology in higher education – an introduction

Yannis Hamilakis and Paul Rainbird

Introduction

The papers in this volume discuss a wide range if issues relating to archaeology in higher education as practised, for the most part, in the UK, but with interventions and experience drawn from elsewhere as well. The majority of the papers were first presented between the 5-7 September 2000 at 'Interrogating pedagogies: archaeology in higher education', the 3rd Lampeter Workshop in Archaeology, organised by the authors, and hosted at the University of Wales, Lampeter. The workshop was the first to examine the teaching of archaeology in British higher education in all its aspects, and all participants agreed that the papers, modified to reflect the workshop discussions, should be disseminated as widely as possible through a demanding editing schedule that would allow the swiftest possible publication. Unfortunately some authors were unable to meet the schedule and are therefore not included in this volume, however we thank them for their contribution to the workshop. Other papers are included that were either not presented at the workshop as the author was unable to be present, have been constructed from transcripts from the workshop audio tapes and edited and approved by the author, or, as in the case of Barker and Halstead, especially invited to comment on the debate generated.

The need for a swift publication acquired a sense of urgency for two main reasons: a) it was generally accepted that the teaching of archaeology in higher education, despite its seriousness and importance as an issue, has not received the attention and the careful scrutiny it deserves; b) the on-going and upcoming dramatic changes in higher education, especially in Britain, seem to be implemented without the required extensive debate, especially in archaeology; it was felt that academic archaeologists should start being proactive in relation to teaching, rather than react to the impending administrative and other measures imposed upon them.

This volume therefore differs from most other edited volumes in the sense that the papers included here are written in the 'heat of the battle'; rather than waiting for long expansions and revisions of the oral presentations, we decided to gather together the slightly revised versions of the papers and maintain, where possible, their dialogic, debating tone.

The aim of this volume is twofold: a) to intervene in the current discussions of the teaching of archaeology in higher education, emphasising the complexity of the matter, and the need to subject all proposed measures to critical analysis and scrutiny; b) to send the message that the teaching of archaeology in higher education is a matter worth discussing seriously in academic sessions and debates, rather than exclusively on administrative committees and working groups; furthermore, as the first volume on the subject to appear in the UK we hope to contribute towards an agenda for the future discussions and debates on the teaching of archaeology in higher education.

The volume

The introductory section, in addition to this chapter, includes a detailed account of the current issues facing teachers in higher education by Hamilakis, where he provides a personal perspective that clearly states the history of thought in relation to the setting up of the workshop and the production of this volume; Hamilakis further suggests a number of programmatic challenges that can usefully be compared to the variety of views expressed elsewhere in the volume. The remainder of the volume is organised into four parts. Part I contains papers which review critically the recent past and present situation, and put forward some broad views, perspectives and ideas of possible future developments. The authors represent different archaeological communities and as a consequence, different points of view. Collis and Pluciennik represent different perspectives within academic archaeology. Collis reviews many aspects of archaeology teaching and examines how the recent enforced changes have altered the experience of undergraduates, especially in relation to field skills. He particularly questions the motivation of universities to provide postgraduate courses at both taught and research level, and wonders whether in most cases the good of the student is not the main objective. Collis concludes by offering a number of suggestions that would make postgraduate degrees more vocationally-oriented, especially in relation to research training and links with the professional sector; in this he equates postgraduate degrees directly with employability. Pluciennik on the other hand, describes, analyses and critiques, the neoliberal and instrumentalist view of higher education, and suggests that engagement with theory may act as resistance and maintain the open space for dialogue and critique. He concurs with Collis, that change is inevitable and in parts ought to be seen as positive, but insists that a positive engagement with theory in archaeology, especially as 'theorised practice' can provide directionality to the change away from growing bureaucracy and instrumentalism.

Grant and Reynier, representing the recently established Subject Centre for Archaeology, Classics and History, discuss the background, remit and future plans of the Subject Centre, and present the results of a recent survey of teaching needs amongst academic archaeologists. In this survey they find that there is a broad array of teaching assessment methods being used, but that lack of time and money is restricting the development of further innovative approaches. Bishop and Roberts represent the professional community (Institute of Field Archaeologists and CADW respectively), pointing to the need for archaeology graduates with practical skills to enable them to carry out the tasks required by the professional sector. In particular Bishop looks to postgraduate qualifications and the role higher education institutions should play in supporting the professional career development of archaeologists. Roberts also considers postgraduate training, but for the most part highlights areas of undergraduate training that she feels are under-represented in the majority of current degree courses; she sees these as essential for students who wish to become employed as archaeologists. Finally, Henson presents the results of a review of archaeology provision in higher education, carried out by the Council for British Archaeology (CBA), revealing some interesting patterns, most notably the widespread provision of archaeology teaching, beyond the known established archaeology departments. Interestingly, the CBA view is one that wishes to promote wide access to archaeology in higher education, which is not solely to provide a product for the 'profession', but one that accepts the needs of the broader constituency that are involved in the 'discipline' at a variety of levels.

Part II is devoted to the discussion of the recent benchmarking statement for archaeology produced by a panel appointed by the academic community (through the Standing Committee for University Professors and Heads of Archaeology - SCUPHA) for the Quality Assurance Agency (QAA). It was felt that the importance of the launching of this document and its potential crucial role for the future (future teaching quality assessment will be based on the document, which will also be used as an internal and external guide for archaeology teaching) is such that merits extensive discussion. Johnson, one of the authors, takes a personal view in introducing the document. This is followed by the document itself, which is reproduced here by permission of the QAA. Following the format of the workshop the document is responded to by commentaries from academic archaeologists (Austin, Sinclair, Hamilakis) and representatives of the professional community (Bishop) and the Council for British Archaeology (Henson). The Chair of the Panel which was responsible for the document (Barker) responds briefly to some of the comments raised (by Bishop, Henson and Sinclair). Practical constraints did not allow him to respond to the commentaries by Austin and Hamilakis. The comments and responses vary, reflecting the broad views of the community of archaeologists within and outside academia, and the diverse needs of different sectors. While professional archaeologists would like to see more emphasis placed on practice, at least some academic archaeologists find the whole move towards potential homogenisation, disturbing. In this discussion, the important point made by Henson, should not be missed: that archaeologists need to justify their role in relation to present-day social concerns and needs.

Part III is more eclectic, containing a range of papers which look at specific aspects of archaeology teaching offering a range of suggestions and views. Holtorf discusses the problems with the conventional ways of carrying out fieldtrips and suggests a number of alternatives, which may provide a much more active, reflexive, and theoretically informed engagement of students and staff. Hingley argues that the teaching of heritage management may help to break the divide between professional and academic archaeologists and between theory and practice, provided that critical, inventive and theoretically-informed teaching of heritage management is developed. Ballin-Smith describes her experience with 'learning contracts' as a supervisory tool for archaeological dissertation projects in an attempt to introduce independent and student-centred learning. Fewster, based on her experience in teaching ethnoarchaeology, questions many of the recent premises of archaeology teaching, such as the narrow perception of accountability, and the emphasis on the quantification of the learning outcomes, and proposes that non-quantifiable values should be at the forefront of any assessment of education. Finally, Smith reports on some of the recent and extensive initiatives on teaching by the Society for American Archaeology (SAA) and in so-doing provides an interesting comparison with the UK.

The volume ends with three brief commentaries/postscripts/reflections. The first of these, by Halstead, provides a highly personal and self-reflexive view of the bureaucratization of higher education as viewed from his own department. The last two, one by Rainbird, and the other by Thomas-Goodburn comment on issues raised by the workshop. Thomas-Goodburn provides her impression of the workshop debate, based on her experience as a recent graduate of archaeology and anthropology.

Interrogating pedagogies in archaeology

What we offer in this volume is a serious debate on the teaching of archaeology in higher education that we believe has been long overdue. It is about time we start reflecting not only on what we teach, but also on how we do it and under which pedagogical framework, as well as on the consequences and effects for students, for us, for society. We hope that this volume will be only the beginning.

Acknowledgements

We wish to thank the UK Council for Graduate Education for financial assistance that made the Lampeter workshop, of which this volume is one outcome, possible. The University of Wales, Lampeter, and its Department for Archaeology supported the workshop. Thanks are due to Sophy Thomas-Goodburn for her help during the workshop, and for transcribing some of the papers. The QAA kindly permitted the reproduction of the archaeology benchmarking statement.

We would also like to thank the contributions of David Austin, Annie Grant, and Jon Humble that are not published in this volume.

Many thanks to the contributors for turning their papers around so swiftly. It is important to note that unless otherwise stated in the enclosed papers all views expressed are those of the individual and not necessarily endorsed by their institution or organisation.

YH (Southampton) and PR (Lampeter)
April 2001

Interrogating archaeological pedagogies

Yannis Hamilakis

The aim of this paper is twofold: a) by way of introduction to this volume, to review critically the current institutional and social context of the teaching of archaeology in higher education; b) by way of contributing to a long overdue and urgently needed debate, suggest some possible issues and concerns that a future agenda on archaeological pedagogy might wish to consider. While the coverage refers to many developments taking place in broader, mostly western contexts, the discussion often focuses on the manifestation of these developments and phenomena in Britain.

The context and the aims of the volume

The workshop from which this volume emerged took place in the background of some significant developments in higher education, both in Britain and world-wide. Obviously, as with everything in education, there is no 'objective' way to outline these phenomena, and depending on where you stand, you may see them as catastrophic or as beneficial. There are certain aspects, however, which need reminding here:

- Most universities in the world, save for some elite institutions relying on private endowments mostly in North America, are characterised by deep financial crisis. As state funds for universities continue to decline and as the principles of capitalist economics seems to become more and more the dominant operational logic, we experience the commoditization of knowledge, the privatisation of the remaining public aspects of the university, and the intensification of links between university research and private capital; this phenomenon has been described by some as the corporatization of the university (see e.g. Castree and Sparke 2000; Kirp 2000; Miyoshi 2000; Monbiot 2000: 281-301; Press and Washburn 2000; Warde 2001). As several commentators have noted, private corporate funding now covers the gaps left by the drastic decrease in public funding. Very often however, 'whoever is paying the piper calls the tunes', as several cases indicate and as staff and students at Berkeley found out recently, when the University accepted $25m by the Swiss pharmaceutical giant, Novartis, in exchange for the first right to negotiate licences on one-third of the benefactor-department's discoveries. Moreover, the company acquired the right to hold two of the five seats on the Department's research committee (Press and Washburn 2001). In Britain, the introduction of tuition fees and the abolition of maintenance student grants two years ago, is only one aspect of the erosion of the public character of the university. There are other, perhaps more disturbing aspects: major corporations such as Shell, BP, Glaxo etc. now fund academic posts and research centres in universities, shaping thus the research agenda by promoting specific topics (e.g.

research on oil rather than renewable resources) (Monbiot 2000). In archaeology this trend is not so prominent as yet (although more prominent than many other fields in the humanities), but we have recently experienced the major sponsorship of fieldwork projects by international corporations (Shell, British Airways, Visa, Glaxo etc.) and, in one case, the direct interference of a corporation in the direction of research and the interpretation and presentation of its results: the case of Visa, a major sponsor of the excavation at Catalhoyuk, requesting an exhibition on the 'evolution of the credit card' from prehistory to the present (Hodder 1999; Hamilakis 1999).

Furthermore, many services which were meant to support research and teaching (student accommodation, catering services, estates) are increasingly run by private companies on a profit basis (cf. Sanders 2001; Radice 2001). This development has immediate and important implications for teaching, research and free debate: as those of us who have attempted to organise conferences recently have found out, the once free space of universities (one of the few remaining public arenas which could be used by academics, students and others) now operates on a commercial basis (charging extortionate rates for hiring lecture theatres, for example), making it extremely difficult for students, unemployed and low-waged people (the vast majority of academic staff) to participate.

- Despite the continuing financial crisis and the cuts to public funding, the student numbers have vastly increased in recent years in Britain and elsewhere (although due to severe financial pressures, the increase seems to have reached its peak: in the last two academic years many universities in the UK failed to fill their allocated places). In the British context, state funding has been linked to student numbers which has partly fuelled the expansion, but has also led to phenomena such as competition, not only amongst different institutions, but also, in some cases, amongst different academic units within institutions.

- As a result of the above developments, universities have now acquired the characteristics of a service industry, where students and their families are seen as customers who demand that the product they are buying should be quality assured. Universities in Britain were included in the wider government 'charter initiative' (cf. the *UK Charter for Higher Education*) which proclaimed as its aim to make universities, as all public services, publicly accountable. As a further consequence we have seen the development of what some have described as audit culture (cf. Shore and Wright 1999; Richardson 2000), with the mass expansion of bureaucratic procedures that are supposed to safeguard the quality of the delivered product. This process is largely driven by government quangos and administrators, as well as some academics, in most cases well-intentioned, who have internalised the discourse of accountability and have adopted a managerial, supposedly neutral communicative code, in the quest for 'efficiency' and 'excellence'. As Kirp put it in relation to the US academia (but which can equally describe the UK one):

> The hoary call for a 'marketplace of ideas' has turned into a double-entendre, as the language of excellence, borrowed from management gurus, dominates in the higher-education 'industry'. Trustees, administrators, faculty, students, business, government - everyone involved in higher education is a stakeholder' in this multibillion-dollar enterprise (Kirp 2000).

- The proliferation of higher education provision (in Britain expressed through the acquisition of University status by the former Polytechnics), coupled by the decreasing public resources and the demand of the 'market' to opt for 'quality assured' product, has led to the formation of distinctive groupings (e.g. the Russell Group, Coalition of Modern Universities etc.) and the establishment of league tables. Research output measured as peer-reviewed publications in prestigious journals and monographs is increasingly seen as the main distinction mechanism for universities, and the main tool through which the remaining state research funding is allocated. Competition for high scores in the audit procedures such as the Research Assessment Exercise, has contributed to the relative devaluation of teaching (despite the efforts and the passion by many overworked and underpaid university teachers), the creation of a poorly paid, academic underclass who carry a significant part of the teaching workload (postgraduate students, teaching fellows, lecturers in short-term contracts; cf. DiGiacomo 1997; Unger 1995; Wojcicka Sharff and Lessinger 1994), and the tendency to divorce teaching from research, with measures such as the proliferation of teaching-only contracts (although in archaeology, teaching and research is still often linked through training in fieldwork etc.).

- On the other end, employers in areas such as professional archaeology, the 'heritage industry' and the 'cultural resource management' sector, an industry that has expanded vastly recently, replacing in some ways traditional industries (Walsh 1992), operate in a similar culture of cost-effectiveness and capitalist microeconomics, especially since over-commercialisation and competition is far more pronounced there than in academic archaeology (cf. Blinkhorn and Cumberpatch 1999). The same is true for most of the other employment destinations that graduates (in general, and in archaeology in particular) will follow. Employers thus demand that their employees should be equipped with the necessary skills to carry out the prescribed tasks (saving resources for in-job training) in the minimum possible

time and at the minimum possible expense. Employers, as well as professional bodies, propose changes in university curricula so that their employees can satisfy these criteria. In the UK, this intervention has been formulated since the late 1980's and early 1990's by schemes such as the Enterprise in Higher Education Initiative, which remarked in one of its reports in 1989:

> 'The need for graduates who are in tune with the enterprise culture, who are aware of the needs of industry and commerce, who know how to learn and have had some experience of the world of work has been highlighted in several major reports' (quoted in Barnett 1994: 90).

In archaeology, the recent formation of the Archaeology Training Forum (mostly by professional associations) is intended to fulfil this function of highlighting the needs of the employers (see below).

Universities thus have recently implemented or are currently implementing a series of drastic changes as a response to financial constraints, the introduction of capitalist maximization strategies and the pressures by employers. These changes include the semesterization of the curriculum to allow for flexible accumulation of credits, an increase in the 'vocational' nature of education, and the discouragement of teaching and learning that cannot be easily quantified and assessed (that is 'accounted for'). In other words, we are experiencing the colonization of the university by neoliberal principles and ideas, by the instrumentalist (or 'banking') accountants' view on knowledge (Barnett 1994; Freire 1972; hooks 1994: 5; cf. Pluciennik, Fewster, this volume) which advocates that everything taught and experienced within the university should lead to a concrete outcome, an investment which should yield significant returns (in most cases in the literal financial sense) in the future. Learning and teaching acquires an operational character (Barnett 1994): the student-customers need to be trained in the specific *modus operandi*, to allow them to function in the modern, complex world order structured to a large degree by the flexible, post-Fordist (Harvey 1990) global capital. The rhetoric is concerned with 'generic skills' (which ignores the fact that skills are context-specific and variable, depending on the aim, and the intended tasks that are geared towards [cf. Barnett 1994: 64]), 'specific learning outcomes' (e.g. flexibility, leadership, teamwork, and communication skills), 'credit accumulation', 'transferability' etc. This neoliberal programme for training the workforce of the future is cast in a neutral objective language and discourse. It hides the fact that the issue at hand is not the philosophical debate on education, but the contest between conflicting agendas serving different social groups and interests. As is often the case, the neoliberal instrumentalist logic is presented as the de-politicized, objectified 'best possible' view.

Moreover, the objectivist instrumentalist notion hides the fundamentally asymmetrical relationships of power in education. In the same way that the so-called performance indicators recently imposed upon schools in the UK hide the class issue, and the fact that the schools in economically deprived areas are disadvantaged from the start whatever the efforts of the teachers, the performance indicators and auditing procedures in the universities mask the fact that the access to resources and to power mechanisms amongst universities were never symmetrical. The refusal of all British governments to date, to abolish the disproportionate funding of Oxbridge through the tutorial system, is only one visible aspect of these inequalities (Austin in press).

This analysis should not be read as a lamenting for the 'good old days' (a nostalgia for a past that never was); it is well known that in the past universities in Britain and elsewhere were posing even more class and other barriers to a large proportion of people, and this author is the last who will support a return to elitism or to the medieval autocratic model of pedagogy (cf. Kirp 2000). The recent changes, however, are dramatic and novel in character. They are also for the first time, at least in the UK, driven not by the academic community but mostly by the 'world of work' (Barnett 1994: 65), that is the employers, and secondarily by the university managers and administrators. The fact that these changes are often justified on the basis of 'social relevance' (meaning, suiting the interests of employers), anti-elitism, and accountability, makes them the more dangerous. Until very recently, little discussion and debate has taken place on these measures prior to their implementation. The whole issue seems to have been treated as simply a matter of objectified, neutral administrative developments, rather than of contested, context-specific and power-related approaches. These ideas acquire the status of 'doxa', which according to Bourdieu (1990) signifies the set of views which become so embedded in certain contexts that are beyond orthodoxy and heterodoxy, beyond critique and contestation. It is only recently, and due in part to the fact that some of the effects and consequences of these measures have now become more prominent, that some academic debate has been generated (cf. some early warnings Atiyah 1992; Barnett 1994, and some recent reactions: Harrison et al. 2001; Shore and Wright 1999; Radice 2001) which may force the British government to reconsider some of its auditing procedures, a move which in an ironic turn, is opposed by student organizations on grounds of accountability (see Elliot Major 2001).

In the context of archaeological teaching there is another paradox, which needs pointing out. While, at least within the Anglo-American tradition, archaeological theory has become a major and important concern which permeates all aspects of our research, the philosophy and methodology of archaeological teaching and pedagogy seems to have remained immune and unaffected by these theoretical developments. Furthermore, while in our research many of us have undermined the premises of objectivism, have emphasized the importance of context, and have rejected the application of maximization

principles in the study of prehistoric economies and societies, in our educational and pedagogical practice and in our life as academics we seem to have tolerated or even endorsed these ideas. We sit back and listen to countless speeches by university administrators on efficiency (abstractly defined) and maximization. Or we ourselves implement willingly the policies of self-policing through structures which are supposed to guarantee accountability, seen in an objectified and neutral manner. How often do we stop to ask, accountability yes, but accountability to whom?

Here is what Sir Michael Atiyah, a mathematician and president of the Royal Society had to say on this matter in his presidential address in 1991:

> 'Over the past decade or so, universities have increasingly been treated like commercial businesses, dominated by accountancy procedure and measured by the products they produce.... The President of the British Academy put it well when he said recently that the great divide in the universities now is not between the arts and the sciences, but between the scholars and the accountants.
> Now there will be those who will say that this is the reaction of unrealistic academics, who do not realize that universities have to be properly managed to the satisfaction of the tax-payer. Perhaps; but I, and I suspect many university colleagues, are deeply uneasy about the present situation, not because we are irresponsible, but because we have little confidence in the foundations on which the great accountancy edifice has been built. As a mathematician I know that the validity of a conclusion rests not only on the accuracy of the argument but also on the truth of the initial premise. In all the intricate discussions that take place on university funding I feel I want to question the initial starting point, not the arcane details of the mechanism.
> So, where do we start? We are told that universities have two functions: to teach (T) and to conduct research (R). These activities are supposed to be more or less independent and their products measured by counting student degrees or published papers. With this simple, not to say simplistic, starting point one then proceeds to work out detailed figures for different institutions depending where they sit in the RT table. It is beautifully simple as an algebraic accounting procedure: but does it correspond to reality?
> All of us have to fill in forms asking us to identify how much of our time, in a given period, has been spent on teaching and how much on research. For many of us this is meaningless and impossible task, especially when one moves from elementary to more advanced teaching. How does one divide, count

or weigh a thought? In desperation we end up filling in some notional figures that give the expected kind of answer. These then are the murky beginnings of the grand edifice that is ultimately constructed, when figures, percentages and graphs are produced to provide a spurious accuracy for the whole process.... Universities, as they have evolved in the western world, are complex intricate structures that cannot adequately be described by two algebraic variables.

If I had to use a two-word definition, I would prefer to say that universities are places of *Learning* and *Thinking*.... If learning is the objective, thinking is the process. Critical and creative thought is the life-blood of universities, the indispensable route to the acquisition of true knowledge, and the essential ingredient in the education of our citizens' (Atiyah 1992: 157-58).

Auditing procedures did result, by default, in some positive effects for universities. The focus on the value of teaching (despite happening through such a distorted and indirect procedure), and the improvement on the teaching support networks and facilities for staff and student are two of them. Whether these positive aspects, however, are enough to counterbalance all the serious negative consequences of the whole procedure, is debatable. Indeed the argument can be made that if the auditing procedures themselves rather than the role of teaching and learning, become the focus of the attention, then there is a serious danger that once this extremely expensive (in time and resources) procedure is over, once the auditors leave satisfied that all the paperwork is in place, teaching will cease to become an issue of serious attention and consideration. The administrative overkill associated with auditing may put off inspiring teachers. The feedback from academics who have competed successfully in the process indicates that the negative consequences far outweigh the positive ones (e.g. Harrison et al. 2001; cf. also Halstead this volume).

The lack of extensive debate on pedagogy, and the gap between the sophisticated approaches in our research and the objectivist and supposedly neutral approaches to our teaching practise and administration, were the two main reasons which led us to organise the workshop 'Interrogating Pedagogies' and produce this volume. It is instructive for a moment to compare archaeology with other disciplines in this respect (cf. also Grant and Reynier this volume). Geographers organise regular meetings and since 1977 have had *Antipode*, an international and highly respected journal devoted to the teaching of geography in higher education. Anthropologists in the UK have had for years an Anthropology Teaching Network which organises regular meetings, and a number of recent critical interventions in their premier journals (e.g. Coleman, and Simpson 1999; Gudeman 1998; Shore and Wright 1999;

DiGiacomo 1997; Wojcicka Sharff and Lessinger 1994) is an indication of how seriously they take the whole issue. Archaeologists are lagging considerably behind; to be fair the last couple of years have seen some discussion in conferences and other fora on these issues (cf. articles in *Antiquity* March 2000; also Chitty 1999), although many of the recent initiatives in archaeology seem to be driven mostly by the needs and concerns of professional organisations. Beyond Britain, the Society for American Archaeology has been particularly active with task forces, meetings and publications (e.g. Bender and Smith 2000; Smith, this volume). The European Association of Archaeology is only now starting to address the issue. To return to Britain, the recent benchmarking document statement (prepared for the Quality Assurance Agency) which is reproduced and discussed extensively in this volume, offers an opportunity to debate these issues further. The establishment of the Subject Centre for Archaeology, Classics and Ancient History (Grant and Reynier, this volume) is an interesting development in that respect, as is the establishment of the Archaeology Training Forum.

This last development however, while well meant and positive in the sense that it raises the issue of archaeological education, needs to be considered within the broader climate of instrumentalism analysed above. Moreover, one of the main aims of this volume is to emphasise that archaeological pedagogy, as all pedagogy, is much more than training. That it has to do with philosophy, reflexivity, politics, critical engagement with the world, life experiences, and not simply with training and transferable skills. We hope that this volume will ignite the debate, therefore, on archaeological pedagogy and education, and not simply archaeological training. On education as a life-transforming experience, rather than simply as an instrumentalist notion (cf. Barnett 1994; Coleman and Simpson 1999; Heyman 2000). On linking critical archaeological theories with critical archaeological pedagogies. On teaching not only skills, methodologies, chronologies and cultural sequences, but primarily critical thinking, ability to question, interrogate common sense and established orders, the ability to not only understand but also change the social conditions of someone's life and experience (cf. Freire and Faundex 1989; Giroux 1988; 1991; 1992; hooks 1994; McClaren 1997 for a large bibliography on critical and reflexive education; cf. Gore 1993 for a critical review of this literature). We also hope that the debate will cover more specific but equally important things, as well. To take just one example, it is surprising that we all more or less use in introductory undergraduate teaching a comprehensive, well known and highly successful textbook now in its third edition (Renfrew and Bahn 1999), and yet apart from one or two engaging book reviews, there is almost no discussion on its epistemological and ideological foundations, on its pedagogical premises, on its authority (on textbooks and authority cf. Johnston 2000).

Towards future agendas

This volume should be seen as only a small contribution to the urgently required present and future discussions and debates on archaeology in higher education. It will be up to the community of teachers, students and all those who support them in the universities to decide on the agendas of this debate and come up with the vision of what archaeology teaching should be about. The thoughts that follow are my initial contributions to the discussion:

1) As Shore and Wright (1999) suggested for anthropology, we should turn our theoretical and analytical tools toward our own communities, and analyze critically and investigate the structures of power that we may reproduce in our teaching, such as the optimization and maximization principles that we may willingly or not, tolerate or even adopt, convey through our teaching and perpetuate. In other words, we should contract a critical and reflexive analysis of our teaching operations and reveal their underlying philosophies and assumptions, and the model of social behaviour and conduct that they perpetuate. This critical analysis requires not only a philosophy of archaeological pedagogy but also an anthropology and political economy of archaeological education, which should cover a broad range of issues, from the production and reproduction of authority in archaeological teaching, to the economy, power relations and inequalities present in our teaching and learning regimes.

2) We should resist the transformation of public universities into semi-private or private spheres of a service industry, which operate on the basis of the dominant (in the present western world) neoliberal logic. In other words, we should strive for universities as public arenas and open spaces, where critical debates and thinking thrive, an arena where dominant, popular and taken-for granted truths are questioned and interrogated.

3) We should raise the debate on accountability, rejecting both the image of the university as an 'ivory tower', an image which is a caricature anyway since universities are in a public sphere, as well as the narrow definition of accountability which implies a 'banking' and accounting view of pedagogy. It is perhaps better to replace the concept with responsibility, and subsequently, explore and debate the different constituencies that we should feel responsible to. The current climate of auditing culture seems to imply that we are primarily accountable to (unaccountable) auditing bodies, whereas we should stress that our primary responsibility lies with our students, the tax-payers who fund public education, the local communities in which we participate (cf. Fewster, this volume), and society in general.

4) We should engage with and explore the implications of recent archaeological thinking and paradigmatic change, not simply for our research and its communication, but also for our teaching philosophy and practice. The plurality and multivocality that many of us advocate for our research agenda and for diverse publics, should also inform teaching, which often follows a monologic, authoritative mode. In other words, as we have problematised (and often partly undermined) our authority as exclusive producers and managers of archaeological knowledges, we should problematise our authority as teachers too (but see below).

5) We should regain the initiative on teaching by being pro-active and setting the agenda on the basis of an archaeological pedagogy which focuses on critical thinking and on a broad definition of education as a life-transforming experience, rather than as banking procedure based on accumulating narrowly-defined skills. The promotion of critical thinking in archaeological pedagogy should go beyond the rhetoric, and forge the methods, the fora and the media (including new terminology and vocabulary) which will allow it to flourish. As Barnett put it:

> 'When, therefore, we hear academics insisting on the importance of critical thinking among their students, there are questions to be asked about the seriousness with which academics take their own rhetoric. Are the students offered an educational experience in which they are encouraged to stretch their legs - intellectually speaking - and engage in their own evaluation of what they encounter? Are they forming the sense that it is their own thinking that counts, and that they should be keeping their own critical distance from all they experience on their course? Are they being given the confidence to form their own ideas and judgements and take up their own stances? A pedagogy of this kind requires that students be given both space, in which to form their own insights, and support, so as to achieve the confidence necessary for forming a viewpoint of their own, when surrounded by the often intimidating weight of authority, in the tangible form of their lecturers and the library shelves (backed up by the computer catalogue)' (1994: 118).

6) We should explore ways of incorporating reflexivity in our teaching agendas, a not easy but hugely rewarding and pedagogically beneficial and important task. By this I mean the attempt to relate our teaching to our lives and those of our students (cf. Coleman and Simpson 1999), and encourage them to view the university experience as an opportunity to trace their own life histories, question their own views, ideas, stereotypes; encourage them to cross boundaries and borders (cf. Giroux 1992), 'unlearn' deep-rooted, common-sensical ideas and perceptions, and patterns of socialization. Not all archaeology teaching is appropriate for a reflexive approach, but a lot of it is. After all, we are in the business of exploring human relationships in the past, and in most cases these are directly linked to present day patterns of living, values, ideas and views.

Reflexive teaching can empower and enable students in many different ways. It will help them to see themselves as active producers of knowledge and ideas, and consider their lives and experiences as being relevant to the aims and practices of archaeology. It has the potential of making education a life-transforming experience for teachers and students, by enabling them to question their own subjectivity, world views and preconceptions, enabling them thus to change the conditions of their social existence. Teaching reflexively involves a more dialogic, imaginative (and as such unpredictable or even risky) teaching, and new forms of teacher-student and student-student communication, interaction, teaching, learning and assessment. The use of student-centred, reflexive journals for certain courses, where student are asked to reflect on the content of knowledge and teaching, on the ideas and thoughts debated, and more importantly on their relevance to their own lives, biographies and experiences, is perhaps one of the most appropriate media for reflexive teaching (cf. Cook 2000; also McCrindle and Christensen 1995; Morrison 1996) although their use is far more complicated than it sounds and it should not be seen as an easy option (cf. Gore 1993: 149-152).

We should be aware however that in forging a new philosophy and methodology of pedagogy based on critique and reflexivity, we replace one regime of truth with another (Gore 1993). Moreover that it is impossible to escape the nexus of power/knowledge, especially in regimented educational structures such as universities. The dynamic of teacher/student with its asymmetries and inequalities will be ever present with everything we do. To give just one example from my own experience, a couple of my students who were asked to write an experiential, reflexive journal, complained that it reminded them of their early childhood when they are forced to keep diaries (cf. Gore 1993: 138). This example brought home to me the realization that in the present educational regime, reflexive, emancipatory methods can be perceived by students as authoritarian. There are no easy solutions to this, and I would not wish to offer any prescriptions on this or any other issue, other than repeat that teaching and learning should be self-critical, and constantly undermine any objectified notion of certainty, seen in a neutral power-vacuum. Furthermore, while we may want to maintain part of our authority and power to allow us to facilitate the educational experience that we believe in, we need to devise ways to weaken our own authority, in order to allow space and opportunity for students to develop their critical thinking and independence. A simplistic valorization of all voices as being of equal status, irrespective of the context and webs of powers in which they are situated, however, is hardly a liberating and emancipatory strategy (cf. MacDowell 1994), and shares many of the problems of extreme relativism (cf. Lampeter Archaeology Workshop 1997). Our responsibility as teachers should include the task of facilitating informed, reflexive and critical judgment amongst multiple and competing voices.

Finally, as many students (and their families and sponsors) in common with many teachers have internalized the discourse of instrumentalist, banking education, they may often resist attempts to experience and engage with critical thinking and reflexivity, not simply because it requires hard work but also because its immediate, tangible benefits are not always apparent. A common complaint is voiced that in dialogic teaching based on thought and self-reflection, students have the feeling that they do not 'learn' (which is usually equated to the number of pages with notes that they have filled in during the class), they do not get 'their money's worth' (in the present regime, meant in its literal sense). A critical, reflexive thinking, thus, requires much more work from teachers and students but its benefits and rewards are recognizable by most students.

7) If we believe that social values such as critical and reflexive thinking, responsibility, co-operation, tolerance of the other and of diversity, compassion and solidarity are important elements of our teaching, then our pedagogies, teaching, learning, and assessment methods and techniques, should be revised accordingly to accommodate and encourage these values. This may mean that we have to dispense of methods and procedures which encourage and perpetuate individualist attitudes (sometimes masked under 'leadership skills'), competitive behaviour, ruthless careerism and self-interest. Development of team-teaching and team-work and group projects is only one possible avenue with many more (e.g. projects involving the local community) remaining to be explored. It would be naive to suggest, however, that teamwork in itself will automatically lead to the appreciation of co-operation and solidarity, especially if it is seen in isolation and not part of a broader pedagogical logic based on critique, reflexivity and collective responsibility. Besides, in a climate such as present-day western society, where individualist, entrepreneurial thinking is held in high esteem and is glorified, attempts to use teamwork are bound to face serious problems, as many of us must have found.

8) We need to problematise the discourse on the 'relevance' of teaching and learning. This notion of relevance has been extensively used within the framework of employability. Despite its broad appearance, however, the concept is often meant and applied in a very limited sense: it very often means relevance to the interests of the employers, in most cases private capital or the privatised public sector. The notion of relevance in its abstract sense is also often used as an argument against curiosity-driven enquiry, or research and teaching which is not seen to be linked directly to quantifiable financial returns. Our challenge will be to show the situated and interest-specific meaning of relevance, and defend teaching and research which is not directly linked to employability and quantifiable returns. At the same time, we should make teaching and research relevant to broader social concerns, emphasising the needs and the problems of wide sectors of the public who, more often than not, lack the means of influencing university teaching agendas, thus making their voices and concerns heard amongst academics and

university managers and administrators. Museum exhibitions which expose the hidden histories of exploitation and of hegemonic strategies, or take a long-term approach to the issue of emigration (cf. Merriman 1993) by showing the artificiality of concepts such as 'self' and 'other', are only a few of the socially relevant teaching initiatives that are open to us.

9) While archaeological research has gone some way towards integrating field and other practical elements with theoretical ones, and there are moves towards a reflexive, theorised practice (cf. Pluciennik, this volume), our teaching still seems to maintain, to a large extent, the opposition between theory and practice, and between field and laboratory-based archaeologists, and theoretical archaeologists. Both elements are now part of the curriculum in most archaeology departments, but their link is still loose and their integration still a matter of serious concern. How can we extend the notion of the 'field' in our teaching, to include, in addition to the excavation or survey locales, the local community, the peer-group, the media? How can we teach theorised practice, how can we overcome in our teaching the binarisms that have proved so problematic in our research and thinking? Moreover, how can we incorporate notions such as social responsibility and the ethics of archaeology and archaeological practice into our field and practical teaching and view them as fundamental to our enterprise rather than as duty requirements like health and safety regulations?

Afterword

While the tone of much of this paper appears rather pessimistic, there are some indications that the consequences of many of the developments discussed here have inadvertently resulted in some reaction which may form the basis of a much more extensive, broad ranging and thorough debate that can subject all present pedagogical practices to the critical scrutiny they deserve, and expose their links to social and political philosophies and world views. In these debates, the teachers of archaeology should go beyond the narrowly-defined training by focusing on education, and imagine, devise and propose alternative pedagogical practices, in tune with the ideas of pluralism, multivocality and ethical practice, that have been endorsed by many in archaeological research and its public dissemination. The broad perspective adopted in this paper, has attempted to show that while subject-specific debates and discussions are urgently needed, many of the phenomena we are experiencing are linked to wider programmes, processes and developments, and they thus require a wider response.

Acknowledgements

Many thanks to Paul Rainbird and Karoline von Oppen for comments on an early version of this paper. Neither them nor any other person or organisation carry responsibility for the personal views expressed here. Thanks are also due to Michael Reynier and Theresa Kintz for bibliographic help.

References

Atiyah, M. 1992. Address of the President, Sir Michael Atiyah, given at the anniversary meeting on 29 November 1991. *Notes and Records of the Royal Society,* 46(1): 155-69.

Austin, D. in press. Archaeology, funding and the responsibilities of the University. In T*he Responsibility of Archaeologists* (ed. M. Pluciennik). Oxford: Archaeopress (BAR series).

Barnett, R. 1994. *The Limits of Competence: Knowledge, Higher Education and Society.* Buckingham: The Society for Research into Higher Education and Open University Press.

Bender, S. J. and Smith, G. S. (eds) 2000. *Teaching Archaeology in the 21st Century.* Washington DC: Society for American Archaeology.

Blinkhorn, P. W. and Cumberpatch C. G. 1999. Archaeology in England 1999. *World Archaeological Bulletin* 9: 45-55.

Bourdieu, P. 1990. *The Logic of Practice.* Cambridge: Polity.

Castree, N. and Sparke, M. 2000. Professional geography and the corporatization of the university: experiences, evaluations and engagements. *Antipode,* 32(3): 222-9.

Chitty, G. 1999. *Training in Professional Archaeology: a Preliminary Review.* Carnforth, Lancashire. (Commissioned by English Heritage on behalf of the Archaeology Training Forum).

Coleman, S. and Simpson, B. 1999. Unintended consequences? Anthropology, pedagogy and personhood. *Anthropology Today,* 15(6): 3-6.

Cook, I. 2000. 'Nothing can ever be the case of "us" and "them" again': exploring the politics of difference through border pedagogy and student journal writing. *Journal of Geography in Higher Education,* 24(1): 13-27.

DiGiacomo, S. M. 1997. The new internal colonialism. *Critique of Anthropology,* 17(1): 91-7.

Elliot Major, L. 2001. A watchdog bitten. *The Guardian* 27 March.

Freire, P. 1972. *Pedagogy of the Oppressed.* Harmondsworth: Penguin.

Freire, P. and Faundez, A. 1989. *Learning to Question: A Pedagogy of Liberation.* Geneva: WCC Publications.

Giroux, H. A. 1988. *Teachers as Intellectuals: Toward a Critical Pedagogy of Learning.* New York: Bergin and Garvey.

Giroux, H. A. 1991. Democracy and the discourse of cultural difference: towards a politics of border pedagogy. *British Journal of Sociology of Education,* 12(4): 501-19.

Giroux, H. A. 1992. *Border Crossings: Cultural Workers and the Politics of Education.* New York: Routledge.

Gore, J. M. 1993. *The Struggle for Pedagogies*. New York and London: Routledge.

Gudeman, S. 1998. The new captains of information. *Anthropology Today,* 14(1): 1-3.

Hamilakis, Y. 1999. La trahison des archeologues? Archaeological practice as intellectual activity in postmodernity. *Journal of Mediterranean Archaeology,* 12(1): 60-103.

Harvey, D. 1990. *The Condition of Postmodernity*. Oxford: Blackwell.

Harrison, M., Lockhood, B., Miller, M. Oswald, A., Stewart, M. and Walker, I. 2001. Trial by ordeal. *The Guardian,* January 30th: 12-3.

Heyman, R. 2000. Research, pedagogy and instrumental geography. *Antipode,* 32(2): 292-307.

Hodder, I. 1999. *The Archaeological Process*. Oxford: Blackwell.

hooks, b. 1994. *Teaching to Transgress: Education as the Practice of Freedom*. New York and London: Routledge.

Johnston, R. 2000. Authors, editors, and authority in the postmodern academy. *Antipode,* 32(3): 271-91.

Kirp. D. L. 2000. The new U. *The Nation* April 17 (http://past.thenation.com/issue/000417/kirp.shtml ; accessed 22/3/01).

Lampeter Archaeology Workshop, 1997. Relativism, objectivity and the politics of the past. *Archaeological Dialogues* 4(2): 164-98.

McClaren, P. (ed) 1997. *Revolutionary Multiculturalism: Pedagogies of Dissent for the New Millennium*. Boulder, Co: Westview.

McCrindle, A. R. and Christensen, C. A. 1995. The impact of learning journals on metacognitive and cognitive processes and learning performance. *Learning and Instruction,* 5: 167-85.

McDowell, L. 1994. Polyphony and pedagogic authority. *Area,* 26(3): 241-8.

Merriman, N. 1993. *The Peopling of London*. London: The Museum of London.

Miyoshi, M. 2000. Ivory tower in Escrow. *Boundary,* 27(1), 7-50.

Monbiot, G. 2000. *The Captive State: The Corporate Takeover of Britain*. London: MacMillan.

Morrison, K. 1996. Developing reflective practice in higher degree students through a learning journal. *Studies in Higher Education,* 21(3): 317-32.

Press, E. and Washburn, J. 2000. The kept university. *The Atlantic Monthly,* 285: 39-54.

Radice, H. 2001. From Warwick University Ltd to British Universities Plc. *Red Pepper,* 81: 18-21.

Renfrew, C. and Bahn, P. 1999. *Archaeology: Theory, Methods and Practice*. London: Thames and Hudson (3rd ed.).

Richardson, P. D. 2000. Audit culture and anthropology. *Journal of the Royal Anthropological Institute,* (N.S.) 6: 721-2.

Sanders, C. 2001. Private lives of public places. *Times Higher Education Supplement,* January 2nd: 6.

Shore, C. and Wright, S. 1999. Audit culture and anthropology: Neo-liberalism in British Higher Education. *Journal of the Royal Anthropological Institute,* (N.S.) 5: 557-75.

Unger, D. N. S. 1995. Academic apartheid: the predicament of part-time faculty. *Thought and Action,* 11(1): 117-20.

Walsh, K. 1992. *The Representation of the Past*. London: Routledge.

Warde, I. 2001. Conflicts of interest on the campus: for sale: US academic integrity. *Le Monde Diplomatique,* March (http://www.monde-diplomatique.fr/en/2001/03/11academic; accessed 21/3/01).

Wojcicka Sharff, J. and Lessinger, J. 1994. The academic sweatshop; changes in the capitalist infrastructure and the part-time academic. *Anthropology Today,* 10(5): 12-5.

PART I

THE PAST & PRESENT

Teaching archaeology in British universities: a personal polemic

John Collis

In the last half-century departments of archaeology in Britain have acquired an enviable reputation as centres of innovation and excellence. Their success cannot only be measured quantitatively – some 25 departments producing 1200 graduates a year (Henson 1999) compared to 40–50 students from 4–5 departments in 1960 – but also in the quality and range of teaching provided. Archaeology has made great inroads into subjects which have traditionally been seen as providing a liberal humanities-based training – Classics, History, English; and in Sheffield for some time the postgraduate school was greater than the rest of the Arts Faculty put together (in this article I shall use Sheffield as an example, as I am familiar with the data, but our experience, I suspect, is similar to that of most of the major departments in Britain).

The popularity is not simply a product of the glamorous image of archaeology presented in the media, especially on television, though a popular programme does much to bolster student applications – I myself am a product of the *Animal, Vegetable, Mineral* generation of the 1950s when Sir Mortimer Wheeler and Glyn Daniel could become 'TV Personalities of the Year'. We have, for instance, benefited in more recent years from Government drives to encourage wide-ranging subjects which cross the boundaries of the Arts, Social Sciences and Pure Sciences. Archaeology scores high in a range of 'transferable skills' – literacy and writing, laboratory and fieldwork training, computer skills, team work.

I have argued on a number of occasions that the success of our universities is not connected with any innate superiority of British archaeology, but more with the organisational structures within which we work. Unlike France, in Britain we are not fragmented into Science, Arts, Medicine and Law based universities, so it is possible for links across disciplines to be encouraged, and departments quite commonly belong to both Science and Arts Faculties (Collis forthcoming). We do not see the best academics siphoned off into primarily research-based institutions like the Archaeological Institutes of central and eastern Europe, or the CNRS in France (Collis 1995), though such academics do commonly assist in teaching. We have also been accepted as a subject in our own right, not forcibly wedded to the histories or art history as in France or Italy, or to anthropology as in the USA. The three-year structure of our degree course has been a help rather than a hindrance, preventing us from following, for instance, the path of German universities where an indulgence in highly specialised teaching such as artefact recognition has been at the expense of a wider concern with techniques and more general theory (it is interesting to note that German universities are now exploring a three-

year system similar to ours). Above all our freedom as a subject has led to our acceptance in the wider world as a science-based subject, not only in name, but also in terms of funding (though a recent initiative in advancing learning skills by the Funding Councils has lumped us together with Classics and History, neither of which are science and fieldwork based – we cannot assume everyone in positions of power understands our subject!). Finally, the British system has been demand led – the more students a subject can attract the more funding it receives, so leading to increases in staff and improvements in facilities, a contrast with, for instance, Spain where larger student numbers simply mean larger classes.

However, the last decade has seen a reversal of some of these trends, as well as new principles being adopted, aimed at improving standards, accountability, and value for money. Many of these changes can only be applauded; importantly, however, they have costs both in terms of time and money, but no attempt has been made by Government to look at these or their long-term effect on the system. Money has become a key factor; as increased numbers of students have entered higher education, so public funding has not been able to provide the support it did in previous generations. Students have increasingly to provide their own funding, and the British Government has generally espoused North American solutions where these save public funds (e.g. student loans instead of grants), without espousing those which cost the Government money (e.g. tax relief for the costs of learning).

Universities are expected to earn money, from profits made from research contracts or from the fees paid by foreign students. Good though this is in providing the 'icing on the cake' to provide better resources, successive governments have seen these funds as providing the 'cake' itself. The dangers of this can been seen in the recent crisis in the 'Tiger Economies' of the Far East which led to a drastic fall in student numbers from these countries, and so of income in some universities. Because funding for British students is not ring-fenced from such entrepreneurial activities, it has led to a drop in the quality of training for local students. At times, because they bring in greater profit in terms of 'fees' we may have to give preference to foreign students. The universities have tacitly played along with these changes. Students mean money, so the more students, the more money. The upsurge in Masters courses in recent years reflects this need to attract more students, sometimes seemingly more important than the needs and interests of the students, or the relevance of the course curriculum to the possibilities of career openings.

It is these changes, and also recent trends in the policies of our Funding Councils and Research Councils (the major dispensers of Government funds to universities) which I wish to explore in this article.

Undergraduate training

For many years the three-year undergraduate course has been seen as the entry point for the profession. A recent survey (Chitty 1999) shows that the majority of people in the profession still think this should be the case, but this has increasingly been rejected by university academics, and also by the professional body, the Institute of Field Archaeologists (IFA). There are several reasons for this. Though the number of archaeological posts has increased considerably, the number of graduates emerging from the universities has always far exceeded the possibilities of archaeological employment. Figures are difficult to obtain, but it may be as few as 10–20 per cent of graduates enter the profession permanently. Thus degree courses have to be oriented towards the 80–90 per cent for whom the course is not vocational. This means that more detailed subject areas which may be essential for professional activity (e.g. the legal framework, identification of artefact sets, excavation and survey techniques) are often only given cursory treatment or even ignored. In any case, university academics may not be the best people to teach some of these fields!

Also, the profession has become increasingly specialised, with specialisms, for instance, such as Planning and Development Officers, Sites and Monuments Officers, university academics, museum curators, people dealing with media and tourism, as well as a range of technical specialists, in ceramics, environmental studies, conservation, etc. No undergraduate course could cover them all in sufficient detail. Thus, undergraduate courses have to be of necessity general, introductory and non-vocational. However, there are some areas which at present tend only to be covered at the undergraduate level, such as archaeological theory, statistics, and the history of archaeology, except in specialist courses on these topics. The reverse side of this means, however, that many graduates are entering other aspects of society with a training and knowledge of archaeology, which can only be good for the subject (we have at least one elected member of parliament with an archaeology degree, Richard Allen, for Sheffield Hallam).

Another peculiarity of the British university training for archaeologists has been the strong emphasis that had been placed on practical aspects such as field survey, excavation and laboratory training, a contrast again with the German tradition with a stronger emphasis on artefact recognition, drawing and site recording. This reflects a social revolution in Britain in the 1950s when the traditional excavation structure of director / student supervisors / paid labourers was replaced by one of director / supervisors / student volunteers. Students thus entered the excavation world not as supervisors / recorders, but as diggers, and

were promoted for their field skills rather than their academic training / social background; in the 1970s it was these people who filled the new professional posts. Many, such as myself, in fact had both the practical and the academic grounding, and I found it strange working in Poland and Germany where, as a student, I was not expected to dig, merely record and draw. In some parts of Europe this gulf between the academics who run the excavation, and the labourers who dig, still exists, indeed, in some countries, it is enshrined in conditions for obtaining excavation permits.

This tradition of practical skills was formalised in archaeological degrees in Britain during the 1970s when the new departments of archaeology insisted on their students having practical experience, and obtained the funding for them to acquire the training. It is this tradition which is now under threat, if not actually being destroyed. The reasons are varied. Only in part is it due to reductions in State funding. Governments rightly claim that they are spending more than ever on higher education, but the *per capita* funding for students has steadily diminished over the last decade – a recent estimate is of 40 per cent reduction (D. Triesman quoted in MacLeod 1999). Thus, in my own department, since funds for fieldwork were devolved to departmental control nine years ago, the lump sum we obtain has remained static despite the effects of inflation and the doubling of our student numbers. We rely increasingly on alternative external funds (grant-assisted projects, etc.), for carrying out our fieldwork training.

The advent of 'Developer Funding' and of a competitive tendering system has led to ground rules whereby student labour cannot be used to undercut the costs of employing professional archaeologists, and generally, within the time and financial constraints under which archaeological units are forced to work, it is not possible for them to undertake the training of unskilled students. If they do employ students, they have to pay the full wage, and naturally prefer to employ experienced excavators rather than beginners who may have no intention of entering the profession, and may not therefore be fully motivated. The result has been more and more students competing for fewer and fewer opportunities to do field work. We are gradually reaching the 'Catch 22' situation of Swedish archaeology (Holmgren 1999): students have legally to be paid on the same scale as professionals and only experienced archaeologists are therefore employed, with no volunteers. So how can an inexperienced student obtain the experience to be employable? The highly centralised French system has been better at dealing with this, with some AFAN excavations taking students for training; a recent move by English Heritage to top up funds of some rescue sites allowing them to take volunteers and students is a move in the right direction.

Another factor has been the shift to modular courses with credits, usually within semesters. What was supposed to give students choice in the combination of modules, and even the possibility of changing universities, has in fact become a straitjacket with strict controls over time-tabling and course length. Under the old system where degree courses in different subjects were largely independent of one another, it was possible to allow time to take students on field courses within term time. Now this is largely impossible, and field and work experience have to be done in the vacations. With the abolition of grants, students have increasingly to earn money to finance their studies. They are thus faced with the 'double whammy': not only can they not earn money while doing their fieldwork, but increasingly they have to contribute towards the costs of completing their compulsory fieldwork.

The reaction of my own department is perhaps fairly typical. We have been more liberal in our definition of 'relevant work experience', and we have decreased considerably the amount of practical work we demand of students (while encouraging them to do more if possible). We have been forced to abandon our much praised six-week 'work experience' programme at the end of the third year, due simply to semesterisation. Students now do about 8–10 weeks of work experience in contrast to the 16–18 a few years ago. If present trends continue we shall have little choice but to reduce this still more, perhaps restricting grants to those who are planning a career in archaeology, and going back to the 1960s situation when field experience was merely 'desirable'.

Another possible victim of the Government's financial policies, with the introduction of 'university fees' is mature entry of students. Sheffield, again typically, always had a high entry of older students, and we were one of only two or three departments which met the university's target of 25 per cent mature intake. In the first year since the introduction of fees, applications from this sector have collapsed, though it may be showing signs of recovery. So much for the Government's commitment to 'lifelong learning'! A final complaint is that intervention by the QAA is not always helpful; for instance their insistence that courses should demonstrate 'progression' from the second to third year, so that teaching and marking second and third year students on the same modules becomes unacceptable. At Sheffield we always put on courses in alternate years to give students greater choice, but this is now frowned upon, and we may be blackmailed into dropping it; on the other hand, in my IFA capacity, I would suggest we should be trying to increase choice so that students can plan their careers more sensibly. I find such interference by the QAA unacceptable, as it has been done, in the case of archaeology at least, with the agreement of neither students, departments, nor the profession.

Taught Masters degrees

In the last decade by far the greatest expansion in both courses and student numbers has been in taught Masters courses (see Henson, this volume). In part this is because a 'market' has appeared as students realise that the Bachelor degree is no longer adequate to obtain a job. The problem is that most of the Masters degrees on offer equally carry no guarantee of employment, and there is no substitute for experience in the field or some other form of work experience. Where Masters courses do come in is for students who are returning after work experience to gain more specialised training in the aspect of archaeology they have chosen. Here is one area where the interests of students, universities and the profession coincide, but at present there is no way of monitoring the content and relevance of these courses in terms of professional development (they are 'accredited' by the IFA, but there are as yet no clear guidelines on how they fit into possible career structures, and at present the 'accreditation' is merely a recognition linked with IFA membership, and is no guarantee of quality). Departments are under pressure to increase student numbers, especially at the postgraduate level as this adds to a department's prestige (and so funding) in 'Research Assessment' (see below). Masters degrees also act as the entry point for the doctoral programme, and there is a very real danger that students could be exploited mainly to meet a university's ambitions.

Doctoral research

In my opinion it is the area of doctoral research that Government policy, as interpreted by the Funding and Research Councils, is going most disastrously astray. The over-riding principle has been 'value for money' with a secondary principle that doctoral research should not be too specialised. While I agree with both these principles, it is the way in which they are implemented that has gone wrong. For me it is the end result that should be the major concern – that is what the student, the profession, and, ultimately, society wants.

Value for money is assumed to be a completed dissertation; as grants from the Research Councils and the British Academy are for three years, so dissertations should be completed in three years. But, as research can be too narrow in focus, so students' research horizons should be extended. Hence there is now a taught element in PhD training. The Research Training Programme (RTP) was initially introduced with the need to complete courses with a value of 30 credits. Thus, the trend is towards an American system in which training becomes a major element, and the PhD itself is seen as 'training for research'. The tradition of the PhD as being the main piece of pure research in an individual's life is thus being watered down. These conditions are imposed by placing the onus on the department to ensure that a certain percentage of students meet the deadline for presentation of the thesis, or sanctions are imposed, with the withdrawal of research funding for future students entering the department.

This scenario presents a number of problems. Firstly there is no onus on the student, the recipient of the public funding, to produce at the end of the period, especially if they already have a job. My own solution would be to treat the grant as an interest free 'loan' for, say, five years, after which either much of it must be repaid, or it will start accruing interest. The original loan can be wiped out by the presentation of the dissertation. Students would also need to pay a 'continuation fee' for tuition if they go beyond the deadline. Sanctions against departments could consist of publishing success rates, and discouraging students from signing on with departments with poor completion rates, for instance, by reducing the value of grants. Sanctions should also only apply for students funded from public funds; the Research Councils should have no right to dictate conditions to students paying for themselves. On the other hand I know of cases of students not applying for jobs for which they are well qualified because of pressures to produce dissertations on time and keep the department's record for submission within the prescribed limits. Sometimes students with grants are ill, but cannot sign off from their research programme, as they would then have no income!

The idea of 'training for research' would be all right if there was any prospect of continuing full-time research. The idea was started in the science-based Research Councils; many scientists, even if they do not continue with an academic career, will take up a research career in industry. Such an option is not generally open to archaeologists, outside universities and a small number of other institutions such as the British Museum; the PhD is thus for the majority the one and only opportunity to carry out sustained research. The advent of 'developer funding' both makes research on archaeological finds difficult, if not impossible, but it is also generating data which needs to be followed up by research and synthesis, and the PhD is one major way in which this could be achieved. The other traditional possibility, the large excavation monograph, is an opportunity that is open to few.

Too many students now look upon the PhD as a stepping stone into a career, when, for some it is more of a blind alley, and experience working in the profession would be more productive. In my view starting a PhD soon after graduation is only relevant for two categories of student: those whose aim is to obtain an academic or research post; or those entering a specialist science or conservation based career, in which cases the PhD is a means of obtaining the skills necessary to practice. For both these groups RTP is irrelevant, if not a positive hindrance. More important is a knowledge of the professional practice of archaeology, but it is precisely this which is being squeezed out of the student's experience because of the pressure exerted by the Research Councils.

As a research student myself, I took the opportunity both to travel in Europe and also to carry out fieldwork. I spent three months each year directing a large and innovative excavation, and it was this experience rather than my research which landed me my first academic post. The connections that I made in Europe at this time also opened up possibilities which my students and I are still exploiting thirty years later. A few years ago a group of our research students started up an electronic on-line journal. At least one student obtained a post because of this experience, but

now, because of pressures of time-tabling, students are less willing to become involved in such 'extra-curricular' activities. The bureaucratic and prescriptive nature of RTP is stifling such initiatives, and destroying the research experience. Much better would be a strong insistence that candidates for PhDs should have at least one or two years' experience working in the 'real world' or better, that PhD programmes should cover at least four years, of which three would be funded for research, and the rest be integrated with a programme of professional experience on field projects, in the laboratory, or other mind-expanding activities such as an Erasmus exchange.

For the majority of graduates who enter the field, management, or heritage branches of the profession, initial research experience might better be learnt through a taught MPhil. The opportunity for intensive research for a PhD could then be undertaken as sabbatical leave when people are in their late 30s or early 40s, perhaps as part of the advancement from middle to senior management. This is the point at which the wider perspective is needed, and also research topics may have already suggested themselves, such as bodies of data which have been excavated or worked on, but where the time and funding to follow up both in depth and more widely were restricted by time and money constraints. This would help to break the monopoly of the PhD as largely something for 'academics' and to build bridges between the profession and academe.

Quality control

In the last decade a whole series of innovations has been introduced into universities, aimed at improving the quality of teaching and research. Most high profile of these has been the Research Assessment Exercise (RAE), under which departments are classified on the basis of a number of criteria (quality of written articles and books, research income, numbers of postgraduates, etc.). The level of the funding for the department is in part based on this classification, which is carried out by a small committee of senior academics for each subject, and so is a form of peer review. A similar exercise is underway for the Teaching Quality Assessment (TQA) and for 'Benchmarking' (quality and content of courses), though at present these bear no financial penalties or rewards. Though they can be criticised in detail, there is no doubt that such aspects as the documentation of courses and their content, have improved enormously. Other similar reforms include anonymous marking, staff appraisal, and staff training (for both teaching and research).

None but a few die-hards would consider these changes as anything other than beneficial, making us more aware of our students as 'customers' and of the quality and cost-effectiveness of what we are doing. The problem has been that their implementation has never been costed in terms of either money or of time. My own experience as an Examinations Officer suggests that simply dealing with anonymous marking takes up two or three days of my time each year because of the need to correlate numbers with names; I have also had bitter experiences of time spent trying to re-route research funds from America to be spent in France via the university's Finance Department so it could be counted for RAE. The amount of paper documentation for RAE, and especially TQA, is immense; for the latter every department has to put aside a room to store examination papers and other documentation! Personally I am aware that 15 years ago I could spend many weekends engaged in research and excavating; now they are spent at the computer producing documentation. Rather than funding these improvements, the Government has continued to cut funds for academic and support staff, or rather I should say that we are expected to make year-on-year 'efficiency savings'. Even the money brought in by charging student fees is swallowed up by the Treasury rather than being used to benefit universities.

The future

Some of the problems which beset archaeological departments are those common to British universities as a whole; the reduction of funding linked with the increasing numbers of students. Certain aspects such as the cuts in student support, the payment of teaching fees, and the 30 per cent drop in staff salaries in relation to other comparable professional groups since 1980, have all been well documented in the media. However, generally the universities have been poor in pleading their case such as the 50 per cent cut in equipment grants introduced for one year by the last Conservative Government, and never reversed. Would a doubling of the student/staff ratio have been accepted in any other sector of education? Though there has been extra funding by the present Government, calculations by the Association of University Teachers show that *per capita* funding of students is continuing to drop; plans for further additional funding are linked with yet another increase in student numbers, rather than any attempt to guarantee and ring-fence an adequate sum per student. Some archaeological departments have suffered the additional blow of cuts in their science funding. Unless the present trends are reversed we are in danger of losing yet more funding by losing our foreign students, faced with American universities starting to deliberately target our best students. We need a guaranteed level of income so that we can make adequate long-term plans, rather then the present continuous crisis management.

Government remedies lie in 'efficiency savings'. The only positive step has been to try to introduce new teaching and administrative procedures via IT, but as the Government is learning from highly publicised disasters in other areas, IT does not lead to reduced staffing and lower costs; it mainly allows us to do more sophisticated things once the data has been input and checked. The Teaching and Learning Technology Programme (TLTP) was meant to provide economies in teaching by producing a range of teaching material, including programmes for Archaeology. To what extent these have now been taken up is still undocumented,

nor what their shelf-life is likely to be; as a member of the TLTP panel for archaeology I urged the making of programmes which could be built on (e.g. animal bone identification) rather than ones which would become dated and need re-writing. Large efficiency savings could only be introduced here by enforcing some sort of national curriculum so that all students used the same programmes, at least in the first year. This would produce an inflexible giant which would stifle variety and innovation. IT provides us with exciting new ways of teaching and learning, but it is a supplement, not a replacement, for more traditional methods.

However, not all is doom and gloom. Negotiations are under way between the universities and the IFA about making 'lifelong learning' a reality (Collis and Hinton 1998; Bishop et al. 1999). With their well-established mechanisms for quality control, universities are a major means by which 'Continuing Professional Development' (CPD) can be implemented. I have already discussed potential roles for taught Masters courses and the Doctorate as part of this new vision of training, but there is even greater potential for providing some of the training needed by those entering the profession, as well as short courses for the training needs of those in post at all levels within the profession. If, as seems likely, a personal training programme will be a condition of individual membership of the professional body, and also a requirement in the Code of Conduct for organisations registered with the IFA, then this will be a large growth area, which only a few universities have really started to explore. University courses and training will need to be accredited by the IFA (probably through the present external examiner system), but this will be a small price in loss of freedom to pay for the gains both to the universities and the profession.

Conclusions

British universities have been going though one of their periodic funding crises, but with hopeful signs that the worst of the cuts may now be over, archaeology departments can start to look for a new and enhanced role within the profession. However, we need to scrutinise carefully what the desired outcomes are, for instance, from our taught Masters and Doctoral programmes, and persuade the Funding Bodies and Research Councils that present policies are not always what is required. We must also continue to remind the Funding and Research Councils and other bodies in government that we need field and laboratory training for our students, and that we are not a mere adjunct to History. British universities teaching archaeology may be having problems, but in the positive ways in which we are tackling these, it is likely we will maintain our reputation for innovation, even though we can expect to see continental departments catching up with us rapidly in the next couple of decades.

References

Bishop, M., Collis, J. and Hinton, P. 1999. A future for archaeologists: professional training a career structure in archaeology. *The Archaeologist* 35: 14–6.

Chitty, G. 1999. *A Rapid Survey of Training Needs.* Archaeological Training Forum/ Institute of Field Archaeologists/ Council for British Archaeology/ English Heritage.

Collis, J. R. 1995. Celts, power and politics: whither Czech archaeology? In *Whither Archaeology? Papers in Honour of Evzen Neustupný* (eds M. Kuna and N. Venclová). Prague: Institute of Archaeology, pp. 82–92.

Collis, J. R. forthcoming. L'avenir de la recherche archéologique française sur l'âge du Fer. In D. Maranski ed. *Actes du XVIIe Colloque de l'AFEAF Nevers – mai 1993.*

Collis, J. and Hinton, P. 1998. Training, training and обучение. *The Archaeologist* 31: 15–7.

Henson, D. 1999. *Guide to Archaeology in Higher Education.* York: Council for British Archaeology.

Holmgren, I. 1999. The lack of practical experience in archaeological education in Sweden. *The European Archaeologist* 11: 10-1.

MacLeod, D. 1999. Peer pressure. *The Guardian Higher Education*, July 13 1999: i.

1.2

Theory as praxis

Mark Pluciennik

Introduction

In Britain during the 1960's, 1970's and 1980's a perceived split arose between academic ('armchair') and field archaeologists. Arguably this was driven by various factors, including the rise in rescue archaeology and hence the prioritising of excavation methodologies and recording, and the expansion in university archaeology departments which promoted various agendas including the need for individual and collective intellectual status and authority. This became connected with a trend towards at first mathematecized quasi-scientific models (New Archaeology), and then abstract and social theory in the humanities (post-processual archaeologies). The academic/public archaeology division was often exacerbated by those seen to be the major figures in the discipline: in the 1980's these tended to be humanistically-inclined archaeologists writing the polemics and the overviews of where archaeology was heading. It was in this latter context that theory courses were developed, often strongly biased towards social theory, despite the marked rise in important and innovative scientific techniques for archaeology and their concomitant funding. At the same time with the decline in large rescue excavations and with recruitment from people who had experienced archaeology in community-based schemes as part of anti-unemployment measures, many 'diggers' entered and passed through academia. Meanwhile those in academia and beyond also became far more concerned with the political ramifications of archaeology, the exploration of which was also part of the post-processual and theoretical agenda. It is these experiences and contexts which have given rise towards British concepts of the nature and role of theory in archaeology in higher education and beyond.

This paper asks what the impact of the new emphases on instrumental reason as ways of measuring learning outcomes and teaching quality means for theory in archaeology. It is argued that many recent directions in higher education can be seen as threats to theoretically-informed archaeologies and academic freedom, and act as forces for conservatism. However, this does not mean that we should seek to retain past approaches to theory. Rather it suggests the need to reintegrate theory and practice in new ways, but at the same time to continue to emphasise a critical approach as essential to a healthy discipline and the higher education sector more generally. This is essential if universities are to have a role beyond that of training people for work and society and producing research with commercial benefits, as narrowly conceptualized by many politicians and government agencies. How to think laterally, investigate a wide range of approaches, and

maintain a critical and radical edge in archaeology (at all levels, from all positions and places) is a key issue for archaeology in higher education and beyond at the beginning of a new century. As perhaps the broadest of all disciplines, much archaeological practice is necessarily multi- and inter-disciplinary. However this requires the ability to think philosophically, theoretically and critically within and about a variety of intellectual frameworks and the wider constitution of archaeology in the modern world. This suggests that we should be encouraging permeability and flux, rather than attempting to police disciplinary boundaries along the lines suggested by benchmarking and a focus on practical skills. This paper argues that we must maintain a critical and reflexive theoretical approach to continually remake the discipline.

The context

Many of us are currently concerned with the ways in which particular forms of knowing, reasoning, evaluation and control all too familiar to non-academic colleagues (Blinkhorn & Cumberpatch 1999) have apparently recently burst through the barrier notionally protecting academia and academic freedom. Nevertheless, my starting point is that we have to understand the changes in higher education, and, within that, in archaeology and attitudes towards theory in archaeology, as part of a much longer and broader framework. One of the obvious places to start is with the growth of instrumental reason, which is seen by many (e.g. Giddens and Habermas, but especially Weber) as one of the characteristics of modernity. The growth of this type of rationality is linked to new types of surveillance within society, typically expressed through bureaucratic systems. Such bureaucracies, although usually founded to administer and achieve instrumental goals, tend to develop their own momentum. Along with the rules and regulations they promulgate for their explicit aims, members of such bureaucracies individually and collectively develop and protect their own interests - their job preservation, and the expansion and colonization of other worlds and systems. How and why have such tendencies impinged on higher education in the UK (and elsewhere)?

Barnett (1994: 22) argues that, beginning after World War II, four general changes are taking place in the relation between higher education and wider society:

> '1.   An overlap of interests and commitments between society and higher education is developing and becoming more pronounced...

2. Knowledge (even high powered and formalized knowledge) is becoming a distinct force independently of higher education.
3. Society is forming its own definitions of knowing.
4. Higher education is being presented with those external definitions of knowledge and is falling in with the requirements being put its way.'

These changes have been expressed in higher education as the extension of managerialism and bureaucracy - the increasing encroachment of not just the State *per se* (strategic interventions of government for the good of 'society as a whole') but also through the insistence of the alignment and measurement of higher education goals and 'outcomes' with those adopted by sectional interests elsewhere in society such as industry, employers, and professional organizations. These outcomes and units of measurement and evaluation have largely been couched in the language of efficiency, of cost-profit accounting, standardization and equivalencing as part of the 'audit' economy. In other words we have seen attempts to commodify learning and knowledge, which is recast in the language of (transferable) skills, competence, outcomes, and credits (Barnett 1994). This has occurred within a rhetorical framework of student ('customer') freedom glossed as 'consumer choice' and the alleged democratization of a mass higher education system opposed to elitism. Such changes have been going on since the 1970's at least, but with a notable acceleration and impingement on academics' daily lives during 1980's and 1990's. When certain inroads have been resisted - and mostly they haven't - such resistance has been expressed in terms of concern about personal academic freedom and autonomy, that is, the freedom to critique, understood as the right to maintain a privileged distance from especially economic and broader societal imperatives. However, this is all too easily glossed by others as merely the self-interest of those within ivory towers. These pressures are not confined to the UK: in the United States, for example, Giroux (2000: 343) argues that:

'asked to define themselves either through the language of the marketplace or through a discourse of liberal objectivity and neutrality that abstracts the political from the realm of the cultural and social, educators are increasingly being pressured to become either servants of corporate power or disengaged specialists wedded to the imperatives of a resurgent and debasing academic professionalism'

By and large however, despite self-interested (even if justified) complaints about workload and increased administration and paperwork, the academic community has largely been willingly co-opted into various processes of self-policing. This has happened in various ways at various levels: firstly, at departmental level with the promulgation and routinization of practices which fit in more easily with other requirements and requests from above; secondly, within institutions through the setting up of various committees and procedures, also involving academics, and the movement of individual academics into certain administrative positions within institutions (and hence who personally no longer have to deal with the effects of the procedures); and thirdly at national level through the supine behaviour of the Committee of Vice-Chancellors and Principals (recently renamed 'Universities UK'), for example, as well as through the participation (and career enhancement) offered for academics in the new bureaucracies.

I like to think of the Quality Assurance Agency (QAA) as one such bureaucracy engaged in surveillance of higher educational activities, including archaeology. By surveillance I here take the definitions offered by Dandeker (1990: 37):

'(1) the collection and storage of information (presumed to be useful) about people or objects; (2) the supervision of the activities of the people or objects through the issuing of instructions... (3) the application of information gathering activities to the business of monitoring the behaviour of those under supervision, and, in the case of subject persons [or institutions], their compliance with instructions.'

Compliance is achieved through various sanctions and mechanisms, of which the most efficient is to get the subject population to administer their own compliance with the imposed rules, and eventually, the bureaucrat hopes, to internalize not only the rules but also the goals and values themselves.

We should note that these processes have been going on for a long time; for example certain forms or parts of higher education have always been considered as more friendly to ideas of education largely perceived as quantifiable, cumulative knowledge and technical competence (for example HNDs, polytechnics, sandwich courses or those which form part of professional requirements such as law and architecture). It was not until the 1960's in the UK that higher education funding shifted from the Treasury (giving block allocations which assumed great institutional autonomy) to the Department of Education and Science, which can be taken as one point at which *strategic* government intervention markedly increased, through the adoption of Reports such as those of Robbins (1963) or Dearing (1997), and the subsequent setting up of quangos. Such intervention has however recently become more and more apparent and is no longer at arms-length under the guise of maintaining independence. For example, in one recent so-called 'consultative circular' on the introduction of foundation degrees, higher education institutions were specifically instructed not to question the merits (or otherwise) of such degrees and their relationship to other courses: instead institutions were told that these WILL go ahead, and comment was only invited on the details. The recent assumption of quasi-total control through mechanisms of surveillance can also be seen in Quality Assurance Agency shifts: 'guidelines' have recently turned into more than 150 regulations governing the measurement of quality; members of that bureaucracy recently spent much effort justifying why excellent teaching will now be known as 'highly commendable'. The Institute of Learning and Teaching aims at quasi-compulsory membership for academics and seems to be more about control than practical assistance or a forum for genuine debate on how to improve teaching. These are clear signs of a typical systemic attribute of institutions including bureaucracies; the proliferation of rules and paperwork which has everything to do with self-justification, self-interest and means of control of the subject population (by getting them to spend time and effort learning to conform with arbitrary decisions and operationalizing methods to do so), but which is often meaningless in terms of the supposed goals of the organization (to monitor and improve the quality and provision of the educational experience). Many academics and others would argue that by far the quickest way to improve the 'education' part of higher education would be to fund it properly, so that staff-student ratios can be dramatically lowered, access to resources (and to higher education in the first place) improved, and staff given time to develop and employ a variety of teaching methods. Yet this most basic of proposals is ruled out of court as a response by these quangos, which often act as a way of deflecting blame from State policies onto the workers, whether in academia, in schools, the health service or in social work. Just as Eric Wolf (1999: 131) notes in the United States:

> 'Many governments are reducing their financial assistance for research and teaching in universities and at the same time establishing cost accounting standards under the guise of "accountability". Institutions of higher education are similarly employing new bureaucratic standards of productivity, which generally means cuts in teaching staff and student support.'

The fact that these changes are thus occurring not just in the UK but also in many other places in Europe (certainly Germany and Italy, to my knowledge), as well as the US, suggest that it is not sufficient to blame 'the government', whether nominally of the Left or Right, but rather that analysis and debate must take place within a much broader context. However, this doesn't help answer the immediate tactical problems. How is one to respond? Are all the procedures and edicts deriving from the state and its quangos therefore always to be resisted?

Few if any would ascribe to a view which claims that earlier practices were always better; that universities as communities and institutions have nothing to learn themselves; and that there should be no change in the conditions, means or ends of higher education. Such a view

would be not only profoundly conservative and arrogant, but also deeply undemocratic. We all recognize that higher education is part of society and that the metaphor of an ivory tower was always partial at best. We might also note that an increasing number of people participate in higher education (and I don't think many would argue against that trend *per se*); and that higher education is in many ways more integrated in broader society than it has been in the past, whatever the persistent problems of differential access and participation by various groups. One can argue that as a consequence higher education should be aware of and responsive to broader social and political constituencies than those of academics and other university staff, though whether that will involve compliance, compromise or resistance should be debated on a case-by-case basis.

One example (discussed elsewhere in this volume) of different perceptions of bureaucratically-driven initiatives and what the nature of our response should be, is the recent production of a 'benchmark' document for archaeology for the QAA. The willing co-operation of archaeologists in the benchmarking exercise has been suggested to be good tactics as a way of safeguarding archaeology (including its special funding base) against future attack, by laying down minimum standards and contents. Others have argued that simply the act of collaboration implies acceptance of the whole notion of the audit economy approach (Shore and Wright 1999) and of control over disciplinary boundaries, and is part of the process of the commodification of archaeological knowledge. In this view benchmarking will in fact act (as the QAA have now declared) as a way of policing and standardizing course content, since compliance with the benchmarking statement will be taken into account in forthcoming quality audits. To my knowledge, various departments have already or are now in the process of restructuring courses in order to comply with the benchmarking statement. Further, the QAA has recently issued guidelines on how to specify and describe 'learning outcomes' for every 'learning experience' for each of the courses they offer (Baty 2000). It is a short step from there to policing the compliance of each module within such a framework. In other words, one could equally propose that, for some reason, archaeologists have willingly set up a framework which could be used for the homogenization or intellectual closure of the discipline, especially through denying access to the academic, bureaucratic and funding playing-fields for new, small and innovative sections or departments. Whatever one's views of the tactical and practical merits of benchmarking - and there are many merits to periodic review and reconceptualization - it is clear that such debates should ideally have occurred within the discipline, higher education and beyond, *before* rushing to comply with the latest edict which was known to emanate from within a system of control and quantification. Such lemming-like behaviour - also seen in responses of the sector as a whole to the Teaching Quality Assessment (TQA) exercises - does not sit easily with notions of critical self-reflection and considered judgements which academics like to deploy elsewhere when defending ideas of academic freedom, for example. At the time of writing, scores of academic archaeologists in England are spending large amounts of time working out not so much how to maintain and improve teaching quality, but rather how to provide paperwork to demonstrate compliance with the TQA rules. Diversity of practice and debate over form and content has been replaced by a rush to conformity. What are the implications for the theoretical aspirations of the discipline?

Theory and archaeology

It was in the 1960's that, through New Archaeology, theory (as in many other disciplines) became the academic battleground. It was not techniques, or fieldwork methods, or even the core activities of archaeologists - though all these issues might become involved - but theoretical allegiance which was at the heart of the debates about archaeology, and usually in the form of competing epistemic claims. In other words, for a long while the debates were really about how to 'do' archaeology in the sense of moving from material remains to explanation and syntheses. Not until the mid-1980s did theory in the sense in which we generally think of it today take off. Despite earlier examples of this new politicized awareness (e.g. Gero 1983; Trigger 1984) I would argue that for many it was Critical Theory, especially as mediated through Shanks and Tilley (1987a, b) which was crucial here, by opening up spaces for tackling theory within archaeology courses and the discipline more widely in terms of cultural politics, through political, social and cultural theories such as feminism, and linguistic philosophy, for example. Now clearly archaeology had been good at borrowing (or open to) theory (and philosophy) from elsewhere before that time, whether Marxism, systems theory, social evolution or whatever. The difference was, I think, that the emphasis shifted from questions such as 'what theory might be relevant to this archaeological question?' to 'what kind of theories are out there and how might they impinge on archaeology?' The factors for this shift are varied and interlinked: they include the continued expansion of (and confidence in) the discipline in terms of numbers of practitioners, and genuine intellectual excitement and exploration, coupled with a marked valorization of 'newness' (or adherence to intellectual fashions in other disciplines) as a prime means of acquiring cultural capital, for example. Importantly, this shift happened at a time when it was increasingly accepted that archaeology was as much about the present as the past. This meant that contemporary social, political and cultural theories, philosophies and intellectual trends were potentially just as relevant to the discipline as those specifically about the past or about the acts of 'retrieving' the past. Whole new fields of legitimate interest opened up to archaeologists, from heritage and museum studies to disciplinary, inter-disciplinary and extra-disciplinary politics (e.g. discourse analysis, feminism, colonialism) and new-style histories and sociologies of archaeologies, for example. Coupled with broader changes such as the linguistic or

interpretative turn across the humanities, it meant that theory broadly construed became perceived not just as an aid to archaeological questions but (at best) a way of reflexively interrogating the nature and expanding the limits of 'archaeology' understood as a discipline. Gradually, during the 1980's for some UK university departments, and during the 1990's for others, theory understood in this sense became a core component of undergraduate degrees.

What this understanding of theory (not just for archaeology, but for other disciplines too) implies, is that the process of engaging with - not just 'learning' - theory will always exceed the question asked and the disciplinary context in which it is posed. Theoretical issues will inevitably overlap with other discourses and other practices; theory is necessarily inter- or cross-disciplinary; it will always demand that we think about why we are posing *this* question in *this* way: it will spill over into the philosophy of politics, of society and education, into ethics, and it will question the frameworks and practices within which questions - and courses, and curricula - are set. Theory is - or should be - a necessarily open-ended and on-going debate, both within the discipline and within ourselves as individuals. It is far from clear that this aspect of theory is best measured by assessed outcomes and credits passed.

I am generally positive about the influence and importance of such theory in archaeological courses and for archaeology as a whole over the last decade or so. But conditions change, and contexts change meanings. It doesn't make so much sense to talk about 'theoretical archaeologists' any more – we are all more aware of and probably more explicit about the kinds of issues I have characterised by theory; the era of specialists in Theory with a capital T has probably passed. Secondly, the pedagogical separation of theory from practice, dealing with theory largely as a series of texts and lectures is perhaps not the best way forward; at least that is what we feel here at Lampeter. Although we do still retain a short theory course, called Thinking Through Archaeology, it is seen rather as a way of introducing students to some ways of thinking about their previous (and potential) archaeological practice in the form of a critical and reflexive set of experiences. In our 'field practice' course these range from ethnographic interviews for the purposes of oral history recording (see Fewster, this volume), SMR recording using the local formats and databases, to more traditional fieldwork and site visits. In other words, we believe that it is now more educationally productive for students to engage with and develop their own theoretical preoccupations through thoughtful practice and reflection upon that practice, rather than merely present them with 'theory' in the lecture theatre. Indeed, whether at Catal Huyuk or in the pages of *Assemblage*, this is the way that many 'theoretical' issues in archaeology are best being explored at the moment (e.g. Chadwick 1999; Cumberpatch & Blinkhorn forthcoming; Faulkner 2000; Fewster forthcoming; Hodder 1999; Lucas 2000) - by thoughtful and sophisticated reflection rooted very much in practice (cf. the turn towards 'grounded theory' in e.g. feminist geographies and sociologies). However, this attitude runs counter to many of the trends in higher education which I described at the beginning of this paper, in which the call is for demonstrable learned units - skills, outcomes, credits, add-ons - which, especially under a fully-modular system, can be 'banked' once acquired, and never need be referred to or drawn upon again.

Theory and academic freedom

I would argue that the sense in which I am using 'theory' is closely related to the concept of academic freedom. Basically academic freedom is to be understood as the *relative* and contextual autonomy, at individual - students as well as academics - and institutional level from 'ideological and managerial pressures' and which enables the exploration, through learning, teaching and researching of unfashionable, unpopular or 'inconvenient' topics among others (cf. Rendel 1988). That is, the concept involves both freedom *from* unjustified interference and a commitment *to* a particular kind of freedom to explore issues within a particular context broadly understood as unbounded and dialogical. It does not mean (bearing in mind the often misunderstood claims about epistemic relativism) completely untrammelled 'anything goes' research or pedagogy. Rather, the precise limits of the boundaries will both change depending on context, and will and should be one of the issues for debate. Thus the promulgation, rather than exploration, of racism may be considered a case for justified interference because it is inimical to the wider idea of freedom; the use of animals for laboratory experiments may be perceived as unethical because it impinges on the freedom of other beings. In positive terms, such academic freedom is seen as allowing the ability to question and explore without the *immediate* pressures often found within the commercial or governmental sphere, for example. More broadly, and beyond its role as a site of the extension of technical and other knowledge,

> 'By examining seriously and disinterestedly the concepts available to society, the university opens and sustains a gap between the civil society and those concepts being examined. The searching examination of beliefs and ideas ... produces a conceptual space between those ideas as ordinarily grasped and understood in that inquiry. This inquisitorial activity is essentially a critical inquiry. The university shows the wider society that its understandings are limited and could be other than they are.' (Barnett 1994: 50).

The benefits, to individuals and to society as a whole, are the enrichment of knowledge and understanding, both practical and theoretical, physical and philosophical; the maintenance of pluralism which enables broader and more nuanced dialogue; and the imagining and proposal of other possibilities. Universities are thus not autonomous and detached, but rather are fertile sources of possibilities for different, as well as critique of existing, practices within society. In this sense the concept of academic freedom overlaps very much with ideas about intellectuals which have been explored elsewhere (for archaeology see e.g. Hamilakis 1999; Pluciennik in press). Indeed, I would argue that any long-term aim of individual and social emancipation should be bound up with the idea of extending 'academic' freedom beyond the academy.

Theory and higher education

I do not believe that many people engaged in academia - often underpaid, overworked and with little job security, just like their counterparts in other sectors - would ascribe to the ivory tower view of higher education, in which universities are largely repositories of specialist knowledge and restful places for contemplation (and other forms of research), protected in part because of their very isolation from society and its attendant pressures and concerns. Firstly, for archaeology - and many other disciplines - there are all sorts of relationships which link the academic archaeological community to other parts of society. Just in our role as archaeologists these may include research interests, consultancies, commercial links, and common interests with and reliance on the work of others in the public and private sectors, for example - museums, local communities. But perhaps the major influence academics have is as part of the (still mainly residential and full-time) university experience of our students: their archaeological and educational experiences will form part of each student who passes through the departments and institutions, become part of their life biography, and help shape their attitudes towards and understandings of archaeology, intellectual and academic endeavour, other people and themselves. Of course, part of that experience will be the acquisition of (or introduction to) particular archaeological and non-archaeological competences, from techniques, facts and skills to initiation into the necessary 'jargon'. However, one may cast the role of higher education in a much more pro-active role, couched rather pompously perhaps as learning for life, rather than lifelong learning. That academic freedom, societal politics, theory and higher education are all bound up together is also suggested by Giroux in his discussion of Stuart Hall's cultural politics: he argues that there can be a 'public pedagogy in which learning becomes indispensable to the very process of social change, and social change becomes the precondition for a politics that moves in the direction of a less hierarchical, more radical democratic social order.' (Giroux 2000: 356).

Whether or not we accept the formation of a 'more radical democratic social order' as the aim, I believe that part of the role of those of us within higher education should be to encourage the acquisition and distribution of, and access to knowledge, understanding and learning more broadly, at least in order to allow more knowledgeable dialogues and debates across a whole variety of spheres. Aronowitz (1990: 34), paraphrasing Habermas, warns that:

'The real criterion of a dynamic society is whether new, noninstrumental knowledge is genuinely valued not only as art, but as the basis for social decisions. Where critical intelligence is shunted to the margins, even in democratic societies, the social formation is destined for decline'

Although we may not wish to cast ourselves as guardians against such social decline, we might well wish to lay claim to both the exercise and promulgation of 'critical intelligence'. Higher education is certainly about enablement, but not only in the narrow sense of job opportunities, earnings potential and technical skills, but also in terms of allowing meaningful participation in disciplinary and wider societal debates about goals and means. However, the thrust of many recent changes and initiatives - the spread of instrumental reason - militates against this understanding of higher education. These include research funding imperatives which privilege, for example, the transfer of knowledge into computer databases, and often over-emphasise originality understood as (potentially commercially-exploitable) innovative *techniques* or other forms of wealth creation. This is coupled with the rise of the 'audit culture' in higher education, with prescriptive formulas such as 'benchmarking' for what comprises archaeology, and with the Government's 'building block' and credit transfer approach to education, which squeezes all qualifications and learning experiences (from primary school to doctorates) into the same supposedly-quantifiable format. We can note, for example, the proposed introduction of 'foundation degrees' which are basically vocational and may be wholly accredited work-experience, and which see the 'higher educational' part of a degree as simply a matter of a one-year add-on; and the desire from those seeing archaeology as a 'profession' to concentrate on quantifiable skills and thus influence the content of degrees at allegedly autonomous universities. All these trends are potential threats to theoretically-informed archaeologies (the diversity of which should be emphasized), and can easily act as forces for conservatism. Higher education should be about enhancing capabilities for debate and decision-making; not just over narrow competences or disciplinary issues, but in terms of what theoreticians might call meta-critique. However this requires the ability to think philosophically, theoretically and critically within and about a variety of intellectual frameworks and the wider constitution of archaeology in the modern world. This suggests that we should be encouraging permeability and flux, rather than attempting to police disciplinary boundaries along the lines suggested by benchmarking and the focus on practical skills. Archaeology has been a dynamic and generally optimistic discipline over the past few decades, clearly helped by buoyant public interest and student numbers. Whatever the details of the theoretical arguments within the discipline, the willingness to look outside the discipline for inspiration, and the relationship between archaeology as a set of both academic and public, and humanities-inspired and scientific practices has helped to maintain a critical and reflexive approach which has continually remade the discipline. To adopt skills-centred learning as the norm and prescribe highly-specified 'learning outcomes' is not ultimately conducive to responsive archaeologies in a fast-changing world. It is in this context that the engagement with theory - whether as 'abstract frameworks' or via 'thoughtful practice' - can and should be the start or enhancement of this process of critical self-reflection, both for academics and students. 'Theory' is a necessary part of desirable academic freedom for both groups. It is a process of internal and external dialogue; and at best it can - and should be - a (democratically) subversive activity.

Acknowledgements

My thanks to Kathy Fewster and Sarah Tarlow for discussion and comments, and to Yannis Hamilakis and Paul Rainbird for providing a much-needed forum for airing these issues.

References

Aronowitz, S. 1990. On intellectuals. In *Intellectuals: Aesthetics, Politics, Academics* (ed. B. Robbins). Minneapolis: University of Minnesota Press, pp. 3-56.

Barnett, R. 1994. *The Limits of Competence: Knowledge, Higher Education and Society*. Buckingham: Society for Research into Higher Education/Open University Press.

Baty, P. 2000. Degree checklist pleases students. *Times Higher Education Supplement* 1446 (July 28th), p. 3.

Blinkhorn, P. and Cumberpatch, C. 1999. Archaeology in England 1999. *World Archaeological Bulletin*, 9: 45-55.

Chadwick, A. 1998. Archaeology at the edge of chaos: further towards reflexive excavation methodologies. *Assemblage*, 3: http://www.shef.ac.uk/~assem/3/3chad.htm

Cumberpatch, C. and Blinkhorn, P. in press. Clients, contractors, curators and archaeology: who owns the past? In *The Responsibilities of Archaeologists* (ed. M. Pluciennik). Oxford: British Archaeological Reports.

Dandeker, C. 1990. *Surveillance, Power and Modernity*. Cambridge: Polity Press.

Dearing, R. 1997. *Higher Education in the Learning Society: Report of the National Committee of Inquiry into Higher Education*. London: HMSO.

Gero, J., Lacy, D. and Blakey, M. (eds.) 1983. *The Socio-politics of Archaeology (Department of Anthropology Research Report 23)*. Amherst, MA: Department of Anthropology, University of Massachusetts.

Giroux, H. 2000. Public pedagogy as cultural politics: Stuart Hall and the 'crisis' of culture. *Cultural Studies*, 14: 341-60.

Faulkner, N. 2000. Archaeology from below. *Public Archaeology*, 1: 21-33.

Fewster, K. in press. The responsibilities of ethnoarchaeologists. In *The Responsibilities of Archaeologists* (ed. M. Pluciennik). Oxford: British Archaeological Reports.

Hamilakis, Y. 1999. La trahison des archéologues? Archaeological practice as intellectual activity in postmodernity. *Journal of Mediterranean Archaeology*, 12: 60-79.

Hodder, I. 1999. *The Archaeological Process*. Oxford: Blackwell.

Lucas, G. 2000. *Critical Approaches to Fieldwork: Contemporary and Historical Archaeological Practice*. London: Routledge.

Pluciennik, M. in press. Archaeology, advocacy and intellectualism. In *The Responsibilities of Archaeologists* (ed. M. Pluciennik). Oxford: British Archaeological Reports.

Rendel, M. 1988. Human rights and academic freedom. In *Academic Freedom and Responsibility* (ed. M. Tight). Buckingham: Society for Research into Higher Education/Open University Press, pp. 74-87.

Robbins, 1963. *Higher Education: Report of the Committee appointed by the Prime Minister under the Chairmanship of Lord Robbins*. London: HMSO.

Shanks, M. and Tilley, C. 1987a. *Social Theory and Archaeology*. Cambridge: Polity Press.

Shanks, M. and Tilley, C. 1987b. *Re-Constructing Archaeology: Theory and Practice*. Cambridge: Cambridge University Press.

Shore, C. and Wright, S. 1999. Audit culture and anthropology: neo-liberalism in British Higher Education. *Journal of the Royal Anthropological Institute (N.S.)*, 5: 557-75.

Tight, M. (ed.) 1988. *Academic Freedom and Responsibility*. Buckingham: Society for Research into Higher Education/Open University Press.

Trigger, B. 1984. Alternative archaeologies: nationalist, colonialist, imperialist. *Man (N.S.)*, 19: 355-70.

Wolf, E. 1999. Anthropology among the powers. *Social Anthropology*, 7: 121-34.

Teaching archaeology, now and in the future: the role of the LTSN Subject Centre

Annie Grant and Michael Reynier

Introduction

This paper provides a brief introduction to the background, roles and remits of the newly established Learning and Teaching Support Network (LTSN) Subject Centre for History, Classics and Archaeology. The second section presents the results of a survey designed to gain an overview of current teaching practices in archaeology and to establish the needs of teaching staff.

The Learning and Teaching Support Network

The Learning and Teaching Support Network (LTSN) was established in January 2000. It is financed jointly by the funding councils for England, Scotland and Wales, and comprises 24 individual Subject Centres around the UK that are intended to act as a focus for teaching and learning, to disseminate good practice, and to encourage networks of practitioners. The Generic Learning and Teaching Centre, which is the centre of the hub of discipline-specific centres, is based in York, sharing premises with the Institute of Learning and Teaching.

Over the last decade or so, there has been a number of centrally-funded, mainly short-term initiatives, that have been designed to promote and enhance teaching at tertiary level and each has had its particular focus and agenda. For example, in the early 1990s Enterprise in Higher Education, which was funded by the DfEE (then the DTI and later the DEE), was designed to enhance students' employability skills and to create partnerships between higher education institutions and industry (DTI 1990). The Teaching and Learning Technology Programme funded in the mid-1990s (HEFCE et al. 1994) was established with a remit to promote the use of technology in teaching, a mission that was in part based on an assumption that computer-aided learning would provide a means to address the teaching of larger numbers of students on a declining unit of resource. Neither of these two programmes had a discipline-specific focus and while the Enterprise in Higher Education programme had an institutional focus and the TLTP project was cross institutional but included some projects that catered to specific disciplines, it was not until the Computers in Teaching Initiative, established in 1999, that discipline-specific centres were established across the UK, in this case to promote the use of computers in higher education teaching (CTI 1999). The LTSN network has followed the model of the CTI centres in recognising the particular needs of different disciplines, but it has a much broader scope, and sees the use of communication and information technology as part of a broader spectrum of approaches to effective learning and teaching. The wide range of disciplines taught across the higher education

sector has been grouped to provide the 24 LTSN Subject Centres, the groupings being determined by the funding bodies. Archaeology shares its Subject Centre, LTSN 18, with history and classics. Although this was not specified by the funding bodies it sees its remit as encompassing the needs of a number of other closely related disciplines, including heritage and museum studies, that are not specifically included in other groupings.

The Subject Centre for History, Classics and Archaeology (HCA) has a distributed structure. The director, Dr Donald Spaeth, the IT co-ordinator and the administrative staff are based at the University of Glasgow, which is the 'home' site, while the other staff are based at Nottingham and Bath Spa Universities (History) and the Open University (Classics). The archaeology strand is based at the University of Leicester and is staffed by the authors of this paper. Each of the three principle disciplines has an Advisory Panel of academics and representatives of relevant professional bodies. The panels meet twice a year and will play a crucial role in helping to ensure that the Centre meets the needs and expectations of the teaching staff and students that it has been established to support.

Exploring the territory: roles, remits and agendas

There will inevitably be suspicion amongst some academic staff about the 'hidden agenda' of any centrally funded initiative. Some have already voiced their opinion that the LTSN is merely one of a number of means currently being used by central government to take away individual responsibility from practitioners and institutions and impose a uniform curriculum:

> 'It is important that this initiative should avoid the temptation (and political pressure) to push the standardization of curricula and content...' (respondent to the survey discussed below).

Rightly or wrongly, such views have been fuelled by experiences of QAA review, the establishment of the Institute of Learning and Teaching, and by the recent Benchmarking exercise (see Johnson, this volume).

It is important to state here that the writers of this paper do not share this view, but denying the existence of any kind of agenda would be disingenuous. There is no doubt that the LTSN has been funded to raise the profile of teaching in a sector in which it has often played Cinderella to research. The strength of the LTSN model is that it is, to a very large extent, owned by and run by the sector itself and the vast majority of those that work in the 24 Centres are practicing academics from the relevant disciplines.

We shall be very concerned to preserve and develop the strengths and uniqueness of the subject and also to respect local needs and individual cultures. Academic staff teach and students learn not only within the context of their discipline but also in the context of their institutions, and what may be effective in one department may be less so in another.

Both the writers teach archaeology at higher education level and we come to the project with our own experiences of teaching and our own strengths and weaknesses. We recognize that in many ways teaching is a highly personal occupation and that there is no clear right and wrong way of being an effective teacher. We do, however, suspect that our experiences are not unique to ourselves but will find resonance across the discipline. Our view of our own role in the Subject Centre is, though, not that of experts but of facilitators, disseminators, and as a resource for others. The Centre will seek to support staff in developing their own teaching; it certainly will not seek to prescribe practice.

It will be important to respond to the needs of staff working at all levels, from professors to recently appointed lecturers. But these latter, together with part-time lecturers and teaching assistants, may have priority in the provision of resources and advice that meet their particular teaching needs. It will also be important to create and maintain effective links with other bodies and organisations. These include bodies such as the Archaeology Data Service, which is also involved in a number of important projects to support teaching through access to primary data, and professional bodies that include the Council for British Archaeology, English Heritage, the Institute of Field Archaeologists and the Museums Association.

SCUPHA, which through heads of departments represents the majority of departments teaching archaeology degrees in the UK, has *ex officio* membership of the Advisory Panel, and played a major role in the establishment of the Centre in its current format.

Working in close collaboration with colleagues who are historians and classicists will broaden our perspectives and provide additional insights and access to resources. The teaching of archaeology, however, presents a number of unique challenges that can best be addressed by archaeologists. These include the teaching of fieldwork, laboratory based skills and the study of the material remains of human societies.

Defining needs and priorities: the Needs Analysis

What is certain is with the level of staffing and funding available to us we will not be able to do everything that we and the rest of the academic community might wish us to do at the same time. Our first step has been to learn more about how archaeology (and its related disciplines) is being taught in HEIs across the UK now and to try to understand how best the Centre can support staff engaged in this teaching in the future. To this end the Subject Centre

produced a questionnaire designed to gain an overview of current teaching practice and needs. The questionnaire was sent out during the summer of 2000 to 52 higher education institutions offering archaeology, heritage management or museum studies programmes, together with a covering letter requesting that it be distributed to all teaching staff. A total of 98 completed forms have been returned to date. This represents approximately 20 per cent of those staff currently teaching archaeology, conservatively estimated at c. 500.

The first three questions (2, 3 and 4) looked at how archaeology was currently being taught in the UK. These three questions asked about teaching techniques, assessment and personal innovations.

Teaching and learning methods

It comes as no surprise to see that most teaching of archaeology in UK Higher Education is based around lectures and seminars/tutorials (Fig. 1, white bars). Similarly fieldwork comprised some element of the teaching of most respondents. Less well anticipated was the degree to which other methods of teaching are employed. Group work, practical workshops and student presentations were all teaching formats used by over 60 per cent of the respondents, and over 40 per cent are using a case study approach. The results show that there is a considerable diversity in the range of teaching methods currently being used, despite the increases in administrative burdens and the declining staff:student ratios that have characterised the higher education environment in recent years.

Respondents were also asked to indicate which areas of their teaching they would like to enhance. Just over half the respondents want to develop computer-based learning (CBL) but there was somewhat less interest in the development of other teaching methods. Nonetheless, around a third of the respondents were interested in further developing the more traditional teaching methods of lectures, seminars and tutorials (see Fig. 1, black bars). There is a concern that the interest in the development of CBL may be based on the misleading view that CBL is an easy means of teaching increasing numbers of students. However, it no doubt also reflects an interest in using the rapidly expanding resources of the internet to enhance student learning.

Assessment methods

Turning to modes of assessment – how students' understanding is tested and graded – a similar picture emerges (Fig. 2, white bars). Once the traditional triumvirate of essay, examination and dissertation is set aside there is considerable diversity in the assessment methods being used by the respondents. Not surprisingly, these include laboratory-based projects and fieldwork reports. However, in addition, seminar reports, library-based projects, group work and skills-based exercises are

What teaching methods do you use?

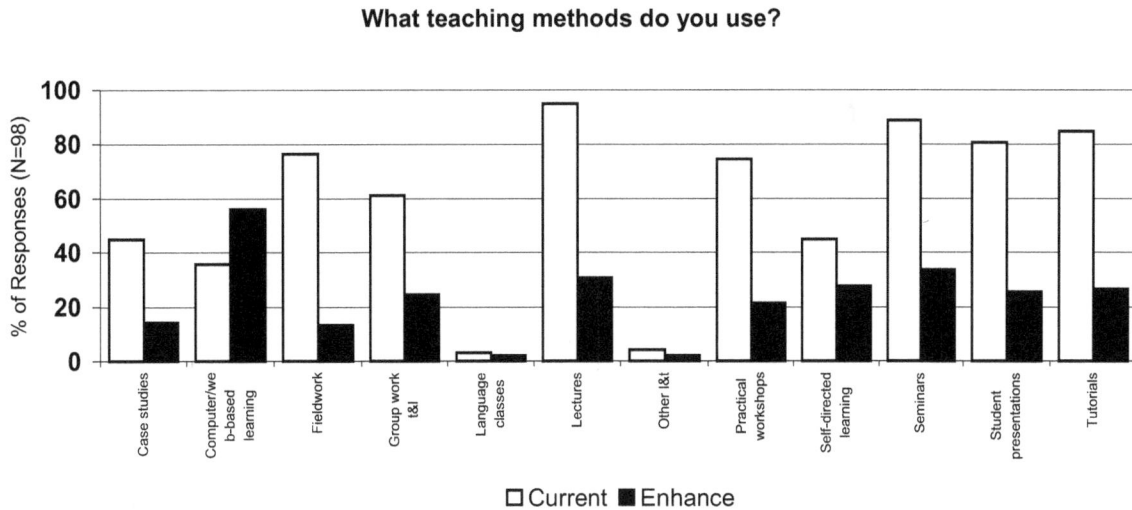

Figure 1. Percentage bar chart showing responses to the questions: a) which teaching methods do you currently use (white bars); and b) which teaching methods would you like to enhance (black bars). (Source LTSN HCA Survey 2000).

What assessment methods do you use?

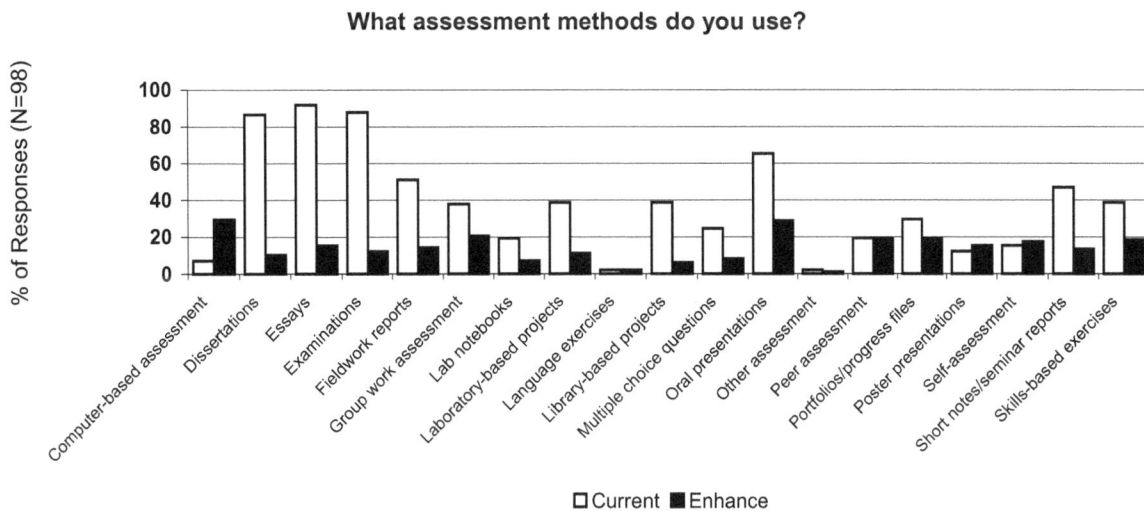

Figure 2. Percentage bar chart showing responses to the questions: a) which assessment methods do you currently used (white bars); and b) which assessment methods do you wish to enhance (black bars). (Source LTSN HCA Survey 2000).

also used by a significant proportion of the teaching staff who completed the questionnaire. Less traditional - and in the view of some, 'trendy' - assessment methods, including peer assessment and progress files, are also being used by approximately 20 per cent or more of respondents. The least commonly used methods of those listed on the survey form were computer based assessment, self-assessment and poster presentations, although all these methods are being used by at least some of the respondents.

Again the impression is that lecturers are using an array of innovative and skills-based modes of assessment alongside more traditional methods. It may be that this is a response to modularization and the concomitant increase in small, single module topics that were often covered but not usually assessed under the old 'course' system. Not surprisingly it is these non-traditional assessment methods that most respondents want to develop, and among these

computer-based assessment and oral presentations are ranked highly, along with peer assessment, progress files and group work assessment (Fig. 2, black bars).

Innovative teaching

Table 1 lists the responses to question four, which asked respondents to outline any innovative teaching practices they currently employ. This question was designed to elicit information about those teaching practices that did not fall into any of the predefined categories specified in earlier questions. A glance through the table gives some idea of the breadth of teaching methods that are being used in the seminar room and lecture hall across the UK. Clearly a priority for Subject Centre staff is to obtain more detailed information about successful teaching methods that have wide applicability and to disseminate this information to lecturing staff.

Examples of Current Good Practice	HEI
'Hands on' experience with artefacts	Southampton
Critical assessment of published works	Bradford
Cumulatively assessed 'spot quizzes'	Bradford
Role Play	Bristol
Agenda-less seminars	Cambridge
Short answer examination questions	Cardiff
Widening access programme	Exeter
Self evaluation	King Alfred's
Buzz Groups	Nottingham
Research Skills	Queen's, Belfast
Key Skills	Sheffield
Slide-tape lectures	Southampton
Film/video	Lampeter
WWW	Lampeter, Cambridge
Seminar-based Modules	Liverpool, Glasgow

Table 1. Examples of good practice reported by HEIs in the LTSN Subject Centre questionnaire.

The role of the Subject Centre

The second part of the survey asked questions relating to the role of the Subject Centre in supporting and promoting teaching and learning in archaeology (questions 5, 6, 7 and 8). Respondents identified two priorities above all others: locating high quality material on the Internet for use in teaching and supporting innovative teaching approaches (Fig. 3). The interest in Internet resources has been highlighted in discussion of responses to earlier questions. As for other roles the Subject Centre might take on, respondents included: serving as a source of information and advice on teaching and learning; developing a network of university archaeology lecturers; and identifying sources of funding to support new teaching initiatives. The request for information on funding sources is interesting in that it suggests that teachers of archaeology are not short of innovative ideas but lack the time and money to develop and implement them.

Teaching support

To draw out the precise nature of support required by teachers of archaeology twelve key areas of teaching and learning relevant to archaeology were listed and respondents asked to select those areas in which they particularly wanted support. Four topics were rated equally highly by all respondents (Fig. 4): using computers in teaching; developing students' transferable skills for employability; encouraging active learning; and

developing students' study skills. All the other areas listed were also seen as important by at least a third of the respondents, including large group teaching, assessment, feedback and course design.

A free format question was also provided (question 8, not shown) to encourage respondents to add topics of their own. Entries here included: copyright regulations for the web; meeting the needs of part-time/mature students; assessment of oral presentations and degree classification.

Delivery mechanisms for teaching support

Respondents were next asked how the support for teaching would best be delivered by rating nine modes of delivery on a scale of 'not useful', 'moderately useful'; and 'very useful'. Figure 5 presents the extreme values for each mode of delivery. Those most highly valued were reviews of resources, case studies, briefing papers and workshops. Very few respondents rated multiple choice question banks, seminars, e-mail discussion groups and bibliographies as useful. Teaching consultancy returned a mixed response with equal numbers in favour and against.

The role of teaching staff in the Subject Centre

A final question was aimed at eliciting to what extent, and in which areas, current teaching staff would be prepared to contribute to the activities of the Subject Centre. Although the response rate for this part of the questionnaire was low,

What should be the top priorities of the Subject Centre?

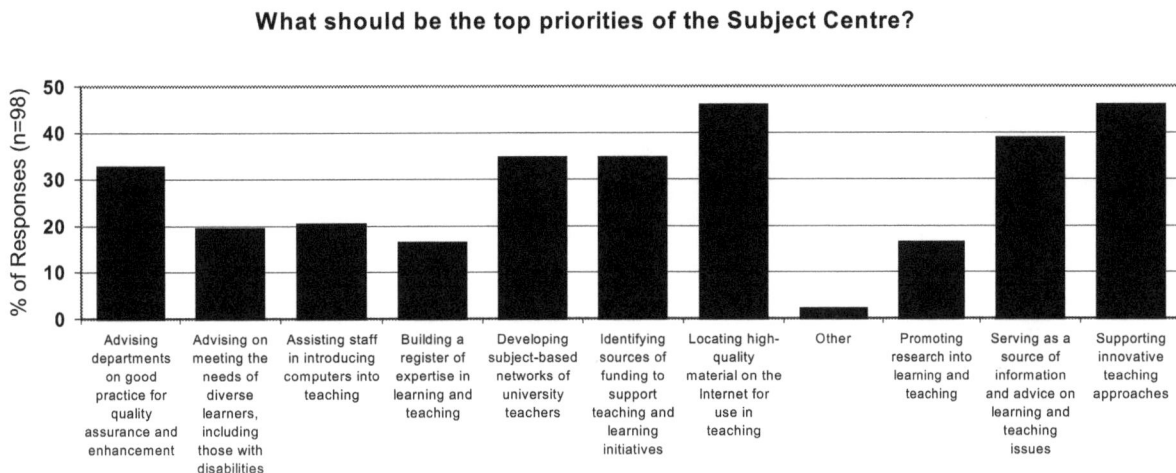

Figure 3. Percentage bar chart showing responses to the question: what should be the top priorities of the Subject Centre? (Source LTSN HCA Survey 2000).

Which topics would you like the Subject Centre to address in workshops, seminars & briefing papers?

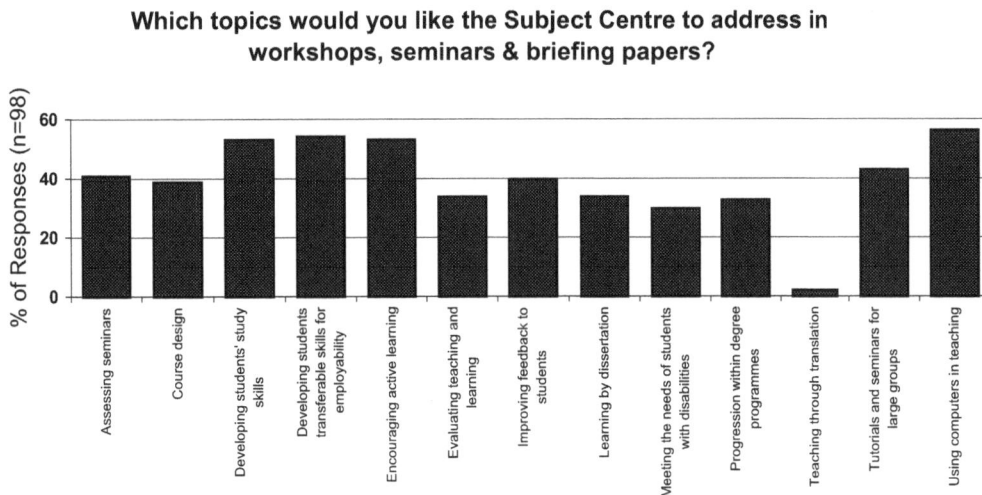

Figure 4. Percentage bar chart showing responses to the question: which topics would you like the Subject Centre to address in workshops, seminars and briefing papers? (Source LTSN HCA Survey 2000).

How useful would you find these services and activities?

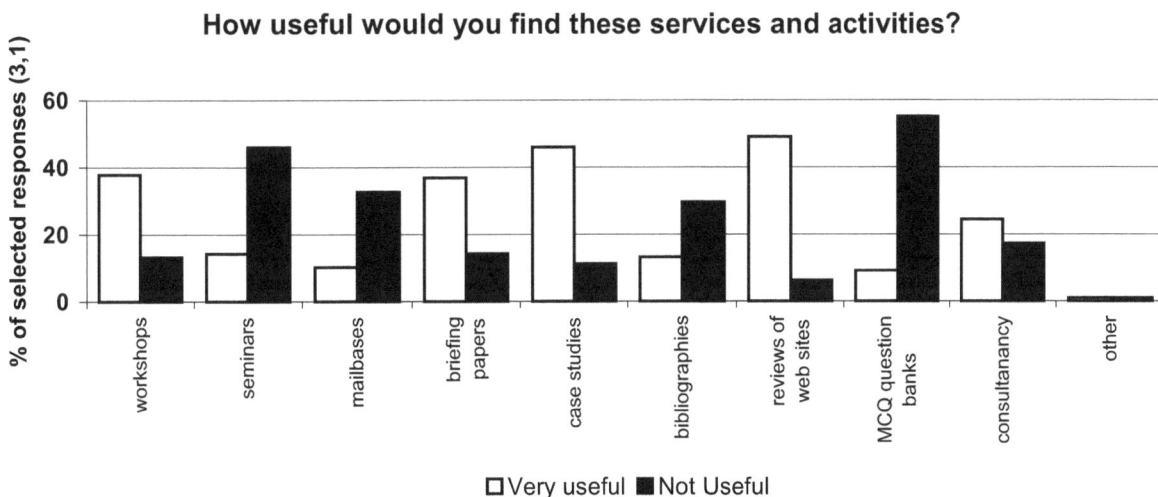

☐ Very useful ■ Not Useful

Figure 5. Percentage bar chart showing responses to the question: rate the use to you personally of the following services and activities which the Subject Centre might provide. (Source LTSN HCA Survey 2000).

those that offered help chose three main areas: forming a network of practitioners; reviewing teaching and learning materials; and reviewing web resources. Many of the respondents also offered to act as a representative for the Centre within their department. Few of the respondents offered to write up their own experiences of teaching or to devote time to research into teaching and learning issues.

Summary of the Needs Analysis

The response to the survey was fairly low, and it may not be entirely representative: it is likely that those who took the time to complete the questionnaire were those who are the most interested in teaching. However, analysis of the survey results has provided a flavour of archaeology teaching, and shown that a broad array of teaching and assessment methods are being used in archaeology departments across the UK. The survey has not only provided a good deal of useful additional information on how archaeology is taught now but has also shown where support may need to be focused in the future in order to provide services of value to practitioners. The main findings of the survey are that:

- a priority of the Subject Centre should be to locate and disseminate high quality teaching resources
- the teaching and learning topics of most interest are using computers in teaching, developing students' transferable skills for employability, encouraging active learning; and developing students' study skills
- the most favoured dissemination methods are product reviews, case studies, briefing papers and workshops.

Concluding remarks

The primary role of the Centre is the support of teaching to promote effective learning. But in doing this we hope to make a broader contribution. Raising the profile of teaching is part of the overall remit of the LTSN and it is particularly important for archaeology. This is not to say that archaeology lecturers are not committed to, or interested in, their teaching role; in fact the results of the survey discussed above indicate the opposite. However, in comparison to many other disciplines, there has been relatively little public debate about teaching. Table 2 includes the results of an analysis of the University of Leicester's Teaching and Learning Bibliography. This is an annotated database of references that has been compiled at Leicester since 1992. It does not claim to be comprehensive, but a wide range of journals and books published each year are searched and abstracted for inclusion on the database; there are currently over 5,000 references. The table gives the number of publications that make reference to the teaching of archaeology, geography and geology. The differences are striking, even if one takes into account differences in the sizes of the constituent bodies.

Archaeology	Geography	Geology
3	162	190

Table 2: The number of articles including references to archaeology, geography and geology published between 1992 and 1999 on the University of Leicester Teaching & Learning Database.

There are, however, already signs of change. The March 2000 issue of *Antiquity* included a special section on teaching with eleven articles on higher education topics. In September 2001 the CBA's annual Archaeology and Education conference will, for the first time, run sessions dedicated to higher education. And, of course, the present volume will also make a substantial contribution to the literature. The Subject Centre will aim to encourage more of this type of debate on a wider range of archaeology-related teaching and learning issues in the future.

Archaeology as a subject deserves a higher profile in the sector. Students are able to acquire skills, knowledge and understanding that cross what the Benchmarking Document defined as the tri-polar range of humanities, sciences and professional practices. Archaeology curricula encompass the intensely theoretical to the thoroughly practical and there are few other subjects that can offer their range and scope. The Subject Centre sees itself has having a role in promoting the value of archaeology as a discipline to other academics, and the value of an archaeology degree to potential employers and prospective and current students. In respect of the latter groups we need to be more articulate about the potential value of archaeology as both an intellectual training and as a preparation for a wide range of careers. Analysis of the 1997-99 First Destinations Statistics gathered by Careers Services through surveys of graduates six months after graduation (Table 3) indicates that the percentage of archaeology graduates who are still unemployed at this time is slightly higher than the national average for all subject areas (HESA 1998; 1999; 2000). The figures undoubtedly reflect the particular difficulty of gaining employment as an archaeologist, but may also indicate that graduates (and indeed employers) are not always fully aware of the range of skills that they have developed and of their applicability to a wide range of careers and contexts.

	Archaeology	All subjects
	%	%
Employment	63	73
Further Study	27	21
Seeking employment	10	7

Table 3. Summary of the first destination of archaeology graduates, 1997 – 1999 (Source: HESA 1998; 1999; 2000).

Developing students skills for employability was highlighted in the responses to the survey, and this is an area that will be addressed as a priority. The writers will be undertaking more detailed investigations of the destination paths of archaeology graduates and postgraduates and also researching and disseminating examples of effective practices in the integration of careers education within the curricula.

This paper has provided a brief overview of teaching and learning in archaeology as it is in 2000. We have identified many challenges but also a great wealth of interest and experience. The LTSN project has just begun; our mandate is clear, let us see what we can achieve by 2003.

The main dissemination point for the future work of the Subject Centre will be through its web site: http://hca.ltsn.ac.uk/.

References

C.T.I. 1999. *Learning and Teaching Innovation in UK Higher Education: Retrospective*, Computers in Teaching Initiative 1989-1999. Computers in Teaching Initiative.

D.T.I .1990. *Continuing Education and Training: The Enterprise and Education Initiative*. The Department of Trade and Industry and the Council for Industry and Higher Education. London: Department of Trade and Industry.

HEFCE et al. 1994. *Institutional Case Studies / Teaching and Learning Technology Programme*. Bristol: Higher Education Funding Council for England.

HESA. 1998. *First Destinations of Students Leaving Higher Education Institutions (1996/97)*. Cheltenham: Higher Education Statistics Agency.

HESA. 1999. *First Destinations of Students Leaving Higher Education Institutions (1997/98)*. Cheltenham: Higher Education Statistics Agency

HESA. 2000. *First Destinations of Students Leaving Higher Education Institutions (1998/99)*. Cheltenham: Higher Education Statistics Agency

1.4

Education for practice

Mike Bishop

Through its membership, the Institute of Field Archaeologists (IFA) represents over a third of the archaeological profession in Britain and speaks for the whole of the profession through its involvement with standards and ethics in archaeological practice that are widely followed by both members and non-members. Since its foundation in 1982, the IFA has been involved in the education of archaeologists, through its Career, Development and Training Committee which was the precursor to the Professional Training Committee, and has been a player and partner with educational organizations and others.

The organization and practice of British archaeology has changed dramatically over the last ten years. Archaeology is now big business, involving sums of money that are paltry by the standards of most other professions but very significant to us in our ghetto – and no less significant to those who have to pay them. Our world is inhabited by archaeological practitioners under a variety of guises – by curators, consultants, contractors – by professional archaeologists who are self-employed or who are employed, and work for a variety of organizations carrying out a variety of archaeological or archaeology related functions – by so called independent archaeologists and (if they are not the same) the traditional amateur archaeologists – and by academic archaeologists. Effectively archaeology has become an industry and its practitioners have become truly professional.

Like any other profession, standards are a major issue to archaeologists and those who buy their services. The keys to standards are knowledge and understanding. One of the reasons for the creation of the IFA was concern about the maintenance of standards, and consequently the Institute must have a regard over the education and training that equips archaeologists to meet the standards expected by the profession and required by its employers. There is widespread concern in the profession about these matters and the need for knowledge and training is a constant refrain to IFA from its members.

The problems come under two major headings. The first is deficiencies in under-pinning knowledge, experience and skills amongst practitioners in general, that leaves them poorly prepared to carry out existing and new tasks, or to adapt to change. The second is that new entrants into the profession so lack basic archaeological knowledge and skills that they are unable to perform satisfactorily in work and have an inadequate foundation to support the development of competencies through training and experience.

The reasons behind these problems are many and complex, and are rooted perhaps far more in three decades of changing social and political expectations in, and of, education in general and in the attitudes of archaeologists themselves, than in the specific defects of education in archaeology. But the result is a mismatch, in perception at least, between education and educators in archaeology and the world of archaeological practice outside of the academic environment. This may be seen in the widely perceived lack of involvement of mainstream academic staff in the practice of archaeology in Britain, which is illustrated by the low numbers of such staff amongst the members of IFA, or by the few numbers of staff or students who make use of Sites and Monuments Records. Conversely, it may be seen in the relative absence of external practitioners contributing to course development or teaching. It may also be seen in the following areas: lack of training excavations in Britain and the scant excavation experience with which many students graduate; lack of knowledge that new or recent graduates present, about the structure, organisation and resourcing of British archaeology, about the law in respect to archaeology, about fieldwork, about principal types of monument and artefacts even; the surprise at the irrelevance of their learning, and the bitterness of unfulfilled expectations in employment and job satisfaction, that is expressed by so many recent graduates – before they leave the profession, and after. Worst of all, it may be seen in the deficiencies in perception and knowledge, and the cynicism about the value of what they do, that can be found in some more experienced practitioners.

This is not to attribute all the ills of the profession to deficiencies in education. Educational institutions bear no major responsibility for the poor conditions of employment in archaeology, for the lack of career structure and poor remuneration, and they are only indirectly influential *perhaps*, in the enduring attitudes of archaeologists towards their profession (particularly the tendency of these to validate their achievements against academic standards and expectations), and in the lack of a satisfactory postgraduate training structure and provision.

Nevertheless, they have a responsibility in the nurture of new archaeologists and there is much truth in the saying that 'the child is the father of the man'. Lack of foundation knowledge and skills can be compensated for in later life only at great personal cost or not at all. Surely it is the role of higher education to ensure that its graduates are equipped with the basic knowledge to relate their learning to the workplace and life experience. In this context, the ancient debate about the distinction between academic and vocational education, about the difference between underpinning general education and training in skills specific to the work place, provides no shelter when it comes to a subject and profession such as archaeology. Wherever it is carried out, under whatever circumstances, archaeology is an academic subject. Its objectives are rooted in academic research and the achievement of these objectives should feed academic research. Archaeology is an activity and a profession that demands the deployment of knowledge and experience and the exercise of practical skills at the same time and in conjunction. Therefore, when it comes to knowledge and skills that are directly necessary to engage with the practice of archaeology there can be no division between academic and practical. This is not an issue, seemingly, in other professions such as medicine, dentistry, veterinary studies, law, or planning. Why should it be an issue in archaeology?

The argument that the majority of students are not interested in a career in archaeology and that courses can not cater for the minority that do want such a career, does not wash either, for two reasons. The first is that an understanding of how archaeology is practiced in the wider world, and may impinge on their working and private lives, is relevant to all engaged citizens of this country. The second is that it *should* be possible to cater for the minority, given the modular structures of modern courses and the choice in selecting modules given to modern students. Nevertheless, the Professional Training Committee of IFA recognizes, even if the majority of IFA members do not, that intended entrants to the profession are a minority, and that many in higher education do not see preparation for the work place as being part of the traditional liberal education that they provide. Therefore, its role ought to be in promoting the development of knowledge and skills within and across the profession, post-graduation.

The IFA vision of this was published in *The Archaeologist* after the 1999 Annual Conference, and is available on the Institute's website (www.archaeologists.net). In that vision, four problems affecting training are identified:

- An underdeveloped professional career structure.
- A lack of formal practical training.
- Inadequate documentation of the skills required to practice (archaeology) in a given role.
- Insufficient value placed on training, and insufficient resources afforded to it.

These are systemic problems to which there are no simple and easy answers. The IFA sees the solutions as lying in the median term and coming from an evolutionary process in which it and others develop approaches and structures in professional training that will serve the needs of the profession, its clients, the discipline of archaeology and the public. Specifically, the Institute wishes all archaeologists to be able to:

- Practice with the skills, knowledge and experience appropriate for the roles and levels of responsibility they hold or aspire to.
- Demonstrate a record of skills, knowledge and experience.
- Obtain appropriate recognition for their skills knowledge and experience in terms of both employment and grade within the professional body.

So, what action towards this vision has there been? In the 18 months since it was articulated, the IFA:

- Has sought, through publication and conference sessions, to promote discussion and debate about education and training.
- Has created a Higher Education Sub-Committee of its Professional Training Committee, to focus on the relationship between higher education and the needs of the profession.
- Has worked, and is working, upon the development of initiatives in partnership with other national archaeological bodies within and through the Archaeological Training Forum.
- Has continued centrally to support and provide ad hoc courses in conjunction with English Heritage and educational establishments.
- Has provided ad hoc courses and training, organized by its regional groups, for members and other archaeologists at the local level.
- Has reworked and republished its scheme for Continuing Professional Development (CPD), providing its members and other archaeologists with a mechanism for identifying their learning needs and to log and record their learning achievements.
- Has published, as part of its CPD Scheme, a statement of the expectations of general underpinning knowledge and experience for archaeological practice at entry level into the profession and above.
- Is undertaking in conjunction with the National Training Body, Cultural Heritage National Training Organisation (CHNTO), and English Heritage, a survey of the roles in, and skill requirements for, practice in archaeology.

The relevance of these to higher education lies in their anticipated outcomes. The roles and skills survey will identify the knowledge, experience and skills in archaeology and other areas that individuals need to function in the variety of situations and at the variety of levels in which they may find themselves. So far as CHNTO, and thereby Government, is concerned this will lead to the definition of occupational standards, that can be translated into National Vocational Qualifications (NVQ). So far as the IFA is concerned this will make explicit the range and levels of knowledge and skills, and thereby degrees of professional seniority required, to be expected of archaeologists in their varying capacities and employment. The identification of these expectations or standards will inevitably redefine the educational expectations of archaeologists and employers, particularly at entry level into the profession.

A start on this has already been made with the IFA's Expectations of General Underpinning Knowledge and Experience for Archaeological Practice. Although published as an appendix to the CPD scheme, this is actually a freestanding document. The intention behind this is not only to assist practitioners in general in identifying their individual learning needs, but also to provide guidance to students and educators about the areas of basic knowledge that entrants into the profession need to have covered. It provides a yardstick therefore, against which students who wish to pursue a career in archaeology may choose courses, and a basis for the design and development of courses to meet the needs of those students. With this intention in mind, it is interesting to compare this statement with the Quality Assurance Agency benchmarks for archaeology (Bishop, this volume, 2.3b).

It is to be expected that as the need for postgraduate entry level training and lifelong learning become established, the demand for learning opportunities will increase. Indeed the lack of these and any mechanism or structure for the delivery of training is already a matter of concern. Traditionally, higher education has been the principal provider of such opportunities, through Masters and extra-mural courses. But evidently, as currently structured and provided, these are not satisfying the existing demands or needs of practitioners. The IFA view is that education in archaeology has not only to be relevant to practice but available to all, irrespective of their entry path into the profession or their status. Currently, the lack of relevance of many Masters courses, the burden of debt upon new graduates and opinion amongst practitioners, militates against making a second degree a prerequisite of entry into, or progression within, the profession. The IFA's Professional Training Committee therefore, does not see Masters courses as being the sole means of delivering postgraduate learning. Rather, it is looking to the development of approaches that will provide access to education and training at a variety of levels and need, through a variety of agencies. We have therefore to look to courses that may be variously recognized by IFA, by say, approval or validation, and qualifications which may range through NVQs, various types of certificate and diplomas, to Masters degrees.

There is a market to be developed here. The demand already extends beyond undergraduates or new graduates wishing to enter the profession, to practitioners in general. In the future not only is demand from archaeologists likely to increase, but this may be extended to other professions and occupations as part of their own CPD requirements and as their involvement with archaeology increases. Indeed, there is evidence of this already.

There should be a significant place for higher education and educational institutions in meeting this need for various types of learning opportunities and in this market –

in debating the intellectual context of courses, in offering qualifications that can be recognised as relevant by the profession, and in delivering structured courses that could be as equally remunerative in aggregate as are current Masters. Achieving this however, may require some rethinking and recognition that much of the knowledge and many of the skills lie not in educational institutions but amongst practitioners working in other environments. For learning experiences to have relevance and vitality they need to be taught by these practitioners. The more common involvement of these in teaching would not only benefit course structures and content, but would also help to bring the fragmented profession of archaeology closer together.

To sum up, the IFA defines the profession as embracing all practicing archaeologists, be they engaged in higher education or be they amateurs. It regards education and training as critical to the maintenance of standards in archaeology. The Professional Training Committee believes that higher education and professional practice are interdependent and that higher education is critical to the development of archaeologists for and in practice. It is pressing forward with the identification of the skills and learning needs of the profession and the development of the means to meet these. Over and above all this however, the IFA sees these initiatives as creating a context within which the profession will be revolutionized – with an established career structure, movement between sectors, less fragmentation, increased respect for the knowledge and skills possessed by archaeologists, and – who knows – may be wages commensurate with that knowledge and those skills!

1.5

Teaching archaeology in higher education

Kathryn Roberts

Introduction

Cadw: Welsh Historic Monuments is an Executive Agency within the Welsh Assembly charged with carrying out the statutory duties of the Assembly with respect to protecting, conserving and presenting ancient monuments and historic sites in Wales. Cadw is not directly involved in the education or training of archaeologists, but as an employer, both directly within its own Inspectorate and indirectly through grant aiding survey and excavation programmes, it has a very strong interest in how archaeology is taught within British universities.

I went to the Lampeter Workshop because I believe that it is important for archaeologists working in university departments and those in professional organisations to maintain contact as much as possible. I would like to add however, that what I have to say comes from personal experiences and is not an official Cadw statement.

Prior to joining Cadw some three years ago I worked as a lecturer in the Archaeology Department of Trinity College, Carmarthen teaching undergraduate students. My particular areas were archaeological science and environmental archaeology although I also was involved in teaching practical archaeological methods and techniques, period based courses and First Year courses.

There are three points which I would like to highlight here:

- undergraduate degrees should provide a springboard for students into all areas of professional archaeology and as such need to continue to place strong emphasis on the development of practical and applied skills alongside academic learning.
- it would be advantageous for both students and potential employers if those skills were to be subject to more structured assessment as part of the degree marking scheme.
- greater contact between archaeology departments and professional field archaeologists is required, and in particular for increased opportunities for post-graduation professional development courses. I am a supporter of the idea of lifelong learning and that training is not something which should only take place at the beginning of a person's career.

The role of archaeology in Britain today

I think we would all probably agree that over the course of the past 20 years the archaeological profession in Britain has changed. Whereas in the past archaeologists were primarily to be found only in university departments, today there are ever increasing numbers of them working in outside organisations particularly as professional field archaeologists and curators. Since the setting up of the national SMR network and as a direct result of PPG16 there are many more opportunities for archaeology graduates to gain employment as professional field archaeologists than used to be the case. Archaeology is now a viable vocation for graduates.

What we need to consider is what these changes mean for the role and function of university archaeology departments. Do we need to change what is being taught or how? Should we be thinking of archaeology as a vocational degree?

I think to an extent, we should. Certainly archaeology graduates have an advantage over their colleagues in other allied degrees of being able to go out and actually practice archaeology. It is therefore reasonable for an archaeology student to expect that their degree course will prepare them to do so. While I do not believe that courses should alter into specifically designed training courses, I do think that the future work activities of graduates must be taken into account in preparing their content, and also the manner in which they are taught and assessed.

Training students to work in contract archaeology and curatorial posts is very important, not because it is fulfilling some vague desire to 'prepare them to enter the work place', although helpfully it is, but because this type of work is so important to the future of British archaeology.

A large number of the archaeology students graduating today will seek employment as fieldwork officers in archaeological units, as SMR and Development Control Officers and County Archaeologists amongst other posts. All these roles are 'front line' involving direct contact with the general public and involving decisions which will affect the future of archaeological sites and the resulting record of information which will exist either in fact, as preserved archaeological sites, or as recorded archives for future generations to use. It is important that university departments do not underestimate or give the impression that they underestimate the importance of this work and that the content of their degree courses reflects this.

The proliferation of archaeological organisations and posts in the last 20 years has been at least in part a response to the greater emphasis placed on archaeology in the planning process, which has in turn had some bearing on the type of work being undertaken by them. Large-scale research excavations are becoming less common while site evaluations, mostly developer funded are increasing in number. Many field archaeologists spend considerable proportions of their time doing desktop and non-invasive field evaluations, advising on site management and preparing reports, often for non-archaeological audiences – some of whom (such as developers) may have little actual interest in the archaeological remains or process of discovery which we, as archaeologists find so fascinating and rewarding.

This is reality and we must consider what training students need not only in order to become involved in this, and to do it well and efficiently, but to ensure that in so doing they do not lose sight of the fundamental need to maintain research and study beyond the specifics of individual threatened sites.

A particularly positive result of the broad range of archaeological posts which exist today is the variety of skills which they require, suiting different people according to their individual abilities and strengths. While archaeological units may be seeking recruits displaying strong practical skills such as surveying and excavation, curatorial posts require computer literacy and the ability to communicate technical information often to a non-archaeological audience. Heritage management posts can require different skills again such as an understanding of the legislation relating to archaeology and the planning process and in many cases practical site conservation techniques.

Obviously many of the skills required are universal, and all can benefit from at least a basic understanding of the work of other areas. For example, as part of its Scheduling Enhancement Programme Cadw grant aids the Welsh Archaeological Trusts to undertake surveys to assess different types of sites and to make recommendations of those suitable for scheduling. This requires the individual involved to be familiar not only with the period being studied, but fieldwork methodology, the legislative background to scheduling, criteria for site selection and how to apply them.

Universities can play a key role by introducing students to this variety of activities helping them to make informed choices for their future careers.

The importance of teaching practical skills

One general expectation of graduates is that they will be competent in the practical skills of excavation, field survey etc., the basic foundation skills of the archaeologist. Universities have always taught archaeological methods and techniques to students – although departments seem to vary in the extent and degree of emphasis placed on this and how it is assessed and marked.

I don't suppose anyone would disagree that we need to teach students these skills but this leads to two questions. Do we need to reconsider how they are taught? Perhaps

adapting to place more emphasis on their application for activities such as site evaluation for planning purposes? Secondly, how should it be assessed and to what extent should the final degree mark be affected by or reflect a student's practical abilities?

For the professional field archaeologist these skills are essential. We have to look critically at what graduates know and are able to do upon graduating and what they have to show for it – in other words – how can graduates demonstrate their level of practical experience, knowledge and ability to potential employers? This is important to both employer and would-be employee. The former needs to be sure that new graduates actually have obtained the archaeological skills required for posts, while the new job applicant would, I am sure, appreciate having tangible evidence of their competence.

More attention should be paid to assessing the quality of a student's fieldwork skills. By this I do not mean scoring them on their ability to present a cleaned section, draw a plan or hold a camera the right way up (although this information could potentially influence their future career choices), but placing more emphasis on practical projects requiring the planning and application of different methods to a problem, be it excavation, survey, or desktop assessment and thereby enabling the lecturer to offer critical training feedback.

When I was a student, assessment was almost entirely through essays and final examination (these were also essays). The emphasis was on developing critique and memorising information and facts. Although undergraduates were encouraged to undertake dissertations there was no requirement for these to be based on practical fieldwork. It was therefore possible for a student to graduate with a degree in archaeology without demonstrating any particular ability to undertake actual archaeological fieldwork or an appreciation of the type of management and planning required of such projects. That was ten years ago, and things have undoubtedly changed since then but I still question the extent to which some universities are actually assessing students on these skills.

Graduates not only need to be taught the methods but they need training in how to apply them. This is particularly so for activities such as desktop analyses and site evaluations. Since effective application develops from experience this is perhaps an area where students could benefit from increased contact with archaeologists working outside of university departments.

Specialist topics such as aerial photography are often taught by external specialists, perhaps this approach could be broadened to cover areas like contract archaeology, site evaluation, heritage management etc. Another method is through group visits and individual work placements. This latter method is often an element of the more 'vocationally based' heritage management courses but remains less common for archaeology students possibly due to their greater numbers and the difficulty this creates in finding suitable placements for all. However, I know from conversations with both students and professional archaeologists that these are often a very useful point of contact between the two from which both sides benefit.

University - archaeological unit contact

There are, of course, a number of universities in Britain which have their own working archaeological units which must offer ideal opportunities to involve students in the realities of contract work. The situation in Wales is somewhat different. Here there are four Archaeological Trusts, none formally connected with the Welsh archaeology departments although there are often quite close links. While I was at Trinity College, Carmarthen the Department enjoyed a close working relationship with the local Dyfed Archaeological Trust through the joint funding of a post – a fieldworker for the Trust, who also worked at the College training students in fieldwork methods and techniques on a weekly basis. I believe that Lampeter now has contact with the Dyfed Trust enabling undergraduates to work alongside archaeologists in field survey projects, and postgraduates to undertake work placements.

Non-specific Skills

I have sometimes heard people casting aspersions on university attempts to impart non-specific or generic skills to students. This is a shortsighted viewpoint. The breadth of work undertaken by archaeologists and certainly those in heritage management roles requires many such skills, not least being the ability to write effectively for a range of audiences, including the general public. This is not a skill which comes naturally to everyone, but is something which should be addressed during the degree training. The ability to reach out and speak to different audiences can be an important skill for archaeologists impacting not just on an individual's work but the profession as a whole. Much as trainee doctors are now taught 'people skills' perhaps archaeologists should be taught written and oral 'presentation skills'?

This brings me to the area of archaeology often referred to as Heritage or Cultural Resource Management which encompasses much of the work of my own organisation. The relatively recent proliferation of such courses recognises that archaeologists working within heritage organisations can require knowledge and skills beyond those traditionally associated with archaeology degrees and including many of the topics which working archaeologists, when asked, can profess inadequate familiarity including monument preservation legislation, conservation, presentation and public perceptions of the past.

Should universities be incorporating more of these areas into the archaeology degrees. If it is a course based on British archaeology then I would argue that they *should* for two reasons. Firstly, because the legislation and practice

of management is inevitably responsible for shaping the archaeological resource itself, and secondly, because it is a career area that many of the students studying archaeology will wish to follow upon leaving college.

What about management training?

Another aspect of a field archaeologist's work is managing projects and people. Again, should management training form part of the undergraduate degree or is this something which doesn't need to be addressed until a later stage? And if this is the case, when and how?

Archaeological units are commercial organisations but they also have an important wider role as part of a research network. I am sure that most archaeologists would agree that we don't want a situation where units are run by non-archaeologists, in other words by professional managers who have no archaeological training. As more work is funded by the developer it is increasingly important to ensure that units and other organisations are able to maintain an emphasis on research and discovering more about the past and to do this we are probably best off keeping them under the control of managers who are first of all, archaeologists.

Obviously, directing archaeological organisations is not the type of job that the average newly qualified graduate is going to be doing, but it may be something which they aspire to, which leads me to my final question; should universities be broadening their teaching and training courses to attract a wider range of consumers and in particular, to provide professional development courses for archaeologists in full time employment?

Who is the consumer and what do they want?

Traditionally universities have taught undergraduates who were more often than not, school leavers. Today I think there is a much broader range of potential consumers. In addition to school leavers there are 'mature students' applying to do degrees, some for the first time, others because they wish to change career. Their needs and expectations are often quite different to those of school leavers. Many of them have studied before and gained skills and experiences which can not only aid them in their studies, but potentially enhance the learning experience of the others on their course.

Postgraduate and extra-mural training

Another potential recipient of university training are professional archaeologists in full time employment who wish to learn new skills, brush up on old ones, or perhaps gain insights into recent developments and research. Their needs can be varied, from short accredited courses providing practical activity based training, for example surveying, sample collection, handling artefacts and field conservation, to career development studies such as project and organisational management skills, marketing, and presenting archaeological information.

There is increasing recognition that to be efficient and successful organisations need to keep up-to-date with current developments and motivate their staff by offering opportunities to take on new responsibilities, many of which will require additional training. It is accepted in most large organisations, including the Welsh Assembly that training is not something which takes place only at the start of a person's career but must continue throughout.

Following the Welsh Assembly lead Cadw recently successfully obtained an 'Investors in People' award. These are only given to organisations which can demonstrate amongst other things a commitment to training and staff development. By helping its employees in this way an organisation, of course, helps itself. By providing for staff development not only does it obtain a better trained and more efficient workforce with a wider range of skills to call upon, but it gains in terms of staff motivation, commitment, loyalty and general satisfaction. Although Cadw is a relatively large organisation the number of professional archaeologists within it is actually quite small and it does not have the means to undertake very much internal training. It therefore has to look to outside organisations to provide it and I am surprised at how few such facilities exist. One exception is the Oxford University Department for Continuing Education which provides a wide range of apparently very popular short courses. At present however, these remain largely unaccredited. I believe that it would be an advantage to the profession if there were more, speaking both geographically and in terms of subject matter. Again, there is the additional possibility that these could act as another forum for contact between undergraduate students and professionals, since many could cover ground of common interest.

Conclusion

In conclusion I believe:

1. University courses must remain wide ranging in subject matter but at the same time provide students with all the necessary skills (and in particular practical skills) to obtain employment as field archaeologists.
2. That marked assessment of practical skills should form a part of final degree results and that students should be able to provide evidence of the skills they have learnt and practised while at university for potential employers.
3. That degree courses based on British archaeology should cover the practice of archaeology in Britain including an overview of the organisations involved, what they do and how it all fits together, preferably including contact with them on either a group or individual basis.

Lifelong learning and professional courses would benefit working archaeologists and enable them to advance while also enabling greater contact between departments and organisations which would bring mutual benefits to all concerned.

1.6

Archaeology in higher education: a review

Don Henson

Introduction

I want to take a very brief and impressionistic look at the state of archaeology teaching in higher education and some of the current and future trends that make the current period one of great and potentially exciting change. Bear in mind I do this from a Council for British Archaeology (CBA) perspective, where we seek to further greater understanding of archaeology among the people of the UK as a whole. A key CBA concern is that higher education in archaeology should be available at various levels and through a variety of teaching modes to allow greater public involvement with the discipline.

The CBA has published an occasional guide to university courses in archaeology since 1979 (1979, 1983, 1990, 1995, 1999). The picture presented in these has been one of growth in the provision of archaeology in universities, although not without setbacks, e.g. the closure of departments in universities at Lancaster, Leeds and St. Andrews as a result of the University Grants Committee report of 1981. This report also proposed that the archaeology department at Reading should be closed, a threat that was happily averted.

It is instructive to compare the information in the guides from 1979 (Roe 1979) and 1999 (Henson 1999) (Table 1). We can see that there has been a dramatic increase in the teaching of archaeology in the university sector. The greatest increases have been in the number of departments that are not named archaeology departments that teach archaeology, and in the number of taught postgraduate degrees in archaeology.

The growth in undergraduate student numbers has also increased in line with the growth in number of courses. Figures from UCAS and its predecessor, UCCA, show that the number of acceptances onto undergraduate courses has more than doubled over the last 25 years (Table 2).

There have been many changes in the academic and financial framework for teaching archaeology during the last 25 years, e.g. semesterisation, student loans and tuition fees, funding arrangements for universities. Perhaps the most important changes have been the result of the Dearing Report of 1997. The importance of the Report can be seen from just some of its consequences: the role of the Quality Assurance Agency in seeking to raise teaching standards, the imposition of tuition fees, a move towards a national qualifications framework, widening access to higher education, greater importance for sub-degree and foundation degree qualifications, and increasing use of work placements for students. All this is making the world of higher education very different to when most lecturing staff were entering higher education as students.

A snapshot of current provision of archaeology in higher education will probably surprise many people by showing just how widely archaeology is now taught. There are 75 separate departments within 54 universities (or university sector colleges) teaching archaeology as part of undergraduate or postgraduate degrees. These comprise 28 departments of archaeology (or named sections of archaeology within wider departments), 10 centres of continuing education and 37 other departments. The degrees being offered by all these departments include 50 single honours BA (or MA in Scotland) degrees, 19 BSc degrees, 257 possible joint honours combinations, and 143 taught postgraduate Masters degrees. The allied field of heritage studies is also becoming increasingly visible as a discipline within higher education, being offered at 45 universities and colleges by a variety of departments, e.g. archaeology, history, museum studies, architecture, and cultural studies. While some of these courses concentrate on leisure and tourism aspects of heritage, others deal with heritage management issues and produce graduates who will wish to find employment in the archaeology sector.

	1979	1999	Increase
universities teaching archaeology	34	54	59%
all departments teaching archaeology	35	75	114%
departments of archaeology	24	28	17%
single honours degree courses	31	69	123%
postgraduate degrees	c.50	143	c.166%

Table 1: archaeology in higher education between 1979 and 1999.

Year	Acceptances
1974	310
1975	357
1976	396
1977	408
1978	426
1994	771
1995	842
1996	924
1997	946
1998	902
1999	950

Table 2: acceptances onto undergraduate archaeology courses since 1974.

Current issues

I will discuss further a few current trends in higher education based on the CBA's traditional concerns, e.g. accessibility to higher education for all, education as a life enhancing experience rather than simply training for work, and a holistic concern for archaeology as discipline.

There is an increasing amount of archaeology being taught in non-archaeology departments and as part of other courses. The types of department involved in teaching archaeology now include departments of art and design, East Asian studies, environmental sciences and mathematics, technology and design, and world art studies and museology. Archaeology modules can now be found in courses like BSc Countryside Management (Aberystwyth), BA Humanities (Barnsley College), BA History of Art (Essex), MA Landscape Studies (Ripon and York St John) and BA Heritage Studies (Worcester College). This means that there needs to be greater awareness by archaeologists of the inter-disciplinary links between archaeology and other disciplines and to accept links with such subjects as heritage studies. Indeed, archaeology is already being treated as part of a cultural heritage sector by the government. For vocational training purposes, archaeology falls within the remit of the Cultural Heritage National Training Organisation, and although training is not the purpose of higher education, the linkage must have some impact on discussion of higher education issues.

Higher education encompasses more than just undergraduate and postgraduate degrees. The proposed national qualifications framework covers a continuous spectrum of qualifications from sub-degree to postgraduate (Table 3). This will have considerable implications for entry into, and progression within, the profession, and for education of non-professionals in the subject. It may enable 'training' at different levels to accommodate the needs of the amateur sector, as well as allowing multiple entry points for anyone wanting an education in archaeology simply out of interest. Archaeology is already available at all except level 3, with 54 separate certificates and 29 separate diplomas in addition to the undergraduate and postgraduate degrees already mentioned.

Level	Description	Proposed qualifications
6	doctorate	PhD, DPhil
5	masters	MPhil, MA, MSc PGDip, PGCert
4	honours degree	BA Hons, BSc Hons Grad Cert, Grad Dip
3	degree	BA, BSc
2	diploma	HNC/HND DipHE
1	certificate	CertHE

Table 3: the proposed national qualifications framework for higher education.

A major growth area for archaeology has been in continuing education (what used to be called extra-mural teaching). Many universities have centres of continuing education (often now called centres for lifelong learning), offering a wide range of qualifications (Table 4): 54 certificates, 25 diplomas, 9 undergraduate degrees and 2 postgraduate degrees. With 88 qualifications available at level 4 or below, continuing education is a major provider of qualified archaeologists. It may be that in future (possibly even already), that full-time degree courses are likely to become a minority way of studying archaeology for a qualification. Greater thought needs to be given to the needs of the part-time sector, e.g. provision of fieldwork and ways of examining students.

One particular method of course delivery for which there is demonstrable public demand is distance learning, which is still in the early stages of development in archaeology. A few universities have developed distance learning courses, e.g. Bournemouth, Exeter, Leicester and Manchester, but curiously not the Open University. There is a continuous stream of enquiries to the CBA from people wanting this kind of course delivery, for whom attendance at part-time classes is impossible due to demands such as shift-work or family commitments. Higher education needs to take more seriously the needs of students for whom traditional classroom-based teaching methods are not appropriate,

Level	Qualification	University
5	MA Archaeology	Birkbeck College London
4	BA Hons Archaeology & Local and Regional History	Leeds University
2	DipHE Archaeology	King Alfred's University College
1	CertHE Industrial Archaeology	Birmingham University
	Foundation Certificate Field Archaeology	Surrey University

Table 4: examples of qualifications available through continuing education.

especially if the sector is to take seriously the social inclusion agenda being set by the government.

The expansion of archaeology courses into new institutions helps to spread the geographical base and enables more people to get involved (those who can't readily move to other areas to pursue their studies), e.g. University of the Highlands and Islands offering archaeology through heritage studies at Moray and Thurso Colleges. Unfortunately, the role of continuing education in serving rural communities has been cut back in recent years with changes in funding and the accreditation of courses leading to a concentration of courses being taught on campus in many cases. An area of future expansion will be the further education college sector, which is increasingly interested in offering courses such as HND or HNC. However, this has considerable resource implications since most further education colleges are not as well provided for as university sector institutions to allow the teaching of a subject like archaeology. Indeed, the teaching of HND Practical Archaeology has recently been transferred from Yeovil College to Bournemouth University for at least partly this reason.

Future trends and issues?

I will now highlight what I think are trends and issues that will become increasingly important in the future. In particular, there are three that we need to discuss more widely: the relationship between interdisciplinary approaches and archaeological theory, use of ICT in teaching, and provision of vocational training.

Interdisciplinary qualifications & theoretical approaches
Archaeology may well become more integrated into wider approaches and schemes of study, e.g. heritage studies that take account of the heritage management aspects of the discipline. What implications does this have for theoretical approaches to archaeology? Might we see a move away from theories concerned with interpreting archaeological evidence to theories concerned with how archaeology is integrated within present day life, e.g. theories of how the past is perceived and manipulated today, or how people engage with and learn from archaeological remains. To some extent, archaeological theory is already engaging with these issues. However, we are likely to see a far greater theoretical concern with archaeology as practice,

rather than archaeology as interpretation. Perhaps we are nearing the point at which archaeological theory becomes outward looking and archaeology begins to provide input into wider concerns (e.g. sustainability and the contribution of heritage to community identity).

New technology

We are already seeing greater use of information and communication technology (ICT) to deliver archaeology to non-traditional audiences. Higher education will increasingly engage with its students in new ways. Perhaps what has not yet been considered is the impact this will have on the content and depth of courses. The Internet (or CD) can provide access to large amounts of detailed information. If that includes information like pottery assemblages, flint collections, stone axe thin sections etc., then the search capabilities of ICT could be used to provide students with self-directed schemes of learning. They could also allow greater in-depth teaching of particular aspects of archaeology that should be basic to archaeological practice in the field, e.g. artefact typologies.

Vocational training

We are already seeing the greater use of work placements as part of degree courses, and considerable debate about the provision of courses for entry level training and continuing professional development (CPD). The work of the Archaeology Training Forum will be important here in enabling that debate and guiding the future provision of training for the profession. Part of that debate must be to address the concern that there will be a split between liberal education qualifications studied for interest and pleasure, and professional qualifications needed for entry to the jobs market. Is professional entry to archaeology to be limited to holders of a Masters degree or will there be a spread of levels for entry to the profession? Will universities be offering qualifications for CPD within archaeology? Oxford and Leeds are already involved in this through continuing education. We should also ask where does the research role of universities fit in the education versus training debate? We should also bear in mind the training needs of the amateur sector. Archaeology is a discipline, not just a profession, and has many practitioners who are not professionally employed as archaeologists. These must remain a vital part of archaeology, with the skills to contribute meaningfully to our understanding of the archaeological heritage.

Conclusion

Archaeology is a popular subject with the public at large, and should prosper in higher education if it acknowledges this and reaches out to the public to offer a wide variety of courses at all levels with a variety of methods of delivery. The impediments to achieving this are both internal (e.g. attitudes within the discipline, motivating and rewarding overworked staff) and external (e.g. funding of courses, resourcing). If the obstacles are to be overcome, this can only be through open debate and willingness to embrace new ways of working.

Questions that need to be included as part of the debate are the really basic questions, whose answers we often take for granted, including:

- who studies archaeology?
- why do they study it?
- what do they do with their qualification?
- what do we teach?

We might want to consider whether the recently issued benchmarking document for archaeology is already out of date in that it addresses the concerns largely of single honours archaeology degrees. We also need to identify potential problems in delivering archaeology in higher education, i.e.:

- resourcing   e.g. ensuring access to equipment, knowledge, skills, research
- fieldwork   e.g. opportunities for field experience before and during courses
- teaching methods   e.g. variety needed to ensure wider access, ensuring comparability of assessment between students taught by different methods.

Many of the above questions and problems are already being tackled, however the whole discipline needs to keep them at the forefront of their minds and engage in discussions about them. The workshop was a good starting point for raising the debate to a higher level. It is to be hoped that a greater proportion of those teaching in higher education will engage with this debate in the future.

References

Henson, D. 1999. *2000 Guide to Archaeology in Higher Education.* York: Council for British Archaeology.

Roe, F. 1979. *Guide to Undergraduate University Courses in Archaeology.* York: Council for British Archaeology.

PART II

BENCHMARKING ARCHAEOLOGY

2.1

The 'benchmarking' document

Matthew Johnson

Introduction

The benchmarking document in archaeology is one of a series of statements defining, or setting a benchmark for, learning and teaching within a given academic discipline. Benchmarking documents have been drawn up by a series of panels meeting under the auspices of the Quality Assurance Agency (QAA); in the case of archaeology, panel members were nominated by the Standing Committee of University Professors and Heads of Archaeology (SCUPHA). The archaeology panel was chaired by Professor Graeme Barker. The informal paper that follows is based on the presentation I made to the Lampeter workshop on the benchmarking document. I write it as an individual member of the panel that drew up the document.

I should start with two preliminary comments. First, this paper is not meant to be a 'defence' of the benchmarking document or indeed of the benchmarking process itself. The document has been opened up for consultation; over the course of its drafting and redrafting, many individuals and institutions wrote in and alterations were made accordingly. The benchmarking statement should therefore not be seen as a text that one group of people within academic archaeology wrote and everybody else passively consumed. I hope that, albeit within the short time scale imposed by the QAA, it has come out of the subject community as a whole. Indeed, far from wishing to 'defend' the document, the reader may find that the comments I make below actually confirm her worst fears about the document. There is nothing inherently wrong in this; it is a document that will have to evolve if it is to serve its purpose within the evolving, self-critical discipline of archaeology. At the very least, it will be revised by July 2003.

The second point is that what I am going to say is very much a personal view. I served on the committee that drew up the benchmarking statement; however, I don't speak officially on behalf of that committee. Many of the comments that I think will interest the reader are actually my subjective impressions of working on the committee. It may well be the case that another member of the committee would comment: 'No that isn't what was in our heads when we were drawing this up; I think Matthew was mistaken…'. What I really want to do is to give a *personal* gloss on the document – to try to critically examine the context of its production.

The aims of benchmarking

The preface to the benchmarking document states that it has three uses for the QAA. It is going to be an external source of reference for higher education institutions in the design of new programmes in archaeology; it is designed to be used as a reference point in pursuit of internal quality assurance; and it is to be used, in part, for the purposes of academic review.

It seems to me that the whole benchmarking exercise does mark a very important shift in the nature of QAA procedures specifically and academic audit generally. It represents an attempt to define the *content* of degrees whether in archaeology or any other discipline. In the current (2000-1) round of QAA Subject Review, at least in theory all academic departments teaching archaeology ('subject providers') set their own aims and objectives within a Self-Assessment Document and are then judged by an external panel on whether these self-set objectives are met. Benchmarking arguably represents the first systematic attempt to specify what academics should be teaching. (David Austin pointed out at the workshop that this was not however the first attempt to define the content of archaeology degrees; various documents did so in the late 1980s, most notably the University Grants Committee review in the context of defining the minimum numbers of staff needed to teach a single honours degree).

There was one central thing that I think the benchmarking committee was conscious of, namely that academic archaeology is a very diverse community. Take any three archaeology programmes at different universities around the country and I predict that you will be looking at three very different views of archaeology and three very different student experiences – all of them excellent. As a community we are very diverse, but equally we hope that we are all very good at what we do. Our intention was to avoid writing a document that leads in ten years time to all or most universities teaching very similar programmes. We did so by forsaking a checklist of what a 'normal' or 'standard' degree should involve, and instead defining a humanities-science-practice 'triangle' within which different undergraduate degrees could be situated at different points. This, we hope, will allow departments maximum flexibility in defining and shaping their own programmes. Perhaps in the longer term we will not succeed; perhaps historical forces may be beyond our control and time will show that we were naïve in believing that such a fate could be avoided.

I have gone through the 'official' QAA agenda, what the QAA want out of the document. There were however several things that as practising archaeologists we wanted to emphasise very strongly. One of these was very simply to protect the funding base of university archaeology. Over recent years, there have been many battles within academe to get archaeology classified with subjects such as geography. Archaeology has in the main been opposed to being grouped with general arts subjects, usually on the basis that our students require fieldwork and a suite of practical and/or scientific skills. Therefore in one form or another, in different political battles down the years we have argued for a higher funding base. We felt it very important therefore that the need for practical and scientific skills to be taught, and therefore for their teaching to be funded, was quite explicit in the document.

More broadly though to identify what can be called the 'value added' in archaeology we wanted to make a very explicit statement that we are an academic discipline that routinely engages undergraduate students in the process of research. When archaeology students participate in training excavations, they actually engage in primary research. As a result, there is a closer link between research and teaching in our discipline than virtually any other. We wanted to head up that link and its educational benefits in terms of transferable skills very clearly. The closest parallel is probably geography; there are field trips and related activities within geography departments, and single honours students generally undertake some original field research in their dissertation topic.

A further aim was not to rule out or inhibit innovation. We wanted to write a document that was enabling rather than restrictive – that did not stop people doing what they wanted to do but that gave them space to maintain and develop distinctive programmes. There was a tension then between being enabling and setting certain standards, because what we also wanted to do was produce a document that did set a certain standard for new programmes. Although I don't think we were conscious of the sheer number of courses on offer in various higher education colleges and other institutions that Don Henson's research (this volume) has revealed, we were conscious of anecdotal evidence of the odd local historian sitting in an further education college deciding it would be nice to do a module or course and calling it 'Archaeology'. In such cases the students might come out with no excavation or fieldwork experience, and actually not having ever been taught by anybody with the degree of expertise that most archaeologists would consider appropriate.

The final thing at the back of our minds was to provide as powerful a statement as we could possibly write not to the QAA, not to our own community but to the outside world. We wanted to say why we were archaeologists, why we are passionate about what we do, why we think archaeology is the most exciting, forward-looking and intellectually challenging discipline in academe. Much of the second page of the document is actually, in many ways, about saying to the world why archaeology is important, why we

want to do it. It is the sort of thing that we hope people can take away and show to their Deans, Vice Chancellors or other administrative heads as well as the wider academic and public community. So, for example in the very first paragraph the idea of 'material remains' being an 'extremely broad concept' is well known to archaeologists but worth re-stating to an audience for whom archaeology and digging are coterminous. So the document is in part a statement to the outside world.

The context of benchmarking

These were some of the things that were in the backs of our minds as we were drafting and re-drafting the document. What I want to do now is put this in the context of the benchmarking process in other disciplines. Several benchmarking documents were the subject of some controversy and met with a mixed response from their subject communities. For example, I imagine that most academic archaeologists would regard the history document as quite an unexceptional document; some academic historians however saw it as dangerously radical. The vagueness of several of the benchmarking documents tells its own story, of benchmarking panels disagreeing so profoundly over the fundamentals of their discipline that a refuge is sought in blandness.

Whether the content of the archaeology document can be deemed controversial or not is another matter, but one of the things that came across strongly to me was this. I went to the first committee meeting thinking that there would be huge arguments about the nature of archaeology, what was to be deemed core and essential and what was to be deemed secondary and ephemeral. Certainly the list of members of the committee represent very different constituencies from the archaeological community, very different theoretical viewpoints, very different outlooks on archaeology. However, I was surprised to find that proceedings were extremely amicable and that 'party lines' were not drawn as I had expected; there were few if any serious moments of irreconcilable intellectual difference.

Such an account sounds a little flippant but I think it leads on to something fundamental and very valuable about our academic community. On the whole, we get on well with each other; we have a sense that, although we have very different views one from another of what we do as archaeologists, very fundamentally different views, we respect each others' views and we think that what each of us does is valuable. If there is one thing that I took away from working on the panel it is that we must not lose that sense of each others' worth, under any circumstances. As academic archaeology expands, the numbers and constituencies will become larger and our discipline runs the danger of becoming more fragmented. We must work to maintain this sense of community that we have.

Such a sense of community is all the more important because it is intellectually very difficult to specify what it actually is about archaeology that leads us to have this coherence. Indeed, I suspect its explanation is at least partly sociological (our reliance on teamwork in the field may be one factor). I was expecting some conflict that in fact did not arise. I suggest that we should hold onto that.

Issues for the future

I'll just conclude by talking around some of the issues that might bear further discussion by the academic community. In trying to assess what we thought a student should know on graduating in archaeology, we adopted a visual metaphor, a base or a platform. On top of that platform, we placed a triangle related around humanities, science and practice. We wanted to do it that way, because, as stated above, we wanted to shy away from giving a specific list of things that students should know in the manner of professional or vocational training. The undergraduate degree, we felt, was not about providing professional training and expertise, but rather about providing such a platform of knowledge and understanding upon which a student could build if he or she wished with a postgraduate degree or professional training.

In any case, in most cases in the first draft of the document where we attempted to specify such a list the exercise began to get picked apart and would fall down before we could get to any kind of general agreement. For example, we began to assemble a list of pieces of British Government legislation the student should be aware of, but it was pointed out firstly that such a list would rapidly date the document and secondly that this was meant to be an international document in some sense. We could not reasonably require someone doing an egyptology degree to have a detailed knowledge of the workings of Institute of Field Archaeologists, for example. Therefore concrete specifications of subject knowledge and understanding tended to get watered down in the statement: for example, 'students should know about the practice of archaeology in the institutional context of that practice', in order to avoid it being an anglocentric document. Some responses to successive drafts felt that we were not specific enough, other people felt that we were far too specific. The fact that those two piles of responses were more or less the same suggests to me that we probably got it about right. It is an open question whether future drafts of the document should be more specific or not.

The second issue was: what should the input be from the Institute of Field Archaeologists? Should there be more explicit reference to IFA in the document? We resolved that a far better strategy would be for this to go forward as a largely 'academic' document and for IFA to produce their own document on their own terms. The community could then look at them beside each other and create a dialogue from that point. My personal view is that this is a far more effective way of creating a positive debate.

The third issue concerns archaeological science. There was some feeling that there should be a very detailed specification of scientific techniques that students should be aware of. This goes back to the age old, thorny question of the role of archaeological science within archaeological study as a whole. Because in Britain and Europe archaeology is generally considered a humanity, science tends to get equated with specific archaeological techniques, despite David Clarke's famous saying that 'the use of a scientific technique no more turns archaeology into science, than a wooden leg turns a man into a tree'. The issue was complicated by the recognition that there were departments that do not have extensive scientific facilities available to provide teaching in such areas, but which by the standards that most of us agree with, are very good departments. Again, there was a funding angle to this issue. If we were going to justify a higher funding base and we were going to do that in part by specifying a body of scientific techniques that students needed to understand, then such a list needed to be in the document; on the other hand we did not want to make it restrictive so that those places that did not have the laboratory and other facilities could not put on archaeology courses. The language was therefore very carefully chosen in the document, for example with mention of 'access to' (rather than ownership of) laboratory facilities.

The fourth issue was that of joint and combined honours degrees. We were asked to write a document that set a benchmark not just for single honours, but also for joint honours and combined honours degrees where archaeology comprised a third or more of the curriculum. This made the drafting of the document especially complex; as a result, all the way through document the reader will find phrases like 'we expect joint honours to acquire some of these but not all of these skills/knowledge/understanding'. Many of the comments on drafts of the document, particularly those which desired a more detailed specification of professional skills and standards, assumed that we were writing solely or primarily for the single honours programmes, which was not the case.

The final issue is that of standards. It was clear from the letters that came back as part of the feedback process that there was some confusion about what was meant by 'threshold' (meaning what a student gaining a bare Pass might be expected to know and be able to do) and 'typical' at the end of the document. Again to take the issue of whether the standards were pitched at the right level, by the end of the feedback process the pile of letters saying that the standards specified were not demanding enough equalled the pile that said they were far too demanding, so we must have got it just about right again. However, I suspect that a student demonstrating a typical standard would probably, nevertheless, be a person who could not write a pottery report without assistance; so typical standard cannot equate to a given level of professional training.

There were also some that thought that the threshold standard was too high. However, there is a very specific context for the positive definition of what a threshold standard was to do; we spent a lot of time thinking about that student, a student who gets a low third or even a pass degree. What can a student at such a level of achievement do? We were constantly reminded, I think rightly, to put such a level in positive terms. There is a very specific reason for this; in the history document the threshold standard is expressed in largely negative terms. A little time after it was published, an article appeared in the *Daily Telegraph*, the burden of which was 'at last the left liberal consensus that runs British universities has been exposed; academics say that *somebody can be this lacking in ability, fail to do all these things and still get a degree*'. Ever since that traumatic experience the QAA has been very specific about defining threshold standards positively. So in the future months and years we might want to talk about whether we are serving our lesser ability students well enough. Again, this is an issue especially relevant to the expanding sector of higher education colleges, where a Pass degree might represent a very positive achievement for a student, rather than to the 'old' universities.

Conclusion

I want to return in conclusion to my initial point which is that the benchmarking statement is a document that will change. It is one that has already been open to consultation; in the future, it will change and change again. It is a document that, for various reasons that I am sure the academic community of archaeology will share, must not be made too specific. If this need for a lack of specificity is not remembered, it is a document that is very easy to criticise in the sense that you can say that such-and-such (knowledge of this piece of legislation or that theory or scientific technique) should be in it. Viewed in isolation, such criticisms are plausible. However, if something goes in, something else has to come out. It's as a coherent statement of the balance in the overall field that I hope and believe that we have got about right.

Acknowledgements

I thank Sophy Thomas-Goodburn for transcribing the text from my recorded oral comments; I then edited this text into a written paper and added several amplifying passages. I also thank Graeme Barker for looking at the text, making comments and correcting several inaccuracies. Any errors or misconceptions that remain are my responsibility.

2.2

Benchmark Statement for Archaeology - January 2000

G. Barker, J. Collis, T. Darvill, C. Gamble, W. S. Hanson, C. Hills, J. Hunter, M. H. Johnson, and E. A. Slater

This document seeks to make explicit the nature and standards of university programmes which carry the word Archaeology in their title, or in which Archaeology is included as a significant component in the programme leading to the award.

1. Introduction

Archaeology provides a unique perspective on the human past, on what it is to be human. As the only subject that deals with the entire human past in all its temporal and spatial dimensions, it is fundamental to our understanding of how we evolved and how our societies came into being. Archaeology can be defined as the study of the human past through material remains (the latter is an extremely broad concept and includes: evidence in the current landscape, from buildings and monuments to ephemeral traces of activity; buried material, such as artefacts, biological remains, and structures; and written sources). Archaeology's chronological range is from the earliest hominids five million years ago to the present day, its geographical scope is regionally-specific but world-wide, its scale of enquiry ranges from distributions and processes of change at the global scale and over millennia down to the actions of individuals.

Archaeology, a subject that has long been of interest to a wide general public, emerged as a separate discipline in the mid nineteenth century, and during the past 150 years has seen many changes of emphasis, but the main focus has remained the discovery and interpretation of the material remains of past societies. Some of the main changes have arisen through improved understanding of the nature of the material record and, thereby, the development of new techniques of recovery and analysis, others from theoretical developments affecting the kinds of questions asked by archaeologists about their material. The result today is a distinct discipline with its own methods and theory drawing on a rich archive of past work. Throughout its history, archaeology has had a close association with a range of disciplines, initially mainly the humanities but in recent decades increasingly also a broad range of social sciences and sciences. Much research and teaching in archaeology are therefore multi - or interdisciplinary: a particular topic or theme may be approached from different perspectives, and with different methodologies. In the sciences there is also a recognition of the quality and significance of archaeological data for other disciplines: one of the key characteristics of archaeological data is time depth, and the ability to examine the effects of process within a tight chronological framework is vital for the study of contemporary concerns such as human impact on ecosystems. The strong links with other disciplines mean

that archaeology is often studied in Joint or Combined Honours programmes and, as with Single Honours archaeology programmes, these degrees can be located in a range of Faculties (e.g. Arts, Social Science, Science).

Archaeology has been taught as a distinct subject in British universities since the early years of the twentieth century. There are currently 28 archaeology departments in the UK, and archaeology programmes are taught at several others. Few incoming students have had the opportunity to undertake formal courses in archaeology, and few departments require previous archaeological experience or specific qualifications in other areas. The educational background of incoming students is extremely varied; this diversity, embracing a range of subjects across the humanities and sciences all with some relevance to archaeology, provides a very stimulating environment for staff and students and is one of the strengths of archaeology programmes. Mature students have traditionally provided a significant proportion of the intake, many entering with non-traditional qualifications but often with practical experience of the subject. The exit routes of archaeology graduates are equally varied: Masters courses (increasingly a prerequisite for research degrees and professional advancement); museums; the burgeoning profession of field archaeology; the wider tourism, heritage, and media sectors; and more general graduate positions. The broad-based nature of the subject and of the skills it gives graduates provide a strong grounding for a wide range of career paths: the archaeology graduate is extremely well equipped with transferable skills from the mix of humanities and science training, engagement with theory and practice, and individual and team-based learning, together with the intellectual curiosity to continue learning, and the skills to benefit from challenging work environments. Archaeology also offers much non-professional involvement, via continuing education courses, local societies, museums, heritage groups and so on, so graduates not employed within archaeology have many opportunities for life-long learning and to share their expertise within the community.

2. Foundations and Contexts of Degree Programmes

Archaeology at HE level firmly aligns itself with a liberal view of education and learning, whilst recognising the practical application of the subject's knowledge base and skills. Understanding the interplay between theories and methods, central to any archaeology programme, is achieved by involving students directly in the recovery and analysis of primary material, usually via involvement in departmental research projects. Departmental teaching and research programmes, therefore, commonly underpin each other. Because all archaeology departments are research active, and Masters courses and postgraduate research students well distributed throughout the sector, archaeology undergraduates learn within lively and stimulating research cultures and work with primary research materials: the undergraduate learning experience frequently involves the same excitement of discovery as that of the professional researcher.

Four contexts provide the foundation on which Archaeology degree programmes are based: social; ethical and professional; theoretical; and scientific.

The social context

Archaeology is embedded in the events, structures, and development of the contemporary world. It is through this close association with contemporary structures such as class, ethnicity, and gender that archaeology derives its power as an intellectual discipline. Archaeology is often a contested discipline, with different stakeholders disagreeing over interpretation and appropriate action towards the remains of the past and their display. The subject provides the material resources through which identity is created at many levels in society.

The ethical and professional context

Archaeology is now recognised in many countries as central to the heritage and tourism industries and increasingly important in the environmental, development, and planning sectors. The commercial and educational opportunities that archaeology is seen to offer have changed many aspects of the subject over the past twenty years. In some countries new areas of employment have opened up, bringing their own requirements for professional standards and bodies to monitor and develop these standards, a prime example in Britain being the creation in 1982 of The Institute of Field Archaeologists. In many countries artefacts, monuments, and landscapes of the past are protected through government guidance, national legislation and international treaty, for example the World Heritage Convention. These developments have not only led to greatly increased employment opportunities for archaeology graduates but encouraged archaeologists to reflect on the role of the past in the present and their own position within the process of gaining knowledge. One of the most important questions posed has been: who owns the past? - a question which reflects how the sources of authority to study and interpret the past have changed.

The theoretical context

Archaeological theory has many facets, almost as many as the traditional divisions by period, region, and continent. Perspectives vary enormously: from Marxism to materiality, from feminist theory to cultural ecology, sociobiology to social theory. The vitality of theoretical debate within the subject is one of its intellectual attractions as an HE subject. It was greatly intensified when the orientation of the subject was redirected towards an anthropological archaeology employing an explicitly scientific methodology. This built on and added to the core tradition of culture history which recognises that archaeology is, in essence, a unique way of writing about the past. The combination of the two traditions has fostered evaluative and interpretative perspectives on the past. The result is a pluralistic approach to the study of the past, yet one characterised by a spirit of intellectual tolerance arising from the strong sense of the discipline as a community of scholarship. Four elements of this anthropological archaeology can be recognised:

- Archaeologists have to recognise many temporal and spatial **scales** from the micro to macro, the individual to the civilisation. Integrating these scales of social and technical activity unites the many period and geographical interests into a study of past human life rather than just past cultures.
- **Social life** is now conceived as inter-connected, a network of relationships rather than a set of formal structures and institutions which need describing. Archaeological theory addresses the question of change and variation within such complex webs. It draws on the immense archive of past societies preserved through material remains to provide interpretations and to seek understanding of variation through comparison.
- As a result, archaeologists now seek to place their findings within a wider **context**. Whether the scale is regional or international, the driving aim is to establish the significance of research within wider frames of reference.
- Archaeological theory is informed by **self-reflection**: the material basis of archaeology, the contested nature of objects, the social relationships that are spun around them and the people who use and interpret them, have led to the conception of the past as an active, rather than a neutral activity, to facts which are theory-laden and to issues of interpretation which cannot be ignored or trivialised because they are 'just' in the past.

The scientific context

Archaeological science is the application of a scientific methodology to archaeological problems, employing a range of techniques whose origins ultimately lie in a broad range of sciences including physics, chemistry, biochemistry, biology, medicine, geology, geography, and materials science. Where possible, thinking scientifically should be part of the armoury of every archaeologist. Many techniques have more than one application, but major research themes include: the formation of the archaeological record; human involvement in landscape evolution within the framework of climatic imperatives; and the origins and development of economic and social systems. Archaeological science has provided the chronometric frameworks which are indispensable to the ordering of our material. Many analytical techniques allow artefact characterisation, composition, manufacturing and exchange processes to be investigated. Environmental science has added fundamental knowledge to our understanding of the human use of landscapes, subsistence and social life. Computing is critical in the analysis, visualisation, and interpretation of the past. Remote sensing and prospection have revolutionised the exploration and understanding of past landscapes and settlements. The archaeological context in which the science is embedded also ensures a healthy reflection on the methods and ethics of the wider science agenda.

Implications for Archaeology Degree Programmes

These four contexts are the four foundation stones upon which all archaeology degrees, whether Single or Combined Honours, are built. However, we expect degree programmes to vary in their aims, objectives, and emphases as a reflection of the diversity, vitality, and confidence of our discipline, though the integration of the humanities and sciences is likely to underpin most degree programmes given that this inter-disciplinarity is as much philosophical as practical/methodological. Particular degree programmes will be located at different points within a triangle drawn between the complementary archaeologies of the humanities, sciences, and professional practice. A department teaching Single and Combined Honours degrees will probably position them at different locations within the tri-polar range. The triangle stresses the contexts, the inter-disciplinarity, and the overarching practice which departments seek to instil in students. The combination of practice, the commitment to primary data, and the focus on object- and landscape-centred learning, provides the means to identify the extent of the discipline.

3. Knowledge and Understanding

Despite the inter-disciplinary nature of archaeology, and the varied pathways through it that different Archaeology programmes can be expected to take, all graduates of degree courses which contain a substantial component (at least 50 per cent) of archaeology can be expected to possess a platform of knowledge and understanding in certain areas. These areas include:

- knowledge and understanding of the origins and development of archaeology as a discipline
- understanding of the intellectual vitality of archaeology, its theoretical basis, current debates over approaches to interpretation, and archaeology's relationship to other disciplines
- appreciation of the social, cultural, and political context of archaeological interpretation
- familiarity with the basic concepts which underpin the subject (such as: archaeological uses of assemblage, culture, and style; approaches to typology, taxonomy, and ancient technology; stratigraphic context; temporality; and landscape)

- understanding of the causes of variation in the reliability of different classes of evidence from archaeological contexts (such as: taphonomy; cultural and non-cultural transformations; depositional processes; and recovery procedures)
- understanding of the relationship between the practice of archaeology and the institutional context of that practice
- appreciation of the importance of the recovery of primary data through practical experience
- critical awareness of methodologies for quantifying, analysing, and interpreting primary data
- understanding of the concepts and application of scientific methods used in collecting, analysing, and interpreting archaeological data
- understanding of the use of analogy and experiment in archaeological analysis
- broad and comparative knowledge of the archaeology of selected geographical regions
- broad and comparative knowledge of the archaeology of selected chronological periods
- from specialised investigation, deep understanding of one or more distinct classes of archaeological material.

4. Skills

The range and depth of the skills acquired by an archaeology graduate will of course vary according to the location of the degree programme within the humanities-science-practice triangle and the number of archaeology modules taken. However, the platform of knowledge and understanding outlined above will ensure that any archaeology graduate will have acquired a broad range of skills. The Single Honours graduate will normally have most, and the Combined Honours graduate many, of the skills identified below. As appropriate to the breadth and depth of the programme they have pursued, they will be equipped to:

- draw down and apply appropriate scholarly, theoretical, and scientific principles and concepts to archaeological problems
- practise core fieldwork techniques of identification, surveying, recording, excavation, and sampling
- practise core laboratory techniques of recording, measurement, analysis, and interpretation of archaeological material
- discover and recognise the archaeological significance of material remains and landscapes
- interpret spatial data, integrating theoretical models, traces surviving in present-day landscapes, and excavation data
- observe and describe different classes of primary archaeological data, and objectively record their characteristics
- select and apply appropriate statistical techniques to process archaeological data, recognising the potential and limitations of such techniques
- assemble coherent research/project designs

- marshal and critically appraise other people's arguments
- produce logical and structured arguments supported by relevant evidence
- present effective oral presentations for different kinds of audiences
- prepare effective written communications for different readerships
- make effective and appropriate use of C&IT (such as: word processing packages; databases; and spreadsheets)
- make critical and effective use of information retrieval skills using paper-based and electronic (including WWW) resources
- make effective and appropriate forms of visual presentation (graphics, photographs, spreadsheets)
- plan, design, and execute a programme of primary research, working independently
- collaborate effectively in a team via experience of working in a group, for example through fieldwork, laboratory and/or project work
- appreciate the importance of safety procedures and responsibilities (both personal and with regard to others) in the field and the laboratory
- (as fieldwork often involves working in new environments with minimal support) appreciate and be sensitive to different cultures, and deal with unfamiliar situations
- to be able critically to evaluate one's own and others' opinions, from an appreciation of the practice of archaeology in its changing theoretical, methodological, professional, ethical, and social contexts.

5. Teaching, Learning and Assessment

Given archaeology's variety of intellectual styles and traditions, the teaching and learning environments developed by different departments will reflect their position within the Humanities-Science-Practice triangle. However, archaeology programmes generally demonstrate a considerable concern and interest in pedagogical developments evidenced in a wide variety of teaching methods, using C&IT where appropriate.

The interactions between teaching, research, and primary data handling are key elements of the environment in which archaeology courses must be taught, to the extent that courses should only be delivered in departments with strong research cultures. Staff teaching within archaeology programmes must be individually competent to deliver those course units for which they are responsible and collectively able to provide the breadth and depth of specialist and non-specialist subjects embraced by the course as a whole.

Students reading for an archaeology degree should be taught within an environment conducive to learning, which is intellectually stimulating, and which embraces intellectual diversity. There should be access to relevant published literature, IT facilities, appropriate primary sources, archaeological materials (such as artefacts, archives, hand-specimens, and comparative collections), and properly equipped and staffed laboratories. Given the importance for archaeology graduates of the development of technical skills in a variety of areas of archaeological practice, institutions should facilitate access to the equipment and technical resources for the pursuit of these within the archaeology programmes they manage.

Archaeology students should be provided with full documentation for their programme of study and on each component within it, including clear learning objectives. Amongst the documentation provided by departments there should be information regarding contextual aspects of the programme, together with health and safety instructions for fieldwork and laboratory analysis, and guidance on ethical issues associated with archaeological practice.

An education in archaeology involves an active engagement with the archaeological community as a whole. Students should be encouraged to participate in archaeological projects within and outside the institution in which they are studying and to be made aware of relevant learned societies and statutory and professional bodies. Fieldwork constitutes an essential aspect of the engagement with professional practice.

Teaching and Learning Methods

The balance of teaching and learning methods will vary between programmes according to departmental missions, aims, and interests. However, it will be characteristic of archaeology programmes in all institutions that there will be a wide range of learning and teaching styles, as befits the intellectual focus of a discipline whose core interest is the evolution and variety of human society. Much of the best teaching and learning in archaeology will be an interactive process from which students and academics gain mutual benefit because of the research-led environment for teaching. Students need to be encouraged to learn through experience, both as individuals and as members of defined teams, with practicals and fieldwork playing important roles in such provision. Directed reading represents a cornerstone for the establishment of the knowledge base. Increasingly, well-designed self-taught materials, many delivered through C&IT, may play an important role in a student's learning experience.

The principal learning and teaching methods that an archaeology student may experience will depend on the aims and objectives of the programme, but are likely to comprise an appropriate combination of the following:

- directed reading within the specialist literature (including books and periodicals)
- field-visits to appropriate monuments, structures, and collections for direct experience of material covered by the course

- field investigation projects including excavations and surveys of various sorts
- hands-on' practical exercises and science-based experiments, laboratory-based demonstrations, artefact handling and identification work
- lectures that inform by capturing interest and exciting curiosity
- placement or workplace experience with an archaeological organisation or museum
- practical exercises and demonstrations (in-door and out) in excavation and survey methodologies
- seminars that provide the context for group work and small-group discussions
- team-based exercises
- tutorials and supervisions for structured regular contact with tutors and supervisors
- a range of self-guided student-centred learning resources, from paper-based materials to IT-based tutorial modules, chat-rooms, message boards, web-sites and so on.

Further developments in teaching and learning methods are to be expected.

Within most Honours archaeology degree programmes there will be a requirement that students should undertake some form of independent research work, often in the form of project work and/or a dissertation presented in the later stages of the programme. Where field-based research is carried out, this represents an area of the student's learning in which mature and intelligent reflection will also be needed on the potential risks and moral and ethical issues associated with a proposed project.

Progression

Few students of archaeology come to the subject with appropriate underpinning knowledge, because archaeology is rarely taught pre-university; some students have practical experience. Accordingly, Level 1 (Levels 1 and 2 in Scotland) of most degree courses comprises core introductory and background studies so that all students, whatever their background, develop appropriate foundations of knowledge and understanding to fit them to embark on Levels 2 and 3 (3 and 4 in Scotland). The end of Level 1 is therefore a key progression or hurdle stage. (Some sub-degree programmes may equip students to enter degree programmes at this level.) The majority of units in Levels 2 and 3 will explore a selected range of themes in greater detail. These may be non-sequential in the sense that the order in which material is presented is a matter for individual departments to determine, but learning needs to promote increasing maturity in the integration of theory, practice, and specialist knowledge.

Assessment

There should be an explicit assessment strategy as part of the curriculum design for all archaeology courses. It is important that the adopted strategy clearly and explicitly reflects the learning outcomes of the course components, supports student learning, and enables students to demonstrate progressive levels of attainment. The strategy should reflect the variety of abilities and skills developed within the curriculum, and be tied to the methods of teaching and learning adopted by the course.

The assessment of archaeology courses should include a mix of assessment methods that are, overall, accessible to students from varying educational and cultural backgrounds within different learning situations. It is essential that the procedures used for assessment cover the subject knowledge (breadth and depth), abilities, and skills developed through the degree programme. The assessment of work undertaken in practical classes is most likely to be through exercise or project submissions. Seminar contributions may be assessed either directly or indirectly. Coursework may be part of the overall assessment of a student, or regarded as a pedagogic device for developing research and presentation skills, with formative assessment and regular feedback being provided by the tutor. Feedback and assessment may also be provided by the peer group. Assessment procedures should be fair, transparent, and externally moderated. The existing system of external examiners ensures rigour and comparability of standards.

Students of archaeology are likely to encounter a range of assessment methods during their course reflecting the range of learning objectives. The following list provides a general indicator of the range of current practice and is not meant to be a specific check-list against which to measure individual programmes:

- an extended personal research project carried out over a prolonged period and involving primary data collection or extensive synthesis of secondary data, to assess powers of data assembly and analysis (including quantitative and qualitative analysis as appropriate), presentation, knowledge deployment, argument, and reasoning
- essays and assignments prepared to a defined timetable to assess communication, analytical, and presentation skills
- examination through unseen and seen papers under timed condition requiring written essays and/or multiple choice questions to assess knowledge-base, understanding, and analytical skills
- fieldwork and/or laboratory notebooks and reports to assess observational procedures, practical skills, and methodologies
- oral presentations to assess presentation and communication skills and group work
- observed participation of practical team-based exercises in the field, laboratory and/or classroom, to assess skills in collaboration and group problem-solving
- on-line examinations and electronic work books
- annotated bibliographies
- creation of WWW pages
- portfolios of work relating to practical exercises
- reports on external placements
- unseen tests

• video, CD, posters, exhibitions, and other media forms.

6. Standards

This statement sets out both the minimum achievement and that which an average student will have demonstrated before she/he is awarded an Honours degree in archaeology. It applies only to those students who acquire at least 50 per cent of the credits for their degree programme in archaeology.

A student at the very bottom of the Honours class will have satisfactorily demonstrated achievement in most of the areas of performance listed below under Threshold Standard on a sufficient number of occasions or over a sufficient range of activities to give confidence that they have the range of knowledge, understanding, and skills expected in graduates in archaeology. The vast majority of students will perform significantly better than the minimum standard, at the Typical Standard listed below (identified here as around the II.2/II.1 boundary in conventional degree classifications). Each institution will have its own method of determining what is appropriate evidence of this achievement, but the external examiner system and the academic review system established by the QAA monitor adherence to these minimum standards.

On graduating with an Honours degree in archaeology, students should be able to:

	Threshold Standard	Typical Standard
Subject specific abilities	• demonstrate knowledge of the archaeology of selected geographical regions	• demonstrate broad and comparative knowledge of the archaeology of selected geographical regions
	• demonstrate knowledge of the archaeology of selected chronological periods	• demonstrate broad and comparative knowledge of the archaeology of selected chronological periods
	• demonstrate understanding of the principles and methods by which archaeological data are acquired and analysed	• demonstrate a good understanding of the principles and methods by which archaeological data are acquired and analysed
	• demonstrate practical experience of the recovery of primary archaeological data	• demonstrate a range of practical experience of the recovery of primary archaeological data
	• describe the variety of approaches to understanding, constructing, and interpreting the past	• evaluate the variety of approaches to understanding, constructing, and interpreting the past
	• describe the problematic and varied nature of archaeological evidence	• demonstrate comprehension of the problematic and varied nature of archaeological evidence
	• describe the development of archaeology as a discipline	• demonstrate an understanding of the development of archaeology as a discipline
	• gather and present archaeological evidence from primary and secondary sources	• gather and appropriately deploy archaeological evidence from primary and secondary sources
	• recognise the range of archaeological data	• analyse and reflect critically upon a range of archaeological data
	• research and present an extended piece of archaeological writing	• design, research, and present a sustained piece of archaeological writing
	• demonstrate knowledge of archaeological field and laboratory skills, particularly in relation to the recording and description of primary data	• demonstrate knowledge of archaeological field and laboratory skills, particularly in relation to the recording, description, and analysis of primary data
	• demonstrate awareness of the social, cultural, and political context of archaeological interpretation and practice	• apply an understanding of the social, cultural, and political context of archaeological interpretation and practice
	• demonstrate awareness of the ethical dimension of archaeology	• demonstrate a critical awareness of the ethical dimension of archaeology
		• apply an understanding of theoretical concepts to other areas of archaeology
		• show an awareness of the issues involved in planning, designing, and executing a programme of field-, laboratory-, or museum-based study

Generic skills	• demonstrate awareness of relevant archaeological concepts and methods in non-archaeological situations	• apply an understanding of relevant archaeological concepts and methods in non-archaeological situations
	• perform assigned tasks as part of a team, participating in discussion	• work as a participant or leader of a team, contributing effectively to decision-making and the achievement of objectives
	• bring together information and materials from different sources	• bring together and effectively integrate information and materials from a variety of different sources
	• identify problems and questions	• identify problems and evaluate answers or solutions
	• undertake the analysis of factual information	• undertake the analysis of factual information in a systematic and coherent way
	• recognise weaknesses in the arguments of others	• make a critical judgement of the relative strengths and weaknesses of particular arguments
	• produce a synthesis of the state of knowledge on a particular subject or topic	• produce an accurate synthesis of the state of knowledge on a particular subject or topic
	• with guidance, undertake tasks independently	• act independently in planning and undertaking tasks
	• reflect on his or her own progress	• reflect on his or her own progress, making use of feedback
	• express her/himself both orally and in writing	• both orally and in writing, express her/himself with clarity and coherence
	• present knowledge or an argument in a way which is comprehensible to others	• present knowledge or a sustained argument in a way which is comprehensible to others, including those unfamiliar with the material
	• use C&IT to select and present information	• use C&IT to select, present, and communicate information effectively and appropriately
	• make oral presentations utilising visual aids	• make oral presentations utilising visual aids effectively and appropriately
	• demonstrate an ability to listen and comprehend when presented with new ideas or information	• demonstrate an ability to listen, comprehend and reflect when presented with new ideas or information
	• demonstrate visual skills in recognising and describing material remains	• demonstrate visual skills in recognising and describing material remains, and recognising anomalies
	• demonstrate classification skills in describing, categorising, and collating data	• apply classification and analytical skills in collating and categorising data
		• demonstrate spatial awareness (both 2D and 3D) in terms of reading plans and landscapes
		• manage her/his time efficiently and effectively in relation to both practical and intellectual skills
		• apply ideas to new situations

2.3

Response and commentary

2.3a

Don Henson

The benchmarking document as it stands is, I think, a very good and very fair statement of what should be expected from an undergraduate archaeology degree. The panel has done an extremely good job given the remit that they had. However, I have two observations about the document.

The first observation is that this document should not be seen as an end in itself. It represents the beginning of a very long process of attempting to monitor, guide and assess higher education by the Government. The discipline of archaeology is really at the beginning of a long journey, and it can take advantage of this by taking every opportunity to press its case for the teaching of archaeology. Indeed, it may find it needs not only to press its case but also to defend itself in a culture that measures educational worth by vocational output.

The other observation is linked to this. The one weakness in the document relates to the need to defend archaeology to those outside the discipline who do not understand what it is and do not perceive it as important. Such people can include university vice-chancellors, politicians, journalists, bank managers etc. There are two places where archaeology is defined in the document. The first says 'archaeology can be defined as the study of the human past through material remains...', while further on it says, 'archaeology is concerned with "writing history" in the sense of narrative accounts of past cultures and societies, both pre-historic and historic.' These are both perfectly fair statements offering a definition of archaeology. However, neither goes far enough, because simply based on these statements, someone who does not like archaeology can come along and say 'What's the importance of studying the past? Why bother?' What is missing from this document is some statement of why archaeology and the study of the past is relevant to people in the present day. Although we can use this document to defend ourselves and promote archaeology, I do not think that it is as effective a defence as it could have been if it had contained a more all-encompassing definition of the discipline.

It is important to realise that having archaeology accepted as worthwhile is a problem not just in higher education, but in society in general. The CBA spent some time, trying to defend Northamptonshire Heritage Education Service from closure. Being interviewed on BBC local radio was part of this campaign and one of the first questions of the journalist was, 'why should the local authority spend money on this heritage education service, rather than on health or social services'. One cannot really reply with 'well, the study of the past is important because we think the past is interesting'. We often forget that, outside the discipline, there are people who (a) do not understand what archaeology is, (b) do not see archaeology as in any way relevant or important, and (c) think that archaeologists are just pursuing a nice private hobby, that we study the past because we like it and because it is fun. Archaeologists need to stand up and declare more often and more widely the reasons why we study the past. We need to show how archaeology is of relevance to people now, and actually come up with concrete examples of how it is relevant to people's lives. It is this that is missing from the document.

2.3b

Mike Bishop

There is no doubt that benchmarks are a feature of modern life for any service provider. In my world of local government there is 'Best Value', which will involve a review of the whole of our archaeological service; in education you have the definition of outcomes set out in the QAA benchmarks. Fear and suspicion are natural human reactions to the setting of standards and the introduction of such means of assessing their attainment. However, viewed positively, they can provide an opportunity to review both what we are doing against what we want to do, and to acquire recognition and support for our objectives.

As I mentioned in my previous paper (Bishop this volume), the IFA has also produced what amounts to a set of benchmarks. This is the statement of Expectations of General Underpinning Knowledge and Experience for Archaeological Practice that is published as an appendix to the Institute's Scheme for Continuing Professional Development (CPD). This is reproduced here in full, because the list must be read against the context of the introductory comments.

Expectations of General Underpinning Knowledge and Experience for Archaeological Practice

This statement is intended to give guidance to archaeologists on the expectations of the profession and on their individual requirements for training and Continuing Professional Development. It is also intended to assist tutors, trainers, training providers, and course managers in developing courses and packages which will meet the needs of archaeologists and the profession in education, training and CPD.

The statement implies that all archaeologists should have a good general knowledge of principles and practice across archaeology with a modicum of experience in excavation and in at least two other areas of activity. Clearly, a wider and/or deeper understanding in particular areas of knowledge or activity will be acquired, and expected, as individuals progress in their career, are employed in particular sectors of the profession or specialise.

Defining 'a good general knowledge' is difficult, for this may vary according to individual and organisational perceptions. So far as this statement is concerned, it may be taken to mean *at least* 'acquaintance', an awareness of principles and significance. This is the first of five levels of achievement proposed by the Professional Training Committee of the IFA.

It is hoped that this statement will assist individual archaeologists to identify their basic needs in preparation for such progression, employment or specialisation, and help those who are already advanced into their career in supplementing and enhancing their underpinning knowledge.

The expectations

- A good general knowledge of the principal types of monument, landscape and artefact of all periods from Palaeolithic to today
- A good general knowledge, understanding and appreciation of the principles of excavation and excavation techniques
- A good general knowledge, understanding and appreciation of the principles of survey techniques, including measured surveys, geophysical surveys, field walking, desk top studies
- A good general knowledge, understanding and appreciation of the law in respect of common law on land and property ownership, scheduled ancient monuments and other statutory designations, planning and planning guidance, treasure, burials
- A good general knowledge of the organisation of archaeology in the UK, and of the roles and functions of organisations and sectors (such as national heritage agencies, professional associations, national organisations, SMRs, curators, consultants, contractors, universities, trusts and societies) within this
- A good general knowledge, understanding and appreciation of the general history and development of field archaeology in the UK
- A good general knowledge, understanding and appreciation of current major concepts and issues in archaeological resource management
- A good general knowledge, understanding and appreciation of the principles of post-excavation studies
- A good general knowledge, understanding and appreciation of finds and other specialist studies, including palaeoenvironmental studies and dating techniques
- A good general knowledge, understanding and appreciation of the principles of interpretation of aerial photographs and uses of air photos
- A good general knowledge, understanding and appreciation of the principles of survey and interpretation of historic buildings
- A good general knowledge, understanding and appreciation of principal historical sources and of information resources, such as SMRs, records offices, National Monuments Records, museums and libraries, and of national survey and overview projects
- A good general knowledge, understanding and appreciation of the principles of project planning, through from initiation to report writing and archiving, including MAP2
- Knowledge, understanding and appreciation of IFA standards, and other standards, such as those for data
- Practical experience (to total at least 16 weeks) in archaeological fieldwork, and any two other knowledge areas above.

IFA and QAA: a meeting of minds?

The document reproduced above is an initial statement only. When the results of the review of Roles and Skills in Archaeology that is being carried out for IFA, together with English Heritage and Cultural Heritage National Training Organisation, have been absorbed the details will doubtless need refinement. The purpose of publishing the document is to give guidance to archaeologists in assessing their own learning needs and attainment today, which may be interpreted as a personal form of benchmarking. But, as the introductory comments make clear, it also provides course designers with guidance over the knowledge that archaeologists need as practitioners. In this sense, the statement also gives would-be students, not only the minority who wish to enter the profession but also the majority who wish to study archaeology for its intellectual benefits, and their mentors, an aid in making choices from the courses on offer.

It may be of interest then, to compare the IFA's Statement of Expectations with the QAA's benchmarks. I have attempted this, in what I concede is a rough, back of the envelope consideration, thus:

QAA	QAA	The IFA Expectations
Threshold Standard	**Typical Standard**	
• Demonstrate knowledge of the archaeology of selected geographical regions	• Demonstrate broad and comparative knowledge of the archaeology of selected geographical regions	
• Demonstrate knowledge of the archaeology of selected chronological periods	• Demonstrate broad and comparative knowledge of the archaeology of selected chronological periods	• A good general knowledge of the principal types of monument, landscape and artefact of all periods from Palaeolithic to today.
• Demonstrate understanding of the principles and methods by which archaeological data are acquired and analysed	• Demonstrate a good understanding of the principles and methods by which archaeological data are acquired and analysed	• A good general knowledge, understanding and appreciation of the principles of excavation and excavation techniques. • A good general knowledge, understanding and appreciation of the principles of survey techniques, including measured surveys, geophysical surveys, field walking, desk top studies. • A good general knowledge, understanding and appreciation of the principles of interpretation of aerial photographs and uses of air photos
• Demonstrate practical experience of the recovery of primary archaeological data	• Demonstrate a range of practical experience of the recovery of primary archaeological data	• Practical Experience (to total at least 16 weeks) in archaeological fieldwork, and any two other knowledge areas above.
• Describe the variety of approaches to understanding, constructing and interpreting the past	• Evaluate the variety of approaches to understanding, constructing and interpreting the past	• A good general knowledge, understanding and appreciation of the principles of excavation and excavation techniques. • A good general knowledge, understanding and appreciation of the principles of survey techniques, including measured surveys, geophysical surveys, field walking, desk top studies. • A good general knowledge, understanding and appreciation of the principles of interpretation of aerial photographs and uses of air photos • A good general knowledge, understanding and appreciation of the principles of survey and interpretation of historic buildings.
• Describe the problematic and varied nature of archaeological evidence	• Demonstrate comprehension of the problematic and varied nature of archaeological evidence	• A good general knowledge of the principal types of monument, landscape and artefact of all periods from Palaeolithic to today. • A good general knowledge, understanding and appreciation of the principles of excavation and excavation techniques. • A good general knowledge, understanding and appreciation of the principles of survey techniques, including measured surveys, geophysical surveys, field walking, desk top studies. • A good general knowledge, understanding and appreciation of the principles of interpretation of aerial photographs and uses of air photos • A good general knowledge, understanding and appreciation of the principles of survey and interpretation of historic buildings.

• Describe the development of archaeology as a discipline	• Demonstrate an understanding of the development of archaeology as a discipline	• A good general knowledge, understanding and appreciation of the general history and development of field archaeology in Britain
• Gather and present archaeological evidence from primary and secondary sources	• Gather and appropriately deploy archaeological evidence from primary and secondary sources	• A good general knowledge, understanding and appreciation of principal historical sources and of information resources, such as SMRs, Records Offices, National Monuments Records, Museums and Libraries, and of national survey and overview projects • A good general knowledge, understanding and appreciation of the principles of survey techniques, including measured surveys, geophysical surveys, field walking, desk top studies. • A good general knowledge, understanding and appreciation of finds and other specialist studies, including palaeoenvironmental studies and dating techniques • A good general knowledge, understanding and appreciation of the principles of interpretation of aerial photographs and uses of air photos • A good general knowledge, understanding and appreciation of the principles of survey and interpretation of historic buildings.
• Recognise the range of archaeological data	• Analyse and reflect critically upon a range of archaeological data	• A good general knowledge, understanding and appreciation of principal historical sources and of information resources, such as SMRs, Records Offices, National Monuments Records, Museums and Libraries, and of national survey and overview projects • A good general knowledge, understanding and appreciation of the principles of survey and interpretation of historic buildings.
• Research and present an extended piece of archaeological writing	• Design, research and present a sustained piece of archaeological writing	• A good general knowledge, understanding and appreciation of the principles of post-excavation studies.
• Demonstrate knowledge of archaeological field and laboratory skills, particularly in relation to the recording and description of primary data	• Demonstrate knowledge of archaeological field and laboratory skills, particularly in relation to the recording, description and analysis of primary data	• A good general knowledge, understanding and appreciation of the principles of post-excavation studies. • A good general knowledge, understanding and appreciation of finds and other specialist studies, including palaeoenvironmental studies and dating techniques • A good general knowledge, understanding and appreciation of the principles of excavation and excavation techniques. • A good general knowledge, understanding and appreciation of the principles of survey techniques, including measured surveys, geophysical surveys, field walking, desk top studies. • A good general knowledge, understanding and appreciation of the principles of interpretation of aerial photographs and uses of air photos • A good general knowledge, understanding and appreciation of the principles of survey and interpretation of historic buildings

• Demonstrate awareness of the social, cultural and political context of archaeological interpretation	• Apply an understanding of the social, cultural and political context of archaeological interpretation and ***practice***	• A good general knowledge, understanding and appreciation of the law in respect of Common Law on land and property ownership, Scheduled Ancient Monuments and other statutory designations, Planning and Planning Guidance, Treasure, Burials. • A good general knowledge of the organisation of archaeology in the U.K., and of the roles and functions of organisations and sectors (such as national Heritage Agencies, Professional Associations, National Organisations, SMRs, Curators, Consultants, Contractors, Universities, Trusts and Societies) within this. • A good general knowledge, understanding and appreciation of current major concepts and issues in archaeological resource management
• Demonstrate awareness of the ethical dimension of archaeology	• Demonstrate a critical awareness of the ethical dimension of archaeology	• Knowledge, understanding and appreciation of IFA standards, and other standards, such as those for data. • A good general knowledge, understanding and appreciation of current major concepts and issues in archaeological resource management
•	• Apply an understanding of theoretical concepts to other areas of archaeology	• A good general knowledge, understanding and appreciation of current major concepts and issues in archaeological resource management
•	• Show an awareness of the issues involved in planning, designing and executing a programme of field, laboratory or museum based study	• A good general knowledge of the principal types of monument, landscape and artefact of all periods from Palaeolithic to today • A good general knowledge, understanding and appreciation of principal historical sources and of information resources, such as SMRs, Records Offices, National Monuments Records, Museums and Libraries, and of national survey and overview projects • A good general knowledge, understanding and appreciation of the principles of post-excavation studies. • A good general knowledge, understanding and appreciation of finds and other specialist studies, including palaeoenvironmental studies and dating techniques • A good general knowledge, understanding and appreciation of the principles of project planning, through from initiation to report writing and archiving, including MAP2

I am not sure what this proves, save that any number of good things can be covered by general statements and *vice versa*. I think it shows that the two documents are not incompatible, and that some or all of the basic foundations of knowledge expressed in the IFA's statement can be covered by the QAA benchmarks. In this, it expresses what ought to be a common understanding that we all belong to the same community of archaeologists, whatever our field of work and study and whatever our particular perspective.

The real test of compatibility however, will depend upon the content of courses and what is actually taught and assessed against the benchmarks. The QAA document states:

'we expect degree programmes to vary in their aims, objectives, and emphases.... Particular degree programmes will be located at different points within a triangle drawn between the complementary archaeologies of the humanities, sciences, and professional practice. A department teaching Single and Combined Honours will probably position them at different locations within the tripolar range. The triangle stresses the contents, the inter disciplinarity, and the overarching practice which departments seek to instill in students.'

So, the principles of academic freedom are properly asserted and maintained. Further, professional practice is recognized as a corner stone of degree programmes. This is good, and we can all be happy. But, how much weight will be placed upon this particular corner stone? Will the positioning of courses be equidistant 'within the tripolar range' or will they be so positioned that professional practice is distant or weightless in relation to its 'complementary archaeologies' of the humanities and sciences? Much responsibility is being placed upon higher education departments here, to choose how they will address *all* the three archaeologies identified in the QAA document. We have to wait upon developments then, to see how the content of courses and their assessment against the QAA benchmarks will relate to the IFA's statement of expectations. However, without wishing to prejudge these developments, I can not but mention that the appearance of practice in only one of the benchmarks (my italics in the list above) causes some faint unease.

Otherwise, the comparison between the IFA and QAA documents shows an interesting difference in vocabulary. As statements of outcomes, that of the IFA might be regarded as the more specific in its expectations, which may be the more easily measured. It can be said of course, that the two documents are addressing different audiences and come from different contexts. Is this – should this – be so? If so, does the difference in specificity and detail then reflect two different archaeological cultures? We live in a world of expanded interest and involvement in archaeology, in which archaeologists are employed in many different capacities and many non-archaeological organisations are involved with archaeology. Consequently, we each could add other archaeologies, according to our perspective, to the three that are recognized in the QAA document. Is it that the differences in vocabulary between the two documents are expressing the new reality at the end of the Twentieth century; that there is on one hand, a culture of 'pure' archaeology within academe, and on the other, a culture of 'applied' archaeology practiced in the wider world? If this perspective is valid, as the debates in this workshop might suggest, then the issue is not about benchmarks. The real question is, who will develop and teach this applied archaeology, and how?

2.3c

Anthony Sinclair

One of the rewards of being a university teacher is that you get the opportunity, and privilege to see in some detail how students develop as both individuals and 'scholars'. Like most junior lecturers, I teach a range of subjects within the portfolio of archaeology, and to students of all levels, from first year undergraduates through to final year undergraduates (with a few above this level). Within my own department, I teach some social anthropology and archaeological theory, some of the legal, employment and ethical issues of modern archaeological practice, as well as more period specific archaeology - the archaeology of the later Palaeolithic and lithic analysis. The comments that follow come from this particular 'chalk-face', or perhaps more appropriately, the smudgy ink of our photocopier and overhead projector. Like my students, I hope, my opinions have developed each time I have read the document, and so I offer, as it were, three readings of the document; each slightly different.

As I started reading the benchmarking document, I was impressed; dare I say it, I even actually enjoyed reading it. I thought, 'this is what I teach', and, 'these are the skills that I learned as a student'. This is of course helped by the fact that from the first page, the benchmarking document notes the centrality of theory, method and practice, and the ethical side of archaeology, and I felt a certain sense of self-importance as my own teaching area was brought to the fore. But more than that, I also thought that if I ended up producing students who possessed all of the specific and generic skills (set out in the appendices at the end), I could feel proud; I would be able to sleep happily at night. In the past I have often questioned whether studying archaeology benefits our students, beyond fulfilling their own personal interest. Indeed, as a Director of Studies, I have also been asked this same question directly by the parents of prospective students, worried that their children are ruining their future life chances. The benchmarking document answers this question well.

By the end of this first reading, though, I also felt somewhat at a loss; and it took me quite a while to understand why. The introductory section notes that, of all the social sciences, archaeology is unique in that it offers a long-term perspective on human history. It is archaeology, it implies, that can identify and detail the big historical questions of human life. No problems, so far. Yet with the exception of a few key contributions of archaeological science to the subject of study, there is no mention of what these big questions might be, or for that matter what the subject of study is at all. I understand that this document has a tight word limit. I also understand that with the extent of television and media coverage offered that archaeology has gained for many years, many people might implicitly know what archaeologists do. Yet the big questions of archaeology are clear. They are covered in most introductory courses to a degree, and previously in the A-level syllabus as well. They are the origins and nature of humankind, the development of agriculture and sedentism, and the origins and development of state societies.

On my second reading through the document, I began to appreciate how it had been 'positioned', how it supports the teaching of archaeology in the modern university and work environment. Specifically, the benchmarking document argues for the value of archaeology as a course of higher education, when it is only sometimes a distinctive career route.

To this end, the benchmarking document has very closely aligned the specific skills that ought to be acquired during an archaeology degree with the generic (transferable) skills that are required for employment after a degree. This is most obvious at the end of the document where two tables outline both the specific archaeological skills and the generic skills. These tables are almost identical, except that one table appears to have had the word archaeological inserted into each skill statement. The impression presented is that during the course of an archaeology degree, students will acquire a whole range of skills that are necessary to understanding the archaeological record, yet each and every one of these skills is valuable in the world of work beyond an archaeological degree. This similarity was even further reinforced in the first web edition of the document in which the list of generic skills was published under both the specific and generic title! Was this simply an administrative slip, or did it reflect the fact that these tables are quite difficult to tell apart to any but the trained eye?

Archaeology occupies a precarious yet interesting position in universities: between degree courses that are essentially vocational in nature (e.g. medicine, veterinary medicine, nursing and engineering) and those which are not (of which history and English might be the most obvious examples). It is possible to become 'an archaeologist', although not easily; it is also very possible to study archaeology with a view to pursuing a career in another field. Our degree courses have to balance the provision of skills necessary to the practice of archaeology alongside providing skills (specifically transferable skills) with which our students may compete in the broader employment market. Moreover, as employees paid from the public purse it is reasonable for the public (students, parents, employers, and so forth) to ask what we are doing for them. If it is not obvious that we are providing a useful service, the public might reasonably wonder why they should continue to support us.

Like most universities, only a small percentage of our graduates will pursue a career in archaeology or the broader field of heritage management. Our students come to study archaeology because they are enthused by the subject either from early childhood, or more recently through the successful expanse of archaeology in the

media. In the case of Liverpool, specifically, many of our students come because of our strengths in the archaeology of Ancient Egypt, or human origins or the Near East. Moreover, for the majority of these students, a degree course at university offers the first and only opportunity within their educational career of learning about archaeology. Despite this real enthusiasm for the subject, many, from the beginning, have no intention of pursuing a career in archaeology. For some their careers advisors will already have informed them that careers in archaeology are few and far between. For others archaeology is a route to a career in the media. Finally a number will make this decision during the course of their degree, as they learn about the current structure of archaeological employment: many other careers offer longer-term security of employment, better working conditions and higher salaries. Despite these problems, archaeology still attracts large numbers of students and especially mature students. It is in this context that the benchmarking document appeared to position itself. We have to make the subject useful for the majority of our students who will pursue a career outside of archaeology.

The close alignment of generic and specific skills in the benchmarking document addresses this state of affairs very effectively. As a Palaeolithic specialist, I can rest easy in the knowledge that although I may be teaching students how to interpret a world that ceased to exist 20,000 years ago, in the same breath I can also be equipping these students with those skills that they will require in the world here and now. It is the same approach that I have often taken when in discussion with prospective students, and more often their parents, who quite legitimately worry whether a degree in archaeology offers a quick route to certain unemployment. The fact that the benchmarking document makes so little mention of our subject of study, those big questions that I alluded to above, helps in the clarity of this approach to the skills. At the end of this second reading, therefore, once again, I felt largely satisfied.

The third reading left me feeling less settled, indeed slightly challenged; but not as an archaeologist, rather as a university teacher. At the moment the School of Archaeology, Classics and Oriental Studies at Liverpool is preparing for the assessment of its teaching provision in the Subject Performance Review (scheduled for October 2001). During increasingly frequent meetings, we consider how far we have got in our production of documentation on modules, student support and guidance, curriculum content and design, and so on. The purpose of this assessment is quite clearly determined by the need for assessors to be able to judge whether we deliver what we say we deliver, and there are clearly rewards to be gained from this focus. But from the inside, this round of assessment feels more like an exercise in paper production rather than teaching improvement. When I talk to friends in other departments and other universities, the same feeling is common. Benchmarking documents, and the subsequent second stage of assessment that they usher in, will change this. We shall now be judged against an idealised provision of archaeological teaching, or history or English teaching.

Liverpool, once again like most universities, has been both modularised and semesterised in recent years. Within a degree programme, students will be offered a range of modules. From this range, students make a choice according to their likes (and dislikes). Directors of Studies help to maintain a balance between choice and structure in these individualised programmes of study. With the emphasis on skills so prevalent in the benchmarking document, this balance will be more difficult to achieve. The tables of specific and generic skills set out a specific portfolio that each student should largely acquire during the course of their degree. These skills emphasise not just the critical thinking of old, but IT, practical skills and data handling, amongst other things. These skills transcend those primary parameters of choice and provision: period, place and topic. And with distinctions becoming clearer between modules offered at levels one, two or three (and even 'M' level for Masters students), module organisers must specifically structure their modules to accommodate not only the provision of specific knowledge but also the provision of appropriate skills. It is here that the challenge presents itself. Specific skills must either be provided in each and every module at a certain level, or students must be required to follow a structured series of modules, through which the provision of these specific skills can be guaranteed. There are skills implications and programme choice implications here.

Lecturers are still primarily appointed according to their research potential. Moreover, lecturers are primarily promoted on the basis of their research output. This is measured in the production of peer-reviewed journal papers, or texts published by reputable academic publishers. In the universities of old, academics might be eccentric, and, perhaps, unskilled teachers, but students still benefited from their close association with people who were so actively involved in research. In the universities of today, staff work the long hours they are known to do, because the research side of their work is both rewarding and vital: it is certainly not the salary. The benchmarking document directly acknowledges the importance and value of this research activity. It notes that archaeology undergraduates are unique in that, during their undergraduate career, they will themselves be actively involved in primary research activities. And it goes further still and argues that archaeology should only be taught in research active departments. When we look at the specific and generic skills set out in the appendix, they are largely those skills that are important to active research. But the successful teaching of these skills is, itself, a highly skilled activity. It requires a considerable investment of time and energy, and for primary and secondary school teachers there are specific programmes of training and continuing professional development. Yet very few lecturers enter universities with such a training.

In addition to this, for most modules, there are few if any dedicated teaching materials that directly address the provision of the diverse range of skills set out in the benchmarking document. For example, for teaching archaeological theory, or teaching the ethical issues of archaeology or the practical structures there are books that currently provide the specific knowledge of these subjects, with varying degrees of success. To successfully provide skills we need to take students beyond a state of knowing or memorising a specific body of knowledge, to the state where they can successfully apply general principles of critical thinking, or data analysis (amongst other skills) in new situations. The best analogy that I can think of at the moment is to suggest that this is like the difference between pure and applied mathematics. But very few archaeology texts adequately provide a framework for the teaching of skills. There are very few 'applied archaeology' texts as such. Moreover, the individual, active research approach of lecturers often means that, whilst they might agree with certain parts of current texts, they usually wish to follow a more individual line in their teaching. Module organisers are, therefore, already largely responsible for developing teaching materials, and for the future these materials will need development to adequately address the provision of skills. This will require considerable co-ordination, and not a few late nights. It represents a challenge not just for individual module organisers, but for the discipline as a whole. And if other benchmarking documents make the same case for skills, it also represents a challenge to universities to reward their staff for producing teaching materials that might not normally have been considered major works of research.

To conclude, the benchmarking document represents a real challenge to the discipline as it is taught in universities. It locates archaeology within a complicated triangle of theoretical, practical and ethical interests. Through its emphasis on skills, it makes a good argument for archaeology as a genuinely useful subject of study, even though most of our students may not follow an archaeological career afterwards. It also values archaeology both for the importance of active research and its teaching as a subject of study.

2.3d

Benchmarking archaeology: comments on Henson, Bishop and Sinclair

Graeme Barker

Matthew Johnson provides an excellent overview of the writing of the *Benchmarking Archaeology* document: of the issues we faced, how we came to decisions, and what we were trying to do in our careful choice of language (for example, the need to bring students into contact with the practice as well as the theories of archaeological science requiring 'having access to', as opposed to 'having' appropriate laboratories, so that a small department, or a strongly arts-based department, would not be penalised). Hence I only want to offer a few short additional comments here.

Unlike the UGC review of the late 1980s which he mentions, where the key parameter of the exercise was to define how many staff were needed to teach a single honours archaeology degree, we wanted to provide a framework for teaching and learning in archaeology in any course in which archaeology was a component. We were mindful of the diversity of the teaching of archaeology courses in 2000, and anxious to celebrate that diversity. But I and others in SCUPHA had also been involved in the negotiations with HEFCE a few years earlier to get archaeology recognised as more expensive to teach than mainstream humanities subjects: we were successful, and as a result HEFCE had placed archaeology in a separate fee band alongside subjects such as geography, midway between the fee bands for the humanities and the laboratory sciences, in recognition of the costs of the laboratory and especially field component in archaeology courses. Hence the Benchmarking panel knew that it was important for us to identify both for colleagues but more particularly for our institutions and their paymasters where the boundaries of our subject lay: in other words, the boundaries within which the archaeology fee band, with all its diversity of course content, was nevertheless appropriately located.

Don Henson's first point is particularly apposite: that *Benchmarking Archaeology* was not meant to be something fixed in stone. It was written as an overview of the teaching of the discipline in UK universities at a particular moment in time, on the assumption that it will be revised in a reflexive manner at regular intervals in the future. His second comment is fair criticism: that we were probably not explicit enough in our introductory remarks about why archaeology matters: being interested in our past (that 'backward-looking curiosity' the early antiquarians wrote about) is important not just in its own right, as one of the defining things that humans do, but also has direct relevance for understanding the present and the future of our species and the world we inhabit. We thought we had trumpeted the unique importance, scale, and

excitement, of our discipline in our opening paragraphs, which were certainly addressed to the world at large rather than to our colleagues. If, even so, we have undersold ourselves, it was certainly not intentional. In the same vein my main criticism of the *Time Team* would be that, whilst it gets across to the general public two key aspects of archaeology, that it is (a) fun and (b) technically complex, it singularly fails to demonstrate that it is also (c) important, capable of tackling big issues about what it is to be human. Anthony Sinclair defines those issues in his comment as the 'Big Three Revolutions' of human history – human, agricultural, and urban – but we can as easily focus on other histories, of gender, class, ethnicities, aggressive versus cooperative modes of behaviour, ecological impacts, and so on, as other important arenas where archaeology is uniquely positioned to inform on their long term histories.

Many of us will sympathise with Anthony Sinclair's points about the challenges of providing a coherent training in archaeology within today's semesterized and modularized systems, that tend to promote a large number of small-scale assessments of gobbet-size learning rather than reflective and joined-up understanding of a subject. But we were clear that, however universities went about it, their archaeology courses had to deliver one key component in terms of learning progression: increasing understanding of archaeological theory, archaeological practice, and in particular of how they interact with each other in the creating of archaeological history. As an aside on the 'transferable skills' agenda he mentions, it would be (as he implies) unrealistic and indeed undesirable for every module to incorporate skills training in a formulaic way, and even allowing for a great deal of student choice it is possible to plan pathways of learning through suites of modules to ensure that each student will develop progressive facility and confidence in transferable skills through the three years of their course. And one of the chief roles of the LTSN Centre for History, Classics and Archaeology is to provide guides to good practice to support departments in course development, the provision of teaching materials, and so on, with the archaeology component in particular operating as a 'one stop shop' of advice about best practice and practitioners to contact (see Grant and Reynier, this volume).

However, all university teachers of archaeology will surely agree totally with Anthony Sinclair's comment in his penultimate paragraph that we are fundamentally concerned with providing not just knowledge and skills but, especially, graduate-level understanding of the discipline (essentially the point above about progressive understanding of theory, practice, and their inter-relationships). And this is where the comments of the university teachers about the benchmarking exercise differ fundamentally from those of Mike Bishop. He endeavours to demonstrate that there is a close match between *Benchmarking Archaeology* and the IFA's *Expectations of General Underpinning Knowledge and Experience for Archaeological Practice*. There seem to me to be fundamental disparities, however. First, the IFA document is based on the premise of the 'archaeology degree', that is, the single honours degree (though do they mean the BA or BSc, which can be very different?), but the benchmarking document deals with all archaeology teaching – and probably the majority of students studying archaeology today is taking joint degrees. Second, the IFA document privileges British archaeology for obvious reasons (I assume that 'a good expectation of the principal types of monument, landscape and artefact of all periods from Palaeolithic to today' is not meant to be worldwide), whereas whilst there are many archaeology courses in British universities that focus on Britain and many others on Britain and Europe, several develop specialist knowledge of the Near East and/or Egypt, and a few on other parts of the world. Thirdly, and most fundamentally, 'understanding' as well as 'knowledge' is required by the IFA under several headings – the principles of fieldwork, the structure and organisation of British archaeology, the history of the subject, archaeological resource management, post-excavation, air photography, buildings, SMRs, MAP2 – but not understanding of the nature of archaeological data and of the complexity of their interpretation.

Being able to 'evaluate the variety of approaches to understanding, constructing, and interpreting the past' is the not the same (as Mike Bishop's table implies) as 'a good general knowledge, understanding, and appreciation, of the principles of excavation, survey, AP interpretation, and surveying historic buildings'; 'comprehending the problematic and varied nature of archaeological evidence' is not the same as the combination of 'a good general knowledge of monument types' and 'a good general knowledge, understanding, and appreciation, of the principles of excavation, survey etc.'; the ability to analyse and reflect critically upon a range of archaeological data is not the same as knowing about SMRs and historic building registers; and few university teachers will recognise 'understanding the principles of post-excavation studies' as equating with the 'critical ability to design, research, and present a sustained piece of archaeological writing' (commonly the final year dissertation). The complexities of the research process identified under the last heading he cites ('awareness of the issues involved in planning, designing, and executing a programme of field-, laboratory-, or museum-based study') are poorly equated with knowing how developer-funded archaeology works in Britain and with the research outcomes of MAP2 as it is currently operating in terms of archiving and report writing (whether or not in relation to regional research agendas).

In Mike Bishop's penultimate paragraph it is also a misunderstanding of the role of UK archaeology teaching at first degree level to welcome our inclusion of professional practice in the 'archaeology triangle' alongside humanities archaeology and science-based archaeology but to worry about how UK archaeology courses will deliver all three components to an appropriate level. Our point in proposing the triangle was to say that

we expected all archaeology courses to include some of all three, but in very different proportions reflecting the variety of institutional, departmental, and course aims. By the time they graduate, all archaeology students need to be aware of the three corners of the 'disciplinary triangle', but they will have selected courses that explicitly position themselves in a particular part of our pleasingly diverse intellectual landscape.

Our primary role as university teachers is to provide a range of broad-based archaeology courses to suit a very wide, and we hope expanding, student body, the majority of whom will not become professional archaeologists. At the same time our courses must certainly provide an appropriate level of familiarity with professional practice for those students who want to progress in the profession. For these professional aspirants, as for all archaeology students, our core business must be in developing intellectual skills at graduate level – 'how to think' in the time-honoured phrase: knowledge and skills, yes, but self-reflective understanding most of all. Our future professionals then need to build on the broad platform of their first degree training with further training to develop specialist skills, commonly by a taught Masters and/or extensive hands-on professional training. It should certainly not be a dichotomy between 'pure' and 'applied' archaeology (and archaeologists?!) as implied by Mike Bishop's final and somewhat depressing comment. Nobody would envisage such a tension between the appropriate content of first degree training in engineering or architecture or medicine, and the appropriate content of professional practice beyond the degree: in these professions it is an effective partnership between universities and professional organisations, and should be the same for us.

2.3e

Yannis Hamilakis

For me, it is the context rather than the content that is more important in the benchmarking exercise; it is clear that the content projects a much more sophisticated and up-to date view of archaeology than previous official documents of similar kind and function, but it is also clear that this view is the product of inevitable compromises amongst the authors, who seem to represent a diverse range (and perhaps opposing sets) of ideas on archaeology, its nature and role. Before I proceed, I should say that I am sure that all of us appreciate the hard work that the colleagues in the panel put into producing it, and I am sure that all of them acted in the interests of the community of academic archaeologists. The most important thing for me, however, is to understand the role of this document in the broader shape of things, and its place within the recent changes in British higher education; to understand its function and future consequences, but also the implicit philosophy of its production and implementation.

This initiative is part and parcel of the whole range of procedures that some critics (e.g. Shore and Wright 1999) have called neoliberalism in British higher education: erosion of the public character of universities, the instrumentalist/banking attitude towards knowledge and thinking, the audit culture under the pretence of accountability, the quantification of academic research and teaching procedures. As I tried to explain in my introductory chapter to this volume, these procedures are presented as neutral, technical and administrative measures which subscribe to abstract notions, such as quality and efficiency; they thus appear to be a 'doxa' (in Bourdieu's sense) which is beyond criticism in its core: after all, who will be against, quality and efficiency? In my introductory chapter to this volume I tried to show that this discourse subscribes to a specific neoliberal philosophy on education and society, masking the highly contested nature of knowledge, and the immense inequalities in the present education system. I have also proposed that our starting point of the evaluation of our teaching should not be an abstract notion of efficiency or quality, but the principle of responsibility (in this case, towards our students and to taxpayers who fund public education).

Within this climate, this document signifies an important development. Leaving apart some earlier, small-scale attempts, it is the first attempt to produce a coherent, national authoritative guide on the fundamental principles of archaeological teaching (defining, for a first time, national learning outcomes), to set the criteria upon which the future national monitoring process of teaching will be based. It is well known that the current QAA assessment cycle is the last one that will be based solely on each departments' own teaching and learning strategy, aims, goals and criteria. The subsequent assessment procedures will be based, to a large extent, on the benchmarking document (in conjunction with internal departmental evaluation). In other words, this is the closest we have come to a 'national curriculum' of university archaeology departments. It is also clear that the government and its agencies such as QAA will take the document very seriously and use it as 'stick to hit the sector', a stick provided by the sector itself. The chair of the archaeology panel, Graeme Barker, in his cover letter states that 'It is clearly vital that we get the document to fit what we actually do, and the kind of graduates we actually produce, as QAA assessors will be using it against which to assess our teaching programmes in the future, beyond the forthcoming TQA'. Additionally, according to the QAA, the benchmarking statements 'are an important external source for reference for higher education institutions when new programmes are being designed and developed in the subject area' (from the introduction to the benchmarking statements).

It is thus anticipated that the two most significant consequences of this development within the broader climate (the neoliberalism and instrumentalism that characterise British academia at present, and the diminishing and centralisation/'rationalisation' of

resources) will be:

a) The closing down of departments or subject groups which do not 'fit the bill'. The Research Assessment Exercise (RAE) is already being used as a mechanism to channel funding into few and perhaps in the future fewer departments. This document will probably be used in conjunction with the RAE scores. After all, it is stated in the benchmarking document that only research active departments should offer degrees in archaeology. This will inevitably mean that, departments which are deemed by RAE criteria to be research inactive, will not be allowed to offer degrees.

b) For the remaining departments, an anticipated consequence is likely to be the drastic change of the curriculum to comply with this document. Both consequences are, to my mind, retrogressive and should be resisted. Rather than enforcing a centralisation of archaeology teaching, the departments or centres which are seen as offering inadequate provision in archaeology teaching, should be helped to improve their resources and be allowed to develop their own vision on teaching, guided by the principles of responsibility towards students and society. As for the rest, the review and the changes in the curriculum, should be the result of extensive consultation and debate, and follow the specific teaching and learning philosophy and aims and objectives of the respective department, rather than the prescriptions of a benchmarking document.

Furthermore, while within academic politics and the present funding regime it may be tactically expedient to define clearly the boundaries of archaeology (see Johnson, this volume), challenging and innovative ideas come from cross-fertilisation and from disrespect towards historically contingent, disciplinary boundaries. Is it not ironic that in our research and teaching we emphasise the fluid, changeable and contingent nature of identities, and yet, we attempt here to produce a clearly defined, concrete and solid identity? The panel was clearly attempting to define archaeology as a discipline, quite distinctive from cognate fields, such as history and anthropology, but have they produced a very narrow definition of the subject as a result? The main emphasis of the document is on the study of the past through its material traces. Yet, while most of us would agree that it is the broadly defined materiality which makes what we do distinctive, the separation between past and present appears more and more problematic in many of the things we do. On my desk at the moment, sits a recent book called, *Archaeologies of the Contemporary Past* (Buchli and Lucas 2001) in which many authors use archaeology in its broadest sense, and deploy archaeological methodologies and techniques to understand the present. I have recently been talking to an archaeology finalist about the possibility of her carrying out a PhD project which will involve the 'excavation' of a present-day neighbourhood in Southampton (soon to be demolished as part of a 'regeneration' project), as a case study on archaeology and social responsibility. But this as an approach is not that new: we only need to think of the 'garbage project' (Rathje and Murphy 1992), perhaps the most famous case of an archaeology of the present, which started in the 1970's and which as an example is taught in many courses in British archaeology departments. Is there room for these ideas and approaches in the document? Shall I say to the student, not to bother and try and do something more 'mainstream' and central to the benchmarking document's vision of archaeology? All major paradigmatic shifts in archaeology since the 1960's happened as a result of re-definition of our enterprise, and of pushing the boundaries of archaeology. There is thus a very real danger that, as a result of the financial and administrative pressures, we may be forced to produce a defensive, averaged out (as a result of inevitable compromises) but, at the end of the day, narrow definition of the discipline; the self-policing of the disciplinary boundaries will inevitably lead to stagnation. All in all, there is a real danger that the implementation of the benchmarking document may lead to stifling of diversity and plurality in the teaching of archaeology.

Before I conclude, I would like to say a word or two on the content of the document. According to the most recent survey (Chitty 1999: 6) approximately 1100 individuals graduate in archaeology annually, and from them, only 10-15% will have a serious interest in pursuing a career in archaeology. The vast majority of people who do archaeology therefore, do it not because they are interested in pursuing a career in archaeology, but because they are attracted by the subject and its broad nature, and want to use the archaeology degree as a broad basis and foundation. We should not forget therefore that we are not in the business of training professional archaeologists as such, although of course we should provide the opportunities for those who wish to acquire the foundations for such a training, to do so. The archaeology curriculum in Britain is not vocational and it should not be. It is likely that a radical change of the curriculum towards a more vocational direction will isolate the subject and deprive it of its wide appeal and popularity that it enjoys, especially at this moment in time, when there are signs that cognate disciplines are facing a recruitment crisis. While many parts of the text give the impression that they indeed promote a broad conception of archaeology, other parts are extremely problematic; to give just one example: the huge question of ethics and archaeology, not simply as a set of professional procedures and practices but as an engagement with the socio-political dimension of archaeology, the conception of archaeological practice as present-day activity with ethical, social and political consequences implicating diverse audiences constituencies and interest groups, is remarkably underplayed in the document. In one or two occasions it is mentioned in the same sentence as the health and safety regulations: it appears thus that ethics, according to the document, is something you have to take into account in order to satisfy some professional standards, rather than a dimension which permeates all aspects of our theoretical and practical work.

But the most worrying thing as far as the content of the document is concerned, is the checklist at the end, which summarises the minimum standards for archaeology degrees. It seems that these will be the most important criteria that the QAA will use to judge departments. The broad and at times inclusive discussion in the main body of the document is summarised and distilled in the checklists at the end. A number of questions can be raised here: is there a hierarchy of importance in the listing? And if so, is the knowledge of periods and regions more important than critical thinking and the understanding of the social, cultural and political context of archaeology (well down the list)? Why is the notion of reflexivity in teaching and learning in archaeology (which is mentioned in the main text) absent? Does this not imply a perpetuation of an objectivist and seemingly distant approach to knowledge and thinking, an approach which many recent theoretical traditions in archaeology have helped to demolish? Finally and more importantly, why are all the words which refer to the critical understanding and awareness of archaeological knowledge missing from the 'thresholds standards' table? Does this imply that only the most 'able' students will be the critical thinkers, whereas the rest just need to be able to memorise and describe knowledges, methods and techniques? What is higher education about, if not the development of critical thinking?

As the document says more than once, archaeology today is an extremely diverse discipline. It is also characterised by a variety of approaches and theoretical paradigms. It is naive to believe that all of us have the same view on what archaeology is or what it should be about, or on what is the most important dimension for research. For example, whereas some of us would say that what is most important is the recovery and interpretation of the conventional primary archaeological material, others would prioritise the critical analysis of archaeology as a discipline and as cultural production, and the study of the consumption of archaeological products in the present. Both approaches are valid today, and should continue to be considered valid and important. Academic freedom should guarantee that all staff and students, and all departments should continue to enjoy the right to pursue their own approaches, and, where appropriate and possible, define common missions and objectives, either as groups and teams or as departments. Benchmarking and the philosophy behind it, despite its authors best intentions, appears to lead to a different direction, that of homogenisation. I suggest that we should regain the initiative by reclaiming our autonomy as an academic community, implementing our own flexible, open, and diverse procedures which guarantee accountability and competence (such as the external examiners system), rather than implementing bureaucratic procedures which restrict creativity and diversity.

References

Buchli, V. and Lucas, G. (eds) 2001. *Archaeologies of the Contemporary Past.* London: Routledge.

Chitty, G. 1999. *Training in Professional Archaeology: A Preliminary Review.* Carnforth: Hawkshead Archaeology and Conservation.

Rathje, W.L. and Murphy, C. 1992. *Rubbish! The Archaeology of Garbage.* New York: Harper Collins.

Shore, C. and Wright, S. 1999. Audit culture and anthropology: neo-liberalism in British Higher Education. *Journal of the Royal Anthropological Institute* (N.S.) 5: 557-75.

2.3f

David Austin

The benchmarking document in archaeology I see very much as a transition point within a process which has been happening through the whole of the time I have been active in universities, was happening long before and will continue long after I am dead and gone. I could define this in Mandelsonian terms as the 'project of archaeology within the academy' of which there have been several significant phases, one of which has been drawing to an end in the last few years, while another has been struggling into life in a somewhat diverse and confusing way. In this perspective the benchmarking document must now become part of the process by which the diffuse archaeological project clarifies and re-defines itself. Thus it has come at an interesting and important time in the development of our subject and will undoubtedly play its part in how it changes and, indeed, in how it survives.

I think that the previous stage of the project was defined in the late 70's and 80's, in very similar circumstances to now. Elsewhere I have defined that project as 'get larger and get smarter' (Austin in press): in other words, archaeology, in the process of defending itself from at least two attempts to narrow its base by rationalization, actually recruited more students into a greater number of departments with an increasingly diverse portfolio of courses and at the same time became more theoretically and philosophically mature, thus justifying its new, stronger position in the mainstream of academic subjects. In a very real sense the benchmarking document is also, therefore, an expression, a summation, of the success of that project, which was conducted, broadly speaking, in the name of a general collective of archaeologists as a whole whether in universities or not. Annie Grant has said in response to this document, that she had read it and felt proud to be an archaeologist: not, note, an academic, but an archaeologist. I would echo that sentiment as a fellow member of the old collective, but what we have to reflect on is whether that is still a realistic proposition and whether it still has a place in the conduct of our profession which the government and circumstance is actively re-defining and making more and more distinct from something which we might call a functioning collective. The benchmarking document is, after all, part of a suite of top-down initiatives which is forcing us to behave more like teachers and secondary synthesizers than archaeologists.

This is part, but only part, of what I see as the fissile tendency in archaeology as a whole. Within the benchmarking document, there is, if we are not careful a potential narrowing of the base of archaeology after a decade in which it has expanded exponentially. It is a kind of reductive puritanism. It begins with the central definition: 'the study of the human past through material remains', i.e. the past **itself** as an objective construct. By contrast for many of us the central proposition of the discipline is that it is 'the study, through material remains, of both the nature and the **uses** of the human past'. This relates not just to what some may try to dismiss as ideology (but what I would call philosophy), but also to the widening practice and vocation of archaeology. Here we seem to be surrendering ground we have already won in selling our discipline to a public and a government wanting more relationship with the world of work. We should not, as the document does, be downgrading the study and experience of 'uses' to a secondary role. Where is museology, heritage practice, graphic animation, integrated land use management, media, environmental conservation and a growing number of other related practices, which can lodge archaeology into the heart of a changing world? The document is written, however subconsciously, from the point of view of the traditional university privileging research, and its associated teaching only, into the past itself. This at a time when we have intellectually constructed the middle ground between us and politics, sociology, psychology, and metaphysics, as well as science and many other subjects. We have made the uses of the material past not just a matter of vocational skill, but important intellectual process for the societies of our contemporary world and thus **central** to what we do as part of the self-definition of what we are as the wider collective. To relegate this is to withdraw us from the truly exciting dynamic of the subject.

At the same time as we seem to be narrowing our ground as academic practitioners, so also the gap between us and our nearest and dearest in the professional practice of field archaeology is widening. This is felt not least in the issue of who is responsible for training the next generation of field archaeologists or artefact specialists. We academics see this task as being fulfilled not at undergraduate level where we must focus much more on transferable and generic skills rather than specific training, but at postgraduate level whether for an MA or, increasingly, I suspect, as short course and distance or e-learning provision. Who, however, pays for this? At the moment the uncomfortable choice for the graduate wanting to be a field archaeologist is to learn on the job at an absolute pittance for an indeterminate period or to find enough to do a course which may (or may not) have a true relationship with the real practice out there. As field archaeology, through the processes of contract, control the resources and expertise of practice, there is not enough money to allow the universities to undertake proper training programmes and fund students, even if they had the will or the mission statement to do so. Until this is resolved and a way is found to resolve the transition the fissile forces in the old collective will continue to drive us further apart. This is compounded at a research level where increasingly universities are not involved directly in the field archaeology of Britain, where our libraries cannot afford even a small proportion of the general output of field archaeology, even where it passes from the grey areas of report into the full light of publication. Consequently increasing amounts of archaeological information are failing to pass into the domains of synthesized knowledge. If this is happening what is the purpose of field archaeology outside of the admittedly vital task of providing information for the narratives and relationships with the material past which sustain local communities?

The benchmarking document is a retraction from the expanding universe or at least a consolidation around a narrow core of methodology and theory and I worry about this. Geography went through this when it separated itself from planning and other hands-on processes, and I sense that the subject is now suffering the consequences of this narrowing and is retracting not least in its reduced role as a school subject. If archaeology goes down this line and 'heritage practice' and other vocational courses are hived off into other domains, then certainly the principles of the old collective will be abandoned forever to our great cost, I feel. As such the benchmarking document cannot be predicated as an archaeology mission statement and it should not be injected into the vacuum that exists in relationship to a corporate archaeology project. Maybe it would be unfair of us to expect that it should, given that it was not the task defined for it, but that it doesn't must weaken us unless we also pay attention to the simultaneous construction of documents and intermediate institutions which successfully maintain and sustain the middle grounds. And I do feel that here was an opportunity missed, perhaps because the committee was dominated by the traditional research-focussed institutions.

If there is to be a corporate archaeology project we have got to find a set of words that will allow the family of archaeology, as Mike Bishop was talking about, to go on constituting itself and keep driving towards a set of common goals. We did succeed with in the previous stage of the undertaking and we are bigger: we are in a vast number of other different kinds of institutions and unless we are careful to be much more inclusive the fissile tensions will tear us apart, perhaps not savagely or violently but nonetheless effectively.

When we were constructing a similar statement, a much shorter and briefer statement, for the subject submission to the Barron Committee, in 1987/8, we were conscious that we were in the business of conflict resolution and we compromised over many areas of difficulty. Then we took it for granted that we shared common cause with the wider professions. Yet I must also admit that we still, at that

time, had a relatively narrow understanding of what archaeology was. Are we about to become victims of our own success and suffer the inevitable consequences of an expanding universe?

Back in the 1980s the tensions already existed in the central definition of our subject, but we felt that this was not the place or forum to address the hard issues and hang out our dirty linen in public. The same thing has happened again with the benchmarking committee and I cannot blame them for that.

On a completely other tack, while I am in reflective and elegiac mode, I can interpose a couple of thoughts about how the benchmarking document will be used. First, whether we like it or not, it will be used as a check-list: from the late 80s the Barron Report document was used as a check-list particularly when we had our TQA investigation, so it will be for the QAA. What worries me is that universities are slowly being brought into line with other sectors of education where the rhetorics of benchmark became all too quickly the rhetorics of judgement which brought the corrosive effects of fear of failure into the system. You can bet your bottom dollar that if the present ethos of government continues then the word failure will be used in the context of universities and departments.

The second thought is not so negative. The other way in which the Barron Report document was used by myself and many others was to take it to Vice-Chancellors and say here are all the things we have got to deliver for archaeology and we cannot do that with three and a half staff and tuppence for a budget. It becomes a tool, maybe the primary tool in negotiating for a better delivery for archaeology as a whole, and we must be prepared politically to use that. If we narrow the project we miss a political trick.

For this reason I, like others, am concerned that there is no enlightened end-user statement, based on clear-cut analysis. In the 80s we worked very hard to provide the data to underpin our assertions of growth and the potential for the subject to be as generic for graduate output as any other major discipline. This was not the task of the benchmarking committee and I am glad, as we have heard in the workshop, that others have taken it on, but we did have some better hooks in the statement to hang the wider project on. Just looking at it in terms of our own self interest, as the 2000's go on increasingly we will be asked what is it that we are delivering for public consumption, and here an end-user analysis which informs the content and the progression within our degrees and which creates a sense of multiple and growing output will become vital, if we are not to ossify.

All of this sounds very critical and I did not mean to be. The document, of itself, is exemplary and I would not take away from anything that has been said. I only wish that it had been a bit more aware of the wider context and responsibilities that such an *ex cathedra* statement has. We, internally, can deconstruct it and take or leave such bits of it as we will, but others externally cannot and will not. Based on my experience I wonder whether we have missed a political trick here and we will live to see the withering away of what we have achieved. I hope not.

Reference

Austin, D. in press. Archaeology, funding and the responsibilities of the University. In *The Responsibility of Archaeologists* (ed. M. Pluciennik). Oxford: Archaeopress (BAR series).

PART III

TEACHING THE PAST IN THE FUTURE

Fieldtrip theory: towards archaeological ways of seeing

Cornelius Holtorf

Fieldtrips in archaeology

Fieldtrips (excursions, visits) are a central element of the discourse of archaeology. They play an important role in the curricula of undergraduate degree courses, the programmes of archaeological societies, and virtually all academic conferences and meetings worldwide. So strong is the desire of archaeologists to visit each other's sites, finds and museums, that their partners and families know that their private holidays too can quickly become small archaeological fieldtrips! As important as such trips can be for individuals travelling with archaeological societies, their families, or on their own, I will restrict my discussion in the following largely to academic fieldtrips organised for and undertaken with students in archaeology.

It is remarkable that to date the archaeological fieldtrip (or visit) as an institution has not been critically studied by archaeologists (for some beginnings of a discussion see Shanks 1995: 25f.; Pearson and Shanks 1997; Lampeter Archaeology Workshop n.d.). This is surprising not only because travel as such has been discussed extensively among archaeologists for a very long time (cf. all the debates about migrations and trade), but also because of the recent interest in discourse analysis and the significance of subjective experiences in archaeology. The notion of 'time-travel' to archaeological sites in the past has been problematised extensively in relation to heritage attractions such as Jorvik in York (UK), but travel to the same sites in the present remains unquestioned in the literature. Until recently, the reason for this was that the educational importance of archaeological fieldtrips was taken to be self-evident. Archaeologists and others organised fieldtrips, or participated in them, without too many reflections about their aims and character: 'you just go and see this-and-that'. The questions asked ahead of a trip were normally restricted to such of costs and exact itinerary ('but we *must* see that site too').

Over the last decade or so, university teachers and other educators (e.g. within English Heritage) have begun to re-think the traditional fieldtrip format and designed new kinds of trips which are often task-orientated. It is, however, difficult to review such innovative fieldtrip formats since there is little or no discussion in print. In geography, on the other hand, where fieldtrips are of the same importance and were traditionally conducted in similar ways as in archaeology (cf. Clark 1996: 386–388), the format and aims of fieldtrips have been scrutinised and become the subject of some debate (e.g. Cosgrove and Daniels 1989; Panton and Dilsaver 1989; Gold and Haigh 1992; Haigh and Gold 1993; Jenkins 1994; Clark 1996; Higgitt 1996; McEwan and Harris 1996; May 1999). As a

consequence, novel ways of teaching geography in the field are tried and tested all the time.

Having been a student in archaeology for ten years, at several universities in Germany and Britain, my own experience as a participant in archaeological fieldtrips ranges from organised day excursions to museums or local prehistoric sites, sometimes as part of conferences, to entirely self-organised trips with friends to archaeological sites in various areas of Europe, to a week-long fieldclass in Andalucía (Spain) arranged and substantially subsidised by the Department in Lampeter. Since then I went on several fieldtrips in Spain, Greece and Britain as a co-leader. Some five years ago, we begun at Lampeter to review critically the aims, methods and outcomes of such trips. These discussions and experiments led not only to the present paper but also to another, as yet unpublished manuscript (Lampeter Archaeology Workshop n.d.).

I will argue in the following that a closer look at the character of traditional archaeological fieldtrips will reveal substantial problems of their set-up and procedure. I wish to propose a way of conducting archaeological fieldtrips which, in my opinion, makes them more valuable and worthwhile. There may also be certain advantages from such an approach for conducting field classes in a contemporary university environment with ever higher student-staff ratios, increasing pressure on teaching staff, and effectively reduced resources (cf. Jenkins 1994; Clark 1996; Higgitt 1996). If similar ideas have already been tested and adopted among colleagues, then so much for the better. My paper will hopefully stimulate these colleagues to put their own experiences into words and then in print too, so that a wider discussion can be conducted for the benefit of the entire discipline.

The traditional fieldtrip format in archaeology

The traditional fieldtrip format in archaeology has been well described by Johnson (1999: 1):

'Every year we get chilled to the marrow or bitten half to death by mosquitoes while visiting some unprepossessing, grassy mound in the middle of nowhere. Miles from a decent restaurant or even a warm bath, we try to look interested while the rain comes down in sheets and some great professor whose best work was 20 years ago witters on in a monotone about what was found in Trench 4B.'

More systematically, such fieldtrips can be described by the following characteristics:

- The participants spend a lot of time travelling in coaches in order to get to archaeological sites. The trips are often late in their time schedule due to a combination of overcrowded itinerary and overcrowded toilets. Moreover, it seems as if most archaeological fieldtrips are undertaken when the weather is extraordinarily poor.

- The trips are led by group-leaders who during the coach journey tend to give long lectures over the microphone system, while the students are looking at the passing landscape and landmarks. During the lecture, the windows take over the function of the projection screen in a lecture theatre and create an experience not dissimilar to that of a standard lecture (Gold and Haigh 1992: 118).

- Fieldtrips are normally documented in specifically prepared handbooks and/or bought travel guides which can be very detailed and usually contain descriptive accounts of why particular places are academically important. In Germany, students are used to compile large volumes summarising the academic literature of each site they are going to visit. They are gaining credits for their course on the basis of this work, which also has to be presented in preparatory seminar meetings and/or during the trip itself. In Britain, the trip leaders are responsible for putting together a handbook, while the students often write essays afterwards.

- Such trips often involve guided tours by local experts, usually 'leading authorities' who are met, after prior arrangements, on the site. They then take over academic responsibility for the visit of the particular site and sometimes also arrange for refreshments or meals.

- Particularly enjoyable are the many opportunities of informal discussions and gossiping they provide. Gossip and anecdotes heard from others or (embarrassing) events happening on such trips become part of the 'social memory' of the discipline and are frequently passed on to other archaeologists. Fieldtrips are also good for making contact with particular individuals and 'networking' (see Grinsell 1989 for many vivid memories of meeting 'famous' archaeologists on fieldtrips, and some brilliant anecdotes).

While many occurrences on fieldtrips are entirely coincidental, others are determined by a variety of constraints and conditions. As it invariably turns out, much that at first seemed desirable or even imperative to do is impossible to put into practice due to the logistics of meals and accommodation, basic health and safety requirements, and financial limits. Often, large group sizes equal more time spent at each location and this can be a severe constraint on the flexibility of groups. In the academic context, decreasing staff-student ratios prevent effective supervision or instruction of small groups and let the teaching experience on fieldtrips become more and more formal and similar to that in the lecture theatres at home. Furthermore, the size of, or access to, some locations such as caves pose strict limits on how it can be visited by groups, in terms of both numbers of visitors at any one

time and particular preservational requirements. In addition, every fieldtrip encounters a variety of further circumstances as a result of which some plans have to be scrapped: unforeseen traffic congestion, delays because of difficulties finding sites, and strikes of museum personnel have all been known to interrupt carefully devised fieldtrip schedules.

Nevertheless, many characteristics of fieldtrips are the result of deliberate choices. General criticism can be raised concerning at least two elements of fieldtrips that frequently create bad feelings or go wrong. One is that travelling long distances is often accepted on the rationale that the sites are 'worth' it. But often it is not clear where the value is in spending hours and hours in the coach in order to visit remote sites about which much more could be learned from spending the same amount of time in a library or, increasingly, on the World Wide Web. The entire idea of visiting sites ought to be questioned and answers need to be found on what exactly the educational benefit is of having seen a famous site. Fieldtrips should be redesigned according to maximise these benefits.

Another criticism that can be made of many trips is that the participants, like other tourists, are often ill-prepared, badly instructed, and little is made of the trip after returning home (cf. Haigh and Gold 1993: 22). One important factor in that is a limited expertise of some academic staff. Given the existing pressures on academics of administration, teaching and completing publications, staff are often not able to invest much time in gaining specialist expertise about every new fieldtrip destination; nor are staff given the possibility for pilot visits in order to identify suitable destinations, establish contacts to local institutions and plan realistic itineraries and schedules (May 1999: 221). Even in the academic context, destinations are sometimes chosen not for any educational benefit but for their popularity among students so that enough participants will sign up (e.g. Panton and Dilsaver 1989: 48). In Britain, where departments receive funding on the basis of student numbers, one important aim of offering foreign and 'exotic' fieldclasses in geography or archaeology is to boost the recruitment of students to degree courses in these subjects (Tilley 1993: 415 and Tables 9.3, 9.4; McEwan and Harris 1996: 413f.). In many cases, the great opportunity which fieldtrips offer for the teaching of important academic skills is thus partly wasted due to pressures within the educational system itself.

But not only 'the system' can be blamed. As far as I can see, archaeologists have failed in recent years to develop an up-to-date format for fieldtrips that could transform them not only into truly educational and exciting teaching methods for students but also into a genuine contribution to archaeological research.

Theorising archaeological fieldtrips

The reasoning which underlies traditional archaeological fieldtrips can be characterised in the following way:

- Archaeological fieldtrips are defined with reference to 'research proper' such as archaeological excavations or studies of historical documents, as they are published in academic monographs or journals. Most fieldtrip handbooks and guide books rely largely on the academic literature and frequently include reproductions of published images, plans, and chronological or typological tables. In many cases, students who have to write an assessed report about the trip are normally expected to submit a standard academic essay. Often they are able to succeed by drawing on the literature alone, without having gained any specific academic benefit from the trip itself. However, in some rare cases, the direct comparison between what was published about a specific site and what is actually there, has led students to criticise the accounts of established excavators.

- Archaeological fieldtrips are site-centred. Often, they look 'inwards' rather than 'outwards', and treat each site as if it was the destination of a single trip. Every site is seen only in its own context; and a week-long fieldtrip becomes de facto the sum of seven separate daytrips. During a visit to a site which has recently been, or still is, under archaeological investigation, the results of the local research project are either presented to the group in a guided tour or collectively remembered with the help of handbooks or guidebooks. The author of the relevant published, academic works is normally considered the best guide to the site – the participants own impressions and experiences count little. The main occupation of the participants is usually to identify their own location on a plan, and to try to identify and verify the actual existence of the various known features of the site. In very exceptional circumstances, new 'discoveries' are made by visitors which add to the academic understanding of the site. As there is normally only one expert to guide the sometimes very large group, most (though not all) members of the group stay together and move across the site as a single unit, like a loose swarm of bees.

- Archaeological fieldtrips often lead to sites where there is actually not much to be seen, and without an expert-guide, reproductions from publications ready-to-hand, or information-boards on site, archaeologists themselves would not know why they came here at all.

- Archaeological fieldtrips are followed by a very strong anti-climax after returning home. This is experienced particularly by students who have to write assessed reports afterwards. Perhaps this is the reason why, unfortunately, many student essays based on fieldtrips I have seen were disappointing. During later re-unions photographs or slides from the trip are shown and nostalgic reminiscences are exchanged, but invariably it all seems to have occurred a very long time ago.

In principle, there is no huge difference between archaeologists and others visiting archaeological sites. 'Academic fieldtrips' are in practice often little more than intensive sight-seeing trips. Archaeologists need the same information boards and written or oral descriptions as other tourists in order to understand what they see. Archaeologists do not learn a particular 'way of seeing' during their education, and if you drop them on an unknown archaeological site they will often be as clueless and dependent on common sense in order to understand what they see, as everyone else would be. The only thing archaeologists may be able to do better, thanks to the many sites to which they have been, is to recognise that a feature in the ground is likely to be an archaeological site in the first place. But this is hardly very much.

If there is at least some truth in my characterisation of archaeological fieldtrips as they are commonly conducted nowadays (which was admittedly in places overstated to make my points clearer), I find several things very puzzling. First of all, what reason is there for archaeologists to visit archaeological sites at all? If all the important aspects of a site can be learned from authoritative works in the academic literature which have either already or soon to be published, it seems hardly worth the effort to go there and confirm what is already known. The educational benefit of simply showing the students the sites is somewhat limited.

There are, however, a few other good educational arguments for fieldtrips (cf. Gold and Haigh 1992: 119; Clark 1996: 386). Fieldtrips provide a change from the ordinary which allows the development not only of more informal relations between staff and students, but also of group dynamics and a team spirit between the students themselves, thus enhancing self-identity and confidence. A confrontation with 'the Other' (in whatever form) can let such processes become even more prominent, and in addition challenges students to question their own positions. Furthermore, in the alien environment of a fieldtrip many activities, as normal as they may seem otherwise, can teach students a variety of transferable skills such as collaboration, problem-solving, leadership, and decision-making. Clearly, all this is very worthwhile, but no doubt it can be achieved without any 'archaeology'. Why, then, do staff on fieldtrips tend to be so anxious to avoid the impression that their trip is a 'holiday' stressing instead its 'academic' value?

Secondly, the conventional fieldtrip format is fundamentally opposed to some of the key contents of recent theoretical arguments and discussions. When visiting archaeological sites, there are usually very few references to:

- the fundamental flaws of positivistic approaches and empiricist methodologies on which both the excavations themselves and later published reports about them are usually based, thus ignoring e.g. the affective and sociopolitical dimensions of these sites (cf. Tilley 1989);
- the benefits of acknowledging pluralism and multiple pasts, although an intensive visit of an archaeological

site by a group of staff and students from another university, perhaps even another country, provides the best opportunity for developing an account of the site which is different from that of the local archaeological authorities (e.g. Hodder 1999);

- the importance of bodily experiences, visibility, and negotiation of power relationships in the landscape, although their recognition has transformed landscape archaeology in recent years (e.g. Bender 1993; Tilley 1994);

- the social and political significances of the past in the present, especially at heritage sites (such as those visited on fieldtrips) which have attracted considerable interest among scholars from various disciplines (cf. Lowenthal 1985).

Could these topics and approaches be reconciled with the idea of the archaeological fieldtrip, and perhaps make them academically more worthwhile?

Some suggestions for archaeological fieldtrips

Having given such a bleak analysis of fieldtrips in archaeology, I nevertheless think that there is a role for fieldtrips in archaeology – even more so if they are conducted in a different way from how we used to know them. I have three key suggestions (which may well coincide with other people's ideas that are however unpublished):

(1) What we need to develop is a fieldtrip format which makes visits important for themselves, and not only as either recapitulations of what has been (or will be) published in the literature or as pure recruitment exercises. Specific aims and objectives need to be defined in order to justify fieldtrips educationally in the teaching curricula of archaeology, especially when a lot of money is spent on them (whether by students or by departments). This need has been recognised for all higher education (Higgitt 1996) and in particular for geography (e.g. Jenkins 1994; McEwan 1996). Moreover, it is of the upmost importance that all participating students are being briefed in full both about the precise aims and particular objectives of a trip, and about the educational and practical principles according to which it will be conducted and assessed. This is a necessary requirement not only for realistically expecting full co-operation of the students but also for the emergence of a team spirit on which so much depends for a fieldtrip to be successful and enjoyable for everyone.

I suggest that on fieldtrips we should (2) foreground certain more general themes and topics in relation to each site rather than deal with the specific details of too many individual sites. A number of topics within larger themes can be investigated by smaller groups of students in independently conducted, task-orientated project work. This will allow a greater student participation and possibly teach some important (transferrable) skills much more

efficiently than is possible in the traditional format of on-site lectures. Such projects can also directly contribute to innovative research agendas (see below for some suggestions of suitable fields). Each project is to be begun and prepared by the students beforehand, supervised during the trip by a member of staff, and concluded in one or more seminars afterwards. Much of the work can be done by the students themselves in small groups. Since 1995, the Department of Archaeology at Lampeter has gained some experience with project work during its annual fieldtrips; the results are very encouraging (Lampeter Archaeology Workshop n.d.).

Finally, I propose (3) that we should focus on the sensual and bodily experiences which can be gained during visits of archaeological sites, and not only on the 'facts' which a guide or guide-book can tell us (Shanks 1992: 5–12, 106, 148–157). It is experiences through which people know the world, and thus also the past. What we therefore need to develop are appropriate qualitative methods and forms of expression through which we can capture our experiences and, where relevant, those of other people (see Eisner 1991: 32–41; Clandinin and Connelly 1994). Someone might object that if fieldtrips are assessed by written work submitted afterwards, the emphasis on subjective experiences may cause difficulties in guaranteeing marks that are fair and can be accounted for rationally. However, it is better to look at this problem from another angle. Foregrounding experience gives us the opportunity to introduce more innovative assessment methods which could reflect, to a much greater extent than conventional essays do, what many archaeologists nowadays think is really important about their subject. Students might be assessed for the sophistication and originality of their individual experiences and interpretations expressed in travel journals or in other literary and artistic forms such as letters and photographs; for the solving of certain practical tasks such as finding, drawing, and describing a particular site (e.g. Fleming 1988: 3); or for submitting a number of site-specific essays, carrying out certain tasks, or answering set questions during the fieldtrip (e.g. Panton and Dilsaver 1989).

Towards archaeological ways of seeing

I would like to discuss five topical fields within which participants can make valuable experiences during archaeological fieldtrips. These fields and the particular experiences associated with them should be seen as first steps towards developing not only an 'archaeology of experience' (cf. Bruner 1986; Shanks 1992), but also distinctively archaeological 'ways of seeing'. The suggested topics are intended to go some way towards a general framework – to be adapted to the particular requirements of each fieldtrip – within which students pursue a series of small research agendas in their own projects. Obviously this list is by no means exhaustive and other fields could no doubt be added.

1. A sense of place

Archaeological sites should be seen within the wider landscape in which they are situated. But the landscape is more than a 'catchment area' filled with different sorts of resources. It is full of meaning and cultural significance (Bender 1993; Tilley 1994). Questions that can be explored during visits of archaeological sites include the following: What is visible from a site, and what impression does a site make from a distance?

What relation is there between natural features of the landscape and the particular design and character of a site? What is the atmosphere of a site, and could that be relevant for its interpretation?

How is the site experienced bodily? How important are different kinds of movement (e.g. different positions and speeds)?

Which bodily senses respond most to a site, and how could these sensations be represented to others?

Such question will help to define and describe a distinctive 'sense of place', thus enabling students to better understand each site but also to compare different sites.

2. Experiencing monumentality

Many archaeological sites are truly monumental, for example prehistoric earthworks and tumuli, megalithic tombs, Roman amphitheatres and architectural remains. In order to comprehend this monumentality it is not sufficient to state lengths, widths and heights, and to admire the surprisingly good state of preservation after so many centuries. A theory of monumentality encourages us to look at monuments as phenomena which require a different set of questions to do them justice (cf. Holtorf 1996).

What are the aesthetics of monumentality at a site? What impression is given to the visitor by the size of a site?

How could the scale of a site be linked to the motivations of its builders?

How is monumentality experienced by modern visitors who look at, walk around, or climb on the monument?

Why can archaeological sites of a similar kind sometimes differ dramatically in their monumentality?

It is the experience of monumentality which matters more than anything else about some of the most impressive (and most often visited!) archaeological sites.

3. The aesthetics of decay

Archaeologists tend to regret any decay and destruction of archaeological sites; their ambition is to preserve and restore sites from the past. But there is also an aesthetics of decay and ruination to which we can all relate in present society (Lowenthal 1985: chapter 4), and to which archaeologists should attend. Shanks (1995: 31, 34) has recently proposed a 'critical romanticism' for archaeology. He argued:

'When a pot becomes part of the ruin of time, when a site decays into ruin, revealed is the essential character of a material artefact – its duality of autonomy and dependency. The ruined fragment invites us to reconstruct, to exercise the work of imagination, making connections within and beyond the remnants.... [T]he task is not to revive the dead (they are rotten and gone) or the original conditions from whose decay the pot remained, but to understand the pot as ruined fragment. This is the fascination of the archaeological.'

'The experiential loss of the past is the condition of gaining other knowledges.... Fragments evoke. Wear and ageing are congenial. Many architectures are designed to age well. Sites to be visited do not have to be "over conserved", where all evocations of ruin and loss are removed.... There should be room for playing on the aesthetic of ruin and fragmentation, because therein is so much of the fascination of the past.'

Questions which can help us appreciating decay and the life-cycles of material culture include the following:

What are the signs of age at a particular site? How do sites age differently?

When do material leftovers from the past appeal to us as 'ancient ruins', and why?

What information can we gain from the way actual material remains of a site have decayed about the intentions with which it was built originally, and about the light in which it has been seen since then?

What are the relationships between material decay, memory and forgetting?

There are many innovative forms in which the aesthetics of decay can be expressed, for example, in poems, photographs, drawings, performance (see e.g. Pearson and Shanks 1997).

4. Accessing the past in the present

Lowenthal stated once that 'the past is omnipresent' (1985: xv). But the past is not equally accessible wherever it occurs in the present. While fieldtrip leaders are used to battle with opening hours and obtaining keys to sites with special access arrangements, these practicalities could also be seen within wider questions of the politics of the past in the present.

Where are material remains of the past situated in the present?

Who owns a site? How do we know?

What rules govern access to archaeological sites in our society? Who sets them and how do we know about them?

How do we approach a site, and behave during the visit? How does behaviour at sites differ?

The very details of how we access archaeological sites during fieldtrips can teach us a lot about the status of the past in the present.

5. The visitor's experience

Visiting an archaeological site involves more than remembering established facts about it, or finding new ones. Many archaeological sites are nowadays 'heritage' attractions and play important roles in defining and expressing the collective identities of human communities (Lowenthal 1985). Archaeologists would do well to reflect the contemporary phenomenon of heritage when they visit sites on fieldtrips. A whole range of important questions can be asked during their stays at archaeological heritage attractions.

How is the past presented to us? What factors and agendas play a role?

In what circumstances can a site retain the presence of another dimension, such as a special aura or sacredness?

What are the cultural meanings and significances of a site in the present?

Where else do we find representations of a site in our own (popular) culture? How do they influence our experience of the site?

Such questions refer more generally to the place of the past in our society. This is what Jörn Rüsen has called the *'Geschichtskultur'* (history culture) of a society. Geschichtskultur encompasses all instances where a given society makes reference to the past. In our society this includes phenomena as diverse as universities, advertising, novels, popular non-fiction books, museums and exhibitions, political disputes, TV documentaries, and tourism (Füßmann et al. 1994).

Where do we want to go today?

I have argued that an educationally worthwhile fieldtrip is not one which first and foremost leads to such sites that are important in the academic literature. I made a case for visiting those sites, whether near or far, at which actual experiences lead students (or other participants) to new insights and interpretations. This will only then be achieved when students are well informed about aims and objectives; highly motivated, e.g. by letting them conduct small research projects in supervised groupwork; and encouraged to take their own sensual and bodily

experiences seriously as potentially rewarding qualitative research methods. None of these suggestions is cost-intensive, and larger group sizes do not put the approach as such in jeopardy. In principle, such fieldtrips could even lead to destinations quite close to 'home'; they are certainly not reliant on visiting 'exotic', faraway places. They can be repeated annually and therefore improved continuously. All this may count in favour of my suggestions.

Moreover, taking the five fields of a sense of place, experiencing monumentality, the aesthetics of decay, accessing the past in the present, and the visitor's experience more seriously on archaeological fieldtrips may have consequences for archaeological research practices at large. Fieldtrips can contribute to current approaches giving significance and attention to place values, the phenomenology of landscape, monumentality, the life-cycles of material culture, the politics of the past, and the significance of archaeological representations in the present. This potential for further developing already promising avenues of archaeological research will make archaeological fieldtrips more important than ever, and truly educational.

Acknowledgements

I would like to thank my former colleagues in Lampeter for intensive discussions on archaeological fieldtrips, especially Ros Coard, Yannis Hamilakis, Greg Stevenson, and Michael Tierney. I have also benefited from discussions of some of my ideas on ARCH-THEORY in 1996. Earlier versions of this paper were presented at the first Lampeter-Sheffield-Southampton Postgraduate Intervarsity Seminar in Lampeter in 1996, in the session 'Applied Metaarchaeology' (organised by Kathryn Denning) at the Theoretical Archaeology Group Conference in Bournemouth, 1997, and at the Lampeter Workshop of which this book is the physical outcome. At each occasion I have learned a lot from the discussions that followed. Detailed comments on the paper were also made by Teresa Chapa and Andrew Jones and I am very grateful for their encouragement and additional insights.

References

Bender, B. (ed.) 1993. *Landscape: Politics and Perspectives*. Oxford: Berg.

Bruner, E. M. 1986. Experience and its expressions. In *The Anthropology of Experience* (eds V. W. Turner and E. M. Bruner). Urbana and Chicago: University of Illinois Press, pp. 3-30.

Clandinin, D. J. and Connelly. F. M. 1994. Personal experience methods. In *Handbook of Qualitative Research* (eds N. K. Denzin and Y. D. Lincoln). London: Sage, pp. 413-27.

Clark, D. 1996. The changing national context of fieldwork in geography. *Journal of Geography in Higher Education* 20: 385-91.

Cosgrove, D. and Daniels, S. 1989. Fieldwork as theatre: a week's performance in Venice and its region. *Journal of Geography in Higher Education* 13: 169-83.

Eisner, E. W. 1991. *The Enlightened Eye. Qualitative Inquiry and the Enhancement of Educational Practice*. New York: Macmillan.

Fleming, A. 1988. *The Dartmoor Reaves*. London: Batsford.

Füßmann, K., Grütter, H. T. and Rüsen, J. (eds) 1994. *Historische Faszination. Geschichtskultur heute*. Köln: Böhlau.

Gold, J. R. and Martin J. H. 1992. Over the hills and far away: retaining field study experience despite larger classes. In *Teaching Large Classes in Higher Education. How to Maintain Quality with Reduced Resources* (eds G. Gibbs and A. Jenkins). London: Kogan Page, pp. 117-29.

Grinsell, L. 1989. *An Archaeological Autobiography*. Gloucester: Alan Sutton.

Haigh, M. J. and Gold, J. R. 1993. The problems with fieldwork: a group-based approach towards integrating fieldwork into the undergraduate geography curriculum. *Journal of Geography in Higher Education* 17: 21-32.

Higgitt, M. 1996. Addressing the new agenda for fieldwork in higher education. *Journal of Geography in Higher Education* 20: 391-8.

Hodder, I. 1999. *The Archaeological Process*. Oxford: Blackwell.

Holtorf, C. J. 1996. Towards a chronology of megaliths: understanding monumental time and cultural memory. *Journal of European Archaeology* 4: 119-52.

Jenkins, A. 1994. Thirteen ways of doing fieldwork with large classes/more students. *Journal of Geography in Higher Education* 18: 143-54.

Johnson, M. 1999. *Archaeological Theory: An Introduction*. Oxford: Blackwell.

Lampeter Archaeology Workshop n.d. Fieldtrips in archaeological education: an exploration of 'Border Pedagogy'. Unpublished Manuscript.

Lowenthal, D. 1985. *The Past is a Foreign Country*. Cambridge: Cambridge University Press.

May, J. 1999. Developing fieldwork in social and cultural geography: illustrations from a residential field class in Los Angeles and Las Vegas. *Journal of Geography in Higher Education* 23: 207-25.

McEwan, L. 1996. Fieldwork in the undergraduate geography programme: challenges and changes. *Journal of Geography in Higher Education* 20: 379-84.

McEwan, L. and Harris, F. 1996. The undergraduate geography fieldweek: challenges and changes. *Journal of Geography in Higher Education* 20: 411-21.

Panton, K. and Dilsaver, L. 1989. Americans in Britain: geographic education and foreign field trips. *Journal of Geography in Higher Education* 13: 45-53.

Pearson, M. and Shanks, M. 1997. Performing a visit: archaeologies of the contemporary past. *Performance Research* 2(2): 41-53.

Shanks, M. 1992. *Experiencing the Past. On the Character of Archaeology*. London: Routledge.

Shanks, M. 1995. Archaeological experiences and a critical romanticism. In Nordic TAG. The Archaeologist and His/Her Reality. Report from the fourth Nordic TAG conference. Helsinki 1992, *Helsinki Papers in Archaeology* 7 (eds M .Tusa and T. Kirkinen). University of Helsinki: Department of Archaeology, pp. 17-36.

Tilley, C. 1989. Excavation as theatre. *Antiquity* 63: 275-80.

Tilley, C. 1993. Prospecting archaeology. In *Interpretative Archaeology* (ed. C. Tilley). Oxford: Berg, pp. 395-416.

Tilley, C. 1994. *A Phenomenology of Landscape. Places, Paths and Monuments*. Oxford: Berg.

3.2

Profession and academic: the teaching of heritage management

Richard Hingley

This brief paper presents a personal view of archaeological teaching and heritage management. It is inspired by my employment at Historic Scotland as an Inspector of Ancient Monuments in conjunction with subsequent work at Durham as a lecturer in Roman Archaeology. The paper seeks to explore two interrelated issues:

- the division between 'professional archaeology' and 'academic archaeology' in Britain, and
- the teaching and researching of heritage management in archaeology departments.

It will be argued that a strict division operates between so-called 'professional archaeology' and 'academic archaeology' and that this divide works against the interests of the archaeological profession as a whole. This division into two camps also has a negative influence on the teaching of archaeology in universities.

Professional and academic archaeologists

Archaeology forms a single profession, yet archaeologists can be divided into various subgroups (Aitchison 1999). I intend to consider the division between professional and academic. My use of the term 'professional archaeologist' is derived from the *Field Archaeologist* (the magazine of the IFA). Professional archaeologists are defined as those who are employed in heritage management – working for archaeological units, central and local government and companies. More specifically, however, professional archaeologists have particular accountabilities. These vary from job to job and may be to central government, to local government, or to clients. In extreme cases they may even in the past have involved the individual in signing the Official Secrets Act (Inspectors of Ancient Monuments were required to sign this Act until recently). The accountability of a professional archaeologist is likely to go beyond the bounds of archaeology as a profession and to include other bodies with differing aims, methods and standards.

The rules that bind professional archaeologists often demand that they convey information in a way that stresses the certainty and stability of the identification of various categories of archaeological material. The theories, methods and language adopted by professionals emphasise the certainty and 'objectivity' of description, classification and analysis. This 'objectivity' provides a firm basis for the decisions of professional archaeologists. These decisions often create impositions on the land, activities and profits of members of the public (including land owners and developers). The 'objective' decisions that are made by professional archaeologists need to be acceptable to the bodies to which they are accountable. In addition, individual decisions are sometimes tested by developers and land owners in a public forum (for instance, in public local inquiries and in the courts) and this stresses the need for valuation to be absolute.

Archaeologists employed in academic jobs, by contrast, are often said to have more autonomy and are primarily responsible for teaching and advancing knowledge in their particular subject. There is increasing discussion about the degree to which academics operate with autonomy from constraining systems, but it remains true that on the whole they are not subject to the same range of legal and bureaucratic rules as their professional associates.

The context of much academic research requires creativity and fluidity. Academic debate and publication thrives upon critique and also on multiple and competing views of the past. Open academic discussion forms a growing part of the educational system as archaeologists employed in academic jobs seek to show students that the past was not simple and that complex accounts are required. This more fluid type of approach to the description, classification and analysis of archaeological materials is often unavailable to the professional archaeologist; the latter has often to strive for an 'objectivity' that the academic cannot accept.

The division between academic and professional is rather arbitrary; some individuals manage to span the divide. Many who work in professional archaeology produce academic work and people employed in academia should be professional – as the Institute of Teaching and Learning are now insisting – even if their professionalism is to lie in a different direction from that of the heritage manager. The simplistic divide between the 'professionals' and the 'academics' is, however, an area that I wish to explore further.

The separation of professional from academic is marked by a division between the professional's pursuit of certainty/description and the academic's interest in theory. Debates in *Antiquity* and elsewhere during the 1970s explored this negative divide but solutions have been slow to develop. It appears that many professional field archaeologists in units and also finds specialists see theory as something that postgraduates and certain university lecturers indulge in at TAG and in seminars at their departments. Theory has no part in fieldwork or finds analysis. Often professional archaeologists appear to feel that theoreticians are careless with the archaeological data and that perhaps they allow their research interests to bias their data collection and analysis. This is felt to make them poor excavators and field surveyors. At the same time theoreticians have been broadly critical of the attitudes of professional archaeologists for a long time.

They have pointed out that you can not collect and study information without using theories, and that it is better to be explicit about research interests so that others can study the materials that you collect and understand the context of your fieldwork or finds analysis.

IFA is symptomatic of the divide. IFA is an organisation for professional archaeologists and there is a general lack of archaeologists from university departments amongst its membership and those who attend its conferences. This is not the fault of IFA, which is led by professionals and reflects professional concerns; it is also not really the fault of university academics, as IFA is not directly relevant to progress in the academic profession. To give an example of this divide, I am one of a small group of university lecturers who are paid-up members of IFA – I have been a member since 1989. When in 1999 I changed employment from Historic Scotland to Durham University and informed IFA of my change of address they contacted me at the Archaeology Unit in the Department, assuming that I had moved to another job as a professional archaeologist.

I accept that the picture that I am presenting is over-generalised, but I would argue that it does hold some truth. At the foundation of the current situation is the observation that people generally pursue a career either in heritage management or in academic archaeology and that archaeologists who span the divide are rare. There is an institutional split that is perpetuating the *status quo*. With the growing professionalism of professional archaeology and the growth of professional teaching and learning qualifications in universities, the two sides are likely to move even further apart as they find it increasingly difficult to communicate and to understand each other's aims and objectives. This is not the fault of either side in the debate but a result of the history of the way that archaeology has developed in the recent past and also of the context in which professional and academic archaeologists operate.

I feel that we should be working to break down this divide. There are some promising signs of change. For instance, the involvement of John Barrett and Gill Andrews in developing a research design for the Heathrow project, a high-quality academic product that has to work in a commercial context. Nevertheless, there is still a great deal to achieve and I suggest that the state of the debate over heritage management teaching is not helping to break down the barriers.

The teaching of heritage management

Professional archaeology is taught both at undergraduate and at masters levels but many archaeology students do not go on to work in archaeology (Chitty 1999: 6). Of the approximately 1100 individuals graduating from degree courses in archaeology annually, perhaps 10 or 15 per cent will emerge with a serious intention to pursue a career in archaeology and/or further vocational training (ibid.). These figures greatly exceed the number of opportunities

for entry level employment in archaeology. This should be a concern to university archaeology departments, since the government are placing increasing emphasis on the role of undergraduate teaching in equipping students for employment. Henson (2000) has argued that subjects that have a low employment base, such as archaeology, may in future be marginalized by changes in government funding. This suggests that we should be working to make our teaching of heritage management at undergraduate level as relevant and up-to-date as possible to make our graduates employable for the archaeology jobs that do exist.

Universities provide an initial training in archaeology for many people who then work within the profession (Andrews 1999; Chitty 1999; Darvill 1999). Undergraduate courses are not, on the whole, designed to equip individuals to enter directly into the workplace without further training (Chitty 1999: 8). Bishop, Collis and Hinton (1999: 15) argue that:

'Archaeology is primarily a graduate-entry profession, reflecting the need for all archaeologists to have a good grounding in academic skills. Equally, sound practical experience is required to practise competently in any area of the discipline. Most first degrees are not intended to provide this experience, nor to cover many of the professional skills required by professional archaeologists.' Some undergraduate courses, however, are more ambitious in offering an archaeology programme which will deliver the fundamental skills that will allow students to subsequently compete for jobs (as in the case of the degree at Bournemouth, Andrews 1999: 93).

Undergraduates generally require further training for a professional career. A few universities offer postgraduate taught courses in heritage management. In addition, some short courses in professional archaeology for graduates in archaeology posts are being developed (Chitty 1999: 9). The Archaeological Training Forum (ATF) has been set up by a number of organisations, including IFA, English Heritage and the Council for British Archaeology (Chitty 1999; IFA 2000). A preliminary review of training in professional archaeology was commissioned by English Heritage on behalf of the ATF in 1998 (published as Chitty 1999). The ATF is currently running a number of training courses for archaeologists at all levels of the profession with the Continuing Education Departments of the Universities of Oxford and Leeds (IFA 2000). Titles available in 2000-1 include 'Archaeological Development Control Reports', 'Business Planning' and 'Financial Management and Control' (ibid.). These courses are taught by professional archaeologists and, on some occasions, by non-archaeologists.

Masters courses in heritage management also exist, and Bishop, Collis and Hinton (1999) have argued that it is vital that these are taught, at least in part, by archaeologists who are currently practising in the field and who have relevant experience. Academics may end up having only a limited contribution to these courses. It is true that while some university lecturers have the interest and background to teach heritage management, others do not. Academics who teach heritage management sometimes do not realise that professional archaeology is a swiftly developing discipline and a very complex one. Professional archaeology in many ways is just as complex a subject to research as the comprehension of past societies through their material remains. The character of heritage management teaching in universities perhaps provides part of the explanation for the concern of professional archaeologists to become involved with teaching.

There are, however, some potential problems with a system that uses only professional archaeologists to teach heritage management to graduates and leaves undergraduate teaching to the academics. Firstly, as the result of conversations with a number of archaeology graduates from various universities, it seems that when students graduate and move into jobs in professional archaeology they realise how limited their heritage management education at university has been. This may help to perpetuate the anti-theory school of thought amongst professional archaeologists and thus to reinforce the existing and deeply flawed system.

Secondly, many professional archaeologists are restricted in the degree to which they can criticise the ways in which heritage management operates. Professional archaeologists are accountable to other bodies and need to create an image of objectivity in their decision-making processes (see above). Academics are not constrained by the same limitations and this should enable them to be more critical and inventive in the teaching of heritage management (Roger Thomas, pers. comm.). Critical and inventive teaching that splits the professional/academic divide is essential if we are to move forward with both teaching and research.

Finally the role of theory in heritage management is currently underplayed, perhaps partly due to the fact that the academic side of heritage management is not being fully developed by the profession. This again is a consequence of the division between professional and academic archaeology. Many of the articles and books that have been written about archaeological heritage management over the past ten years contain relatively unchallenging views regarding for instance, valuation, ethics and the relationship between archaeologists and the community. As a discipline archaeology's professional side is not keeping up with developments in sociology and environmental ethics, where developments in valuation and community involvement are occurring swiftly (for instance, Environment Agency 1998). Professional archaeologists are generally unlikely to be at the cutting-edge of social analysis. There appears also, however, to be a lack of interest in heritage management as an academic subject within universities. University archaeology departments should be able to provide access to expertise in these areas through teaching that spans a number of academic departments within a single university.

Universities must have a part to play in developing the training for heritage managers. IFA and the National Training Organisations can not achieve this unaided and academic input to the process of teaching is required if we are to create a dynamic and challenging discipline for our future students and professionals.

Lessons for interrogating pedagogies

Academic archaeologists have a duty to provide high-quality and relevant education for the students that they teach. The government is pushing vocational training and we have a duty to our students (both undergraduate and postgraduate) to provide this. Universities should aim to train students for jobs as well as giving them a sound academic training. This education should use professional expertise wherever possible, to create a co-operative educational environment. Undergraduates and postgraduates who aim to work in archaeology may require more training after they obtain their academic qualifications. Universities should offer training to a certain level using up-to-date theory and practice. If we do not, we are failing our students and, perhaps, as I have suggested, acting to perpetuate the unhealthy division between theory and practice in British archaeology.

In addition to improved teaching we need to develop heritage management theory. Indeed, a focus upon a better-informed theory of heritage management may lead in due course to this sub-discipline becoming more acceptable in the university syllabus. This may help to create more posts in heritage management teaching and research in universities that, in turn, may also generate a more challenging approach to the subject. Future research in the theory of heritage management should be focused upon whether our existing approaches to the valuation of the heritage can be justified.

Acknowledgements

I am very grateful to Roger Thomas for the considerable assistance that he provided with this paper. The ideas expressed in it, however, are my own.

References

Aitchison, K. 1999. *Profiling the Profession*. Council for British Archaeology, English Heritage and IFA.

Andrews, K. 1999. University archaeology: ivory tower or white elephant? In *Communicating Archaeology* (eds J. Beavis and A. Hunt). *Bournemouth University School of Conservation Sciences Occasional Paper* 4, pp. 91-9.

Bishop, M., Collis, J. and Hinton, P. 1999. A future for archaeologists: professional training and a career structure in archaeology. *The Archaeologist, Summer 1999*: 14-6.

Chitty, J. 1999. *Training in Professional Archaeology: a preliminary review* (http://www.britarch.ac.uk/training/survey.html).

Darvill, T. 1999. The IFA: what it means to be a member of a professional body. In *Communicating Archaeology* (eds J. Beavis and A. Hunt). *Bournemouth University School of Conservation Sciences Occasional Paper* 4, pp. 35-48.

Environment Agency 1998. *Valuing the Environment.* Preliminary Report on a seminar held at Church House, London, 7th July.

Henson, D. 2000. Archaeology in higher education. *The Archaeologist, Spring 2000*: 19-20.

IFA 2000. *Learning Opportunities for Archaeologists* (http://www.archaeologists.net/news/item7.html).

Learning contracts and supervision in archaeology – the undergraduate experience

Beverley Ballin Smith

Summary

Research on undergraduate students, their dissertations and supervision, highlighted important educational issues and broader concerns. In continuing the research into the dissertation process a pilot programme using an educational innovation, that of a learning contract or agreement, was introduced for a limited number of students and their supervisors in the 2000-21 academic year. Although the pilot programme is not complete, certain issues and facts concerning the teaching of archaeology are coming to light, some of which were generally discussed at the Lampeter Workshop. This paper aims to explore some of these issues and the use of learning contracts in the light of the benchmarking statement for archaeology in higher education.

Introduction

In the Department of Archaeology, University of Glasgow all single honours and some joint honours students undertake a dissertation as part of their final degree mark. Through researching the process of supervision of dissertations it became apparent that there are important problems, such as the selection of suitable subjects for research, allocation of supervisors, time, management etc. Often, the dissertation is squeezed in between course requirements, last minute fieldwork, holidays and now, the necessity to earn money.

Problems are compounded with the commencement of course work after the summer recess, where contact between student and supervisor can either be minimal, or too great. Earlier research led to the instigation of the present pilot study into the introduction of learning contracts between the students and their supervisors, with the aim of reducing some of the problems and possibly improving standards. The learning contract is intended to explore the aims of individual student's piece of original research, their research/working methodologies, the eventual outcome(s), and finally the assessment (Appendix 1). Not all students will need a learning contract, but the pilot study is in the process of exploring the usefulness of the document for those who need early support as well as confirming its role as a grounding document for the student/supervisor relationship.

Undergraduate project supervision appears to be a neglected area of higher educational research in comparison to the postgraduate situation, where literature on project research supervision is prolific (see Dawson 1996; Hockey 1996; Krokfors 1996; McQueeny 1996; and Pole 1998). It is hoped that through the pilot scheme learning contracts can be critically analysed as a viable means of assessing supervision and of improving students' potential at the undergraduate level.

Reasons for the innovation

The problems associated with the dissertation as a means of learning became apparent through the informality of the dissertation set up. In some cases, the lack of communication, contact and management between student and supervisor, and even a breakdown in their academic relationship, can lead to lower results than expected. Often it is the borderline student who is in need of academic support and help, but will not seek it. With the dissertation the department gives students the responsibility for their own learning. One aim of this research is to explore whether there are adequate mechanisms in place to assist with the informing, development and support of that responsibility. The introduction of the learning contract was one means of exploring the interaction between student and supervisor and the mechanisms that exist.

The educational issue in context

Academic issues – the benchmarking document

The dissertation is probably one of the most important learning elements in the archaeology degree course. To quote from the *Junior Honours Handbook* 2000, the dissertation 'provides an opportunity to carry out a piece of first-hand research, in your (the student's) own time, on a topic of your own choosing, and thus to demonstrate your mastery over a parcel of archaeological evidence.' A dissertation of 'high quality will increase the possibility of a good degree and may open the way to postgraduate research.' The undertaking and successful completion of the dissertation provides a means of assessing whether the student has assimilated the transferable skills that are part of what archaeology is. These transferable skills are noted in the benchmarking document as the blending of 'humanities and science training', the integration of theory and practice, and the pursuit of intellectual curiosity, among others.

Through the dissertation the student has the opportunity to explore and analyse the fundamental elements of the archaeology degree programme in the topic they choose to research. The benchmarking document lists these elemental contexts as: historical and social, ethical and professional, theoretical, and scientific. In addition, the benchmarking document outlines and lists the 'platforms' of knowledge and understanding and the broad skills required of the student at the 'Threshold' and 'Typical' standards. Completion of the dissertation is a means of providing appropriate evidence for some, not necessarily all, of these elements with assessment being the means of examining the level of achievement and the standard reached.

Practical issues – the dissertation in practice

For some students the jump between formal learning in a lecture or seminar situation and undertaking their own research is a large one (R. Jones, pers. comm.). Their academic abilities may not be in doubt but the application of their skills and knowledge for undertaking a dissertation is one that is potentially problematic. During my research, concerns were raised by both staff and students identified as:

- defining roles, especially that of the supervisor
- general expectations
- the amount of student/supervisor contact time
- instituting dialogues rather than traditional teacher-learner relationships
- timetabling the dissertation
- the workload expectations
- student self-organisation
- pastoral issues

These issues are not in any particular order or priority, nor do they reflect the needs of every student and supervisor. They were raised as causing general problems during the dissertation process. For some students and supervisors, none or only some of these issues are problems, but for others, all will apply. It is often the student who lacks confidence, or has problems of organisation so cannot maintain a supportive academic relationship with their tutor, or who may be an academic borderline case, that needs to be identified and assisted. There is also the issue of the supervisor who may, through pressure of work and volume of students, not identify potential learner problems early in the dissertation process. Contingency arrangements such as student/supervisor meetings do not always function as they should, and the situation can be fraught with problems.

Aims of this research

The main aim of this research is, having identified problems in the student/supervisory element of the dissertation process, to put forward and examine a possible solution. If an innovation in academic practice could be instituted into a department of archaeology early on in the dissertation process, it could be of benefit to both staff and students, and possibly help eliminate the annual perpetuation of the same or similar problems. If that innovation could draw students' attention to the dissertation as a valuable, (student-centred) piece of individual research which could demonstrate their knowledge and skills, it could be a means of generally improving the standard, quality and the marks awarded.

The innovation proposed and explored in this module, is the application and use of 'learning contracts'.

The innovation – the learning contract[1]

Learning contracts are not new innovations in educational practice (see Anderson et al. 1996: vii) but have not been used previously in the Department of Archaeology at Glasgow University. They can be described as a document between a student and their supervisor where the learning needs of the student and the learning objectives of the course are addressed, and where the methods of achieving (in this case) the dissertation (i.e. the study strategies and resources needed), the outcome of the work (the dissertation) and the criteria for assessment, are set out.

In general, a learning contract is a negotiated agreement between the student and supervisor which sets down the course and achievement strategies for the work, as well as a list or statement of the expected outcomes. In order to be a useful document, communication, negotiation, respect and commitment by both parties is required. Discussion of the roles, responsibilities and expectations of the student and supervisor is also necessary in the drawing up of the document. The contract can also provide a means of gaining student commitment to the dissertation and its agreed activities, it can focus on learner needs rather than those of the subject or the supervisor. It should also embrace the supervisor's responsibility to challenge and extend the learner and ensure that new learning occurs or new skills are developed.

The document is signed by both parties concerned and although it cannot be entirely open-ended, it can be flexible enough to allow renegotiations if necessary after reflection on its various elements. Where necessary, learning contracts can be the foundation for a positive learning experience not only for the student but also for the supervisor. There is 'a general social expectation that there should be more consultation and participation by (students) in decisions which affect their lives' (Anderson et al. 1996: 12) and a learning contract can be a means of achieving this.

Aims of introducing the learning contract as an innovation

Highlighted above are issues that have been raised by students and supervisors during the undergraduate dissertation process. By introducing the learning contract for certain student/supervisor groups, it is hoped that the following aims can be realised:

- to give the students the responsibility for their own learning and enable them to be active participants in

---

[1] It was suggested at the Lampeter workshop that the term *learning contract* could be misleading or have different connotations for different users. The term *learning agreement* was suggested as being more 'friendly'. For the purposes of this paper, and for consistency of terminology, the word 'contract' is used throughout.

the decision-making process, as far as is allowable under the course requirements i.e. designing their own learning strategies, to set down means of communication and negotiate contact time.

- to acknowledge students' individual needs and differences in learning and organisation etc. Although following a precise set of criteria for the dissertation process, each supervisor will have different expectations of their students and a learning contract will 'enable (supervisors) to respond to the diverse needs of a wide range of students and the contexts in which they operate and hence promote improved access and equity' (Anderson et al. 1996: 12), as well as fulfilling their own needs and that of the course.
- to allow the learning process to be 'tailored to the specific needs and interests of each learner' (ibid.: 10), within the confines of the dissertation exercise. This can mean allowing students alternative approaches to the exercise, perhaps choosing their supervisor etc. Above all it is intended that the learning contract supports student learning.
- to allow the student and the supervisor to evolve a more democratic relationship, where they become partners, and not adversaries, in the learning process.
- to allow students to be analytical and reflective early on in their dissertation project about their needs etc., rather than after the event. A learning contract will help 'focus (their) learning and provide clear goals and directions' (ibid.: 11) and provide a formal framework for carrying out the dissertation.

Expected benefits

The flexibility of the learning contract should allow students to identify and acknowledge their own learning needs and experience a more worthwhile research exercise and dissertation process. The student should also be better motivated, having taken part in the decision making process and be committed to the dissertation. It is hoped that the expectations of students and their supervisors will be similar and that any wide divergence can be eliminated. A further benefit for students who are borderline cases will be the aim to raise their academic standards from threshold to typical achievements, and for others to 'demonstrate progressive levels of attainment' as stated in the benchmarking document.

Possible problems

One problem likely to be encountered is the lack of desire from the supervisor to empower the student. Another potential problem is the lack of willingness of both student and supervisor to participate in constructing and using a learning contract, especially when the advantages will not be immediately obvious to them. A problem highlighted by Anderson et al. (1996: 13-4) is whether the parties will have the skills to plan and write contracts, especially as neither in the case of undergraduate dissertations, may have used them previously. This lack of familiarity with

learning contracts may create problems of stress or anxiety as some students may not know what they need, their learning contract may take some time to evolve into a workable document.

After the presentation of this paper at the Lampeter workshop, the question was asked, how does one ensure that the contract will be honoured by both parties. Using the pilot scheme with archaeology students and providing them with the opportunity to empower themselves, ensures that they can positively invest in the document and the dissertation process. Communication and familiarity of use may be further keys to eliminating this problem. However, both negative and positive outcomes of the pilot scheme will be discussed (in a future document) at the end of the project.

The preliminary results

It is not the intention of this paper to outline the methodology behind the introduction of learning contracts nor to discuss the detail of the documents in practice. However, the outline of the contract which has been introduced can be found below in Appendix 1.

The learning contract, for all intents and purposes is a simple, but complex, document. The logical exploration by both supervisor and students of the contractual elements highlighted several important issues:

- the shortcomings of the students' dissertation topics (the choice, the scope, the archaeological periods etc.)
- the quality of advice they received from the supervisors (i.e. topics that were too large for undergraduates in the permitted timescale etc.)
- the problems of the students' timetables and summer commitments (holidays and earning money)
- management, planning and study strategies
- the outcome(s) of the dissertation

If introduced early in the dissertation process there is time for some of the critical issues to be addressed, such as the student who needs to rethink the topic, or its scope. Working through the document provides the opportunity for students to logically think through their fieldwork – when are they going to do it, for how long, what resources they need, what cost or equipment would be involved, who would they need to contact? etc. By asking straightforward or even searching questions, the supervisor can facilitate a better understanding of what learning strategies, skills and knowledge the student needs to achieve their dissertation objectives, without setting themselves unrealistic targets. This process also enabled the aims of the dissertation to be made clear, some fundamental problems voiced and others lessened, by discussion and dialogue.

The learning contract is also a document which expresses future needs. This became apparent in meetings, when students requested regular contact with the supervisor, and that they should read and comment on dissertation chapters prior to submission. As the pilot scheme will not be completed before March 2001, it is expected that other issues will be raised which may better inform when the document should be introduced, how it is to be negotiated, and what factors influence renegotiation.

Evaluation

Although the learning contract is intended to be a negotiated agreement between the student and supervisor, there were certain elements of the document that were non-negotiable – the completion date and the assessment criteria – both of which are determined by the Department and the Faculty. In general, the learning contract is valuable in providing the means to clarify aims, objectives and other elements which students, embarking on project research for the first time, will not have thought clearly about. The contract also enabled uncertainties to be aired early in the dissertation timetable. It also allowed for deeper communication and commitment towards the research project, by both students and supervisor who share a common goal, than has been experienced previously by the supervisor. The flexibility of the contract has allowed individual documents to be drawn up and will allow renegotiation where warranted.

The important questions which need to be asked about learning contracts as an innovation in practice within the Department of Archaeology, are:

1. how does the contract affect the student's planning and design of their project?
2. how does the contract affect the supervisor's support of the student?
3. how does the contract affect the student management of the project?
4. how does the contract affect the supervisor's management of the student?
5. does the learning contract help support student learning, and the integration of theory, practice and specialist knowledge?

1. The students' planning of their research projects were much more thorough and had greater depth with the learning contract than without it. Unfortunately, the contract was not put in place early enough for one student's design of the dissertation to be significantly revised. Another student's project scope required alteration, and an attempt was made to achieve a more balanced approach using the learning contract.
2. The use of a learning contract integrated supervisory support of the students by negotiation. The supervisor's responsibilities and commitments were discussed as were their expectations of the students. Although not expressed in written form in the current contracts, it is expected that specific reference will be made to the availability and role of the supervisor in supporting the students in document revisions.

3. The learning contract clearly brought out practical issues of conducting fieldwork and management concerns in both researching and writing the dissertation. These were issues which students had not thought about in beginning their research project. By highlighting these shortcomings early in the process, solutions could be discussed and solved. These issues may not have been clearly addressed without the use of the learning contract.
4. It is much easier for the supervisor to manage the student and their work when clear aims, strategies and outcomes are set down in the form of a learning contract. The document provides guidelines for the student to follow and the supervisor to support. The goal posts are kept from wandering and misunderstandings about the production of the project should be kept to a minimum. To summarise: management of the student should be much more straight forward with a contract than without one.
5. The final evaluation of the success of the learning contracts will be made during the assessment of the students' dissertations. Higher than expected standards and marks will not always guarantee the success of the innovation, but student appraisal of the learning contract at the end of the dissertation process, will be an important evaluation and learning exercise. For the purposes of this study, can the introduction of learning contracts into educational and archaeological practice be demonstrated to have been successful or worthwhile? From the feedback received from the students and supervisors on the use of learning contracts, it is suggested that they are a valuable and worthwhile tool, for all the reasons given above. Although the learning contract is still under trial, and the present evaluation is somewhat limited, the usefulness and effectiveness of the document has already been demonstrated. However, fine tuning of the design and the timing of its use will need to be considered more directly for the next Junior Honours students.

The dissertation remains a valuable exercise whereby students can demonstrate their mastery over the integration of theory, practice and knowledge of a specialist subject by undertaking an original piece of research. It is hoped that by the introduction of the learning contract that students can raise their standards, especially border-line students, who can improve their 'data assembly and analysis, presentation, knowledge deployment, argument and reasoning' by having clear learning objectives.

The evaluation of the learning contract must also review the academic standards set out in the benchmarking document, to include whether the contract succeeds in providing (positive) 'interactions between teaching, research, and primary data handling' in 'departments with strong research themes', and whether the students, and the supervisors, find the use of the contract to be 'intellectually stimulating'. However, this research has highlighted the fact that use of a learning contract is 'an interactive process from which students and academics gain mutual benefit....' Further evaluation of the use of learning contracts as innovatory educational tools in the Department of Archaeology will take place over a longer time scale than is available for this piece of research. However, it is the intention of this research to follow the students through the complete dissertation process and evaluate the learning contact more thoroughly at the end of their Senior Honours year. Independent evaluation of the use of learning contracts for undergraduate dissertations will also be made by the departmental Honours Convenor, who will have advised on this project from its inception to its end. Preliminary discussion with the Convenor on the drafting and implementation of the contracts indicate that problem areas or worries about individual students, may be alleviated with the use of the document.

Preliminary conclusions and recommendations

The learning contact has been introduced within the Department of Archaeology, on a small scale. It has been demonstrated to have been of use after being put into practice, and is therefore considered, even with limited evaluation, to have been a worthwhile innovation.

However, there are some practical considerations which need to be addressed if the use of learning contracts are to continue. If learning contacts could be introduced even earlier in the dissertation process, at the time the students are thinking of their research project topics, rather than afterwards, the document may be of more value. Often the rationale behind the choice of topic is lacking but this could be discussed through the learning contract if brought in earlier. Perhaps a redrafting of the guidelines in the *Junior Honours Handbook* with emphasis on learning contacts may be beneficial for future student planning.

Working through the learning contract elements is not easy, and equity between student and supervisor may not exist initially. For successful negotiation, clarity of thought, good communication and especially time is needed by both parties. Searching questioning, patience, commitment and a certain amount of empathy are also required of the supervisor. Knowing when to listen and allowing time for empowering the student, are supervisory attributes which need to be available or to be learnt. Management of the negotiation process also needs to be undertaken, and not all parties will be able to do this successfully. Refinements and renegotiation of contracts could lead to problems which may have not been foreseen and may require arbitration by a third party. Many of these issues have been noted by Anderson et al. (1996: ch. 9), who suggests that a pre-dissertation seminars or workshops on 'the theory and practice of using learning contracts' could be of great benefit to both students and supervisors.
Another consideration is that of the assessment of the dissertation. The criteria for assessment are only vaguely mentioned in the student guidelines. It may be possible in the future for the criteria to be stated and critically evaluated so that different forms of dissertation presentation could be allowed and negotiated with the learning contract.

The immediate effects of the introduction of the learning contact seem to be successful, but a more critical awareness of these effects for both student and supervisor will need to be evaluated by both, and by the Honours Convenor, at the end of the dissertation process. One suggestion is a questionnaire to be filled in by all the Junior Honours students and their supervisors, to indicate the successes, failures, satisfactions, problems etc. of the research project and working with, or without, a learning contact.

It is an undoubted problem of the dissertation timetable that this research, in its current form, is limited both in scope and value. As stated above, the research into the learning contract innovation will continue and its results will be presented to the Department, possibly in the form of a seminar in 2001. Only at this stage will the merits of the learning contract be fully tested over the whole dissertation process, and the results and statistics of those students who negotiated a learning contact be available for study and comment. The resources required of supervisor will also be taken into account, as this is considered to be a management factor with cost implications (see Anderson 1996: ch. 13).

This research could have also been improved by the formalisation of numbers of supervisors and students working with a learning contact and having another formal group of students working without, for comparative purposes. However, this was not a practical consideration in this current academic year. For those students, and the supervisor, the experience of using learning contacts has been extremely valuable. For the student it has served as an apprenticeship for future research projects. For the supervisor it has served as a valuable innovation which could be used in other teaching and research areas.

Afterword

The Lampeter workshop allowed some of this research and its findings to be aired and discussed. In the spirit of the workshop this paper has tried to show that by the adoption of an initiative, a potential solution to specific problems in the teaching of archaeology in higher education can be tested and evaluated. The learning contract defines learning outcomes and promotes the acquisition and use of generic skills which can be transferred to the postgraduate level and to working within archaeology in the wider world. There is little published discussion of the problems of teaching archaeology to undergraduates nor of the broader concerns and external factors which have increasing call on student time, their learning and their demonstration of skills and knowledge. It has been possible through this workshop to critically examine some of the specific issues which concern students and supervisors and to do this with reference to the benchmarking document. The learning contract will not hold all the answers but it is a method of exploring changes and reforms which can only have benefit for the individual student, the archaeology department and the teaching of archaeology as a whole.

Acknowledgements

Students and staff at the Department of Archaeology and the Teaching and Learning Service, Glasgow University are thanked for their co-operation and time in aiding this research project. Especial mention must be made of Dr Richard Jones and Dr Erica McAteer for their continued support and advice. Valuable comments were also made at the Lampeter workshop and further information was given to this author by Dr Michael Reynier, The Subject Centre for History, Classics and Archaeology.

References

Anderson, G., Bond, D. and Sampson, J. 1996. *Learning Contracts*. London: Kogan Page.

Dawson, V. 1996. The (r)evolution of my epistemology: my experience as a postgraduate research student. *Educational Action Research* 4: 363-74.

Hockey, J. 1996. Strategies and tactics in the supervision of UK social science PhD students in Qualitative Studies. *Education* 9: 481-500.

Krokfors, L. 1996. The character and quality of supervisory discourse: linking the beliefs and actions of supervisors. *European Journal of Teacher Education* 19: 35-45.

McQueeney, E. 1996. The nature of effective research supervision. *A Journal for Further and Higher Education in Scotland* 20(1): 23-30.

Pole, C, 1998. Joint supervision and the PhD: safety net or panacea? *Assessment and Evaluation in Higher Education* 23: 259-71.

Appendix 1.

Learning Agreement Form
For undergraduate dissertations

Student:

Date agreed: **Completion date:**

Learning Objectives
1.
2.
3.
4.

Learning Resources and Strategies
1.
2.
3.
4.

Outcomes
1.
2.
3.
4.

Assessment Criteria
1.
2.
3.
4.

Signed:
Student: Supervisor:

Teaching ethnoarchaeology: taking the unquantifiable into account

Kathryn Fewster

Introduction

In this paper I will explore an aspect of my experience of teaching ethnoarchaeology at the University of Wales, Lampeter and use this as the basis for a wider discussion of the changes that are taking place in higher education in Britain. These changes include the increasing presence of auditing in teaching in general, and I shall be addressing in particular the implications for archaeology of the benchmarking document. It came as something of a surprise that at the workshop, the benchmarking statement was hardly questioned for its very existence, or for the implication of it once it becomes programmatic in the QAA, but rather discussion focused on negotiating the fine detail of the statement so better to represent the interests of individual groups. More generally, the discussion has tended to shy away from the wider issues – such as what exactly it is that the benchmarking statement represents and what is meant by 'accountability' with regard to universities. While it is acknowledged that universities, as recipients of public money, must make themselves open to government audit, there are other groups to which universities might also be said to be accountable – to the communities in which universities are located, and to university students and teachers. The expectation that universities may channel all accountability through government institutions is to neglect the broader pedagogical role of universities and I will try to show that in some cases the requirements of the QAA stand in direct contradiction to those other responsibilities.

Last year, before the stage at which the subject benchmarking statement was finalised in many disciplines, anthropologists formed a co-ordinating committee to formalise their response to the proposals as they concerned them. The impetus for such action in anthropology was a result of the dissent within the discipline that had been caused by the attempt of the QAA to place anthropology in the same subject area as sociology, thus effectively disengaging the field of physical anthropology. Although the original protest from anthropology was one of subject definition alone, at that time Shore and Wright (1999: 572) widened the debate to argue that:

'there are no effective sanctions (as yet) if a discipline as a whole asserts, and reorganises itself around, its own definitions of quality and accountability, even if they diverge from those of the QAA ... the audit system seems to rely largely on fear, expectations of compliance and a lack of imagination regarding the possibility of alternatives.'

Unfortunately Shore and Wright's observation does not seem to have registered profoundly within the academic body as a whole, with the result that little or no resistance has been actively displayed by academic subject groupings across the board. Why might this be? After all, the university is an institution which has been until now protective of both its academic freedom and its right to sustain independent critique of the very formal institutions of politics which seek to impose explicit structures of monitoring 'quality assurance'. There must be many answers to the question, the anecdotal evidence suggests the powerful combination of a variety of conflicts of political interest between individual academics as well as pressures levied at the collective level to comply in the name of pragmatism.

Furthermore, I shall argue in this paper that in terms of pedagogy itself, universities have paved the way for the arrival of the auditors into their ivory corridors by having already institutionalised a system of bureaucratic assessment of their own students which has not been difficult for the QAA to convert into a bureaucratic assessment of teachers. If an alternative is to be offered in the current climate of accountability it would necessitate a broader evaluation of the way that value is assessed in higher education at all levels; including the means by which university teachers ascribe value to the work of university students. This of course relates to the philosophy of education itself which is an enormous topic; all that can be offered here is a selective reading of the literature which relates most directly to a personal observation generated by my own experience of teaching ethnoarchaeology at the University of Wales, Lampeter this summer.

Education and the social order

In 1932 Bertrand Russell argued that opinions on pre-university education policy were divided between those who considered that the social goal of education was to train good individuals and those who thought that the end product should be good citizens. Russell was very much in favour of the education of the individual, which he described as LT, 'licensed to think'. His opinion of the other was low; Russell (1932: 14) described the well-educated citizen as a person who is:

'likely to be incapable of discovery, since he will respect his elders and betters, reverence the men of the past generation, and look with horror upon all subversive doctrines.'

Russell argued that governments aim to produce good citizens by their systems of education to the exclusion of any other educational end-product, because good citizens are most likely to admire the status quo and not criticise the very government institutions which funded their production. It was on these philosophical grounds that Russell set up his own educational experiment in the form of an independent school which encouraged individual and personal responsibility and growth in its students by its non-authoritarian organisational structure and alternatives to formally assessed work.

The political role of education has been critically assessed more recently by left-wing intellectuals especially in countries where government is proactive in setting educational agendas, again, the argument is that educational institutions, including those of higher education, are used to play a part in social control to such an extent that their primary aim is to actively discourage critical thinking, academic freedom and personal growth and development because such qualities in individuals would lead to a critique of government itself, a challenge to the status quo (Giroux and McLaren 1994). Freire and Faundez (1989) argue that a curriculum of which government has played a large part in determining the content, whether by the promise of funding or the threat of funding withdrawal, facilitates this process of social control. As such they argue that curricula should be kept 'slippery' enough to make it difficult for government intervention at the level of pedagogy itself:

'education should be regarded as a process, as a process of self-transformation, as a process which must itself be in a constant state of change ... it should not cling to preconceived ideas or models' (ibid.: 77).

The implication of this is that in the case of the benchmarking statement, which itself is a form of model, or template for an archaeology degree in Britain, it is the very existence of this template that makes it eligible for increasing government intervention in what is taught in higher education, available for appropriation and for use in social control. Secondly, and this is the point I shall develop here, it also creates a list of expectation which has the effect of 'standing in' for the personal responsibility and creativity of teachers. Rather than improving quality it may serve to reduce quality by stifling innovation (see Pluciennik, this volume, for the possible effect of the benchmarking statement on the teaching of archaeological theory) and personal development, creativity of both students and teachers. I shall continue with the theme of personal development in particular.

Education and personal development

Coleman and Simpson (1999) made a study of the ways in which anthropology penetrates university students' lives and affects their personal development; comparing students from prosperous middle class families at Durham University and less privileged students from the Stockton

campus. They suggested that there are a number of ways in which students use the anthropology they learn; some used anthropological knowledge purely as a means to fulfilling the assessment procedures required to gain a degree in the subject, while others, most often the underprivileged students from Stockton, used their anthropological knowledge of subjects such as gender and power to re-examine their own lives. Such reflexivity often led to personal growth and change and brought about transformations in family relationships, in aspirations and in world view.

Reflexive learning is nurtured in institutions of anthropology where the dominant theoretical paradigm emphasises the dynamic of the encounter between the observer and the observed; the learner and what is learned. Importance is given to the reflexive nature of the experience of anthropological fieldwork; considering the personal development of the observer as the result of the encounter with 'other' as illuminating as the responses of the subject him or herself (Clifford and Marcus 1986; James et al. 1997). Thus Coleman and Simpson (1999) concluded from their study of Durham students that it would be equally valid, if not more so, to assess anthropology students in terms of this personal development rather than the standard formal means of assessment. This idea was much influenced by the work of Mascarenhas-Keyes and Wright (1995) who advocated a move away from substantivist strategies of teaching, in which the acquisition of knowledge is the goal, towards imaginationist strategies, in which the greater emphasis is given to the student's personal development. They advocate this despite the inherent difficulty in quantifying, or assigning a numerical mark to different levels of different aspects of personal development.

A case study in teaching ethnoarchaeology - the Project

The observations outlined above are relevant to any pedagogical experience which involves the student encountering 'other' for the first time, or during the course of their work, such as for example, in the following case study with which I was involved, in which the project was ethnoarchaeological in nature.

Last summer I taught ethnoarchaeology in the field to groups of undergraduates as part of a larger project currently being run by the Department of Archaeology at the University of Wales, Lampeter. The Project has as its underlying pedagogical philosophy the idea that archaeological theory can and should be taught as an integral part of practice and in keeping with this the ethnoarchaeological part of the Project itself had two elements in which students were involved.

Firstly students ran a questionnaire-based survey of visitors at various tourist sites in the research area, the Upper Teifi Valley. Information about visitors' needs and wants regarding the development of tourism in the area – especially with regard to its archaeological heritage – was collected and will potentially be used in the creation of a heritage management project for which European funding will be sought. The valley is in a designated Objective One area and the proposal which comes out of the Project aims to meet the funding criteria in that it involves partnerships between public sector, private enterprise and the community in an attempt to create a heritage management plan which will bring about sustainable economic development in the valley.

Secondly students were required to conduct extended interviews with specific (named) local people in order to record information about their perceptions of the local past and their own personal histories. This, the oral history project as it will be termed for the purposes of this paper, also aimed specifically to collect information that people had about local archaeological sites, such as sites on their land, sites with which they were familiar, and so on. This information was to be added to the SMR so that local knowledge of sites would be recorded as oral testament and thereby enhance the SMR. It was also anticipated that the information would be made available and accessible to the community from which it came for use by, for example, schools and local history groups.

It will have become clear by this point that the ethnoarchaeology referred to here is not the logical-positivist ethnoarchaeology with which the word has become associated, but is rather ethnoarchaeology in its widest sense – the exploration of the relationship between living people and their material culture informed by recent theoretical developments in the subject of archaeology as well as in anthropology (Clifford and Marcus 1986; James et al 1997; Gazin-Schwartz and Holtorf 1999). In both its objectives the ethnoarchaeological project aimed to be 'accountable' to the local community: by facilitating the economic development of the area in the case of the visitor survey, and by 'giving back' an enhanced version of the SMR to the community through the oral history project. For the students, the project aimed to deliver a field experience that related to employment in the sector of public archaeology and facilitate growth in confidence and personal responsibility. More generally, the ethnoarchaeological project was a way of building links between the university and the community.

Teaching oral history recording - the experience

I shall concentrate here on the second element of the ethnoarchaeological project – the oral history project – to demonstrate the importance of those aspects of the learning process that were discussed at the beginning of this paper – the qualities of the learning experience, such as personal growth and development, that are so difficult to quantify they tend to get ignored altogether.

There are so few guidelines for teaching ethnographic interviews in archaeology that first-timers are usually directed to the anthropological literature on methodology (e.g. Agar 1980; Ellen 1984; Tonkin 1992). Some of this can be quite daunting, for example, Naroll and Cohen (1973: 3) suggest that it has long been believed that 'the incumbent must do it the hard way by going through exactly the same experience as those who are the acknowledged professionals in the field.'

As the anthropological literature suggests, it is not easy to teach a student how to do an ethnographic interview. What is more, in keeping with the aims of the project in general, it was decided to allow the learning process to take place out in the field as much as was possible. So those on the oral history project were given just a two-hour session in the classroom and were then invited to do their interviews 'the hard way'. They were given a tape recorder, an appointment with their interviewee, and a list of questions about the local archaeology which they could refer to if the interview veered dramatically off course or if they got 'stuck'. This list turned out to be significant. The rest was up to them and I personally felt quite anxious about letting undergraduates loose on the local community, especially those students who had in the past missed lectures, handed work in late and not received good marks (in short, those who had struggled in the formal quantifiable assessment procedures of the institution). After all, these students were 'representing' the university and it was a matter of trust on our part that they would comport themselves well in their interviews, probably drinking tea in the kitchen of a Welsh farmer, talking about that farmer's memories and aspirations for the future; it was an encounter with the 'other' that they would experience, not least in terms of language and culture.

Despite my misgivings, all the students found their interviews a positive experience; they came out 'buzzing' and chatty, obviously having been affected quite profoundly by the encounter in one way or another. But what was most unexpected was that it was the so-called less able students who performed their interviews much better than did the ones who had up until then got good marks: on listening to the tape recordings, it became clear that the students who had received higher grades until that point tended to interview according to what they felt was expected of them by often referring to the list of 'back-up' questions and occasionally performing an interrogation of the subject, which led to awkwardness, protracted silences and a lack of rapport between interviewee and interviewer. The so-called less able students on the other hand, took a very different approach, they seemed less duty bound to refer to the pre-set questions and instead engaged their interviewees in general conversation about their subjects' lives, showing genuine interest in their responses and establishing a rapport that made it obvious the interview had been an enjoyable and rewarding experience for both observed and observer. While their interviews did not reveal as much 'hard core' quantifiable SMR-related information as did the more formal interviews, what those students had done in terms of an ambassadorial role, in terms of relationships between the community and the university, and in terms of their own personal development, was equally valuable for a project in which an explicit aim was the development of good relations between the university and community.

Unfortunately, this year, the interviews themselves will not be formally assessed. We had not anticipated that personal skills and development would be such a large part of the students' experience or that this encounter with 'other' would lead to such a stark differential response. As Coleman and Simpson (1999) suggest, such qualities as, for example, the ability to establish rapport are notoriously difficult to quantify, and the means by which we will incorporate them into the assessment procedure in the future will need a great deal of working out. Mascarenhas-Keyes and Wright (1995) advocate imaginationist teaching strategies and I think it would be interesting to see a further exploration of these ideas on a wider scale. It is obvious that in the case described here, the fear of formal assessment and the written list of questions that we had given all the students actually stifled the so-called better students' performance in their interviews, blocking creativity, responsibility and their own personal sense of accountability. Russell would suggest that they had behaved like good citizens, and in so doing had rendered themselves 'incapable of discovery'.

Conclusion - moving the benchmarks

Russell might also argue that the benchmarking statement for archaeology and the formal expectation of the QAA will do the same to university teachers. Many lecturers see teaching as an intensely creative process, one that could be made awkward and stilted by the imposition of an external template. This is not to deny the need to seek high standards, merely to raise the point that the implicit assumption of that standard as defined by the QAA is that university teachers will improve their performance as a result, i.e. come 'up' to that standard. It should be considered that, as with the student interviews described above, what is prepared formally might well be below the personal best of some teachers and the very existence of a homogenising document may well remove personal commitment to the profession, thus impeding some of the most inventive and inspiring teaching.

One of the good things about the benchmarking document for archaeology is that it has forced a re-evaluation from a variety of sectors of what it is that is important in higher education. From the point of view of liberal pedagogical philosophy the very imposition of quantification and account in teaching life paradoxically has served as a reminder of the importance of the non-quantifiable values of higher education. Because there has been little formal reaction from academics against the benchmarking statement, or indeed the QAA of which it is a product, it is important to react by exploring alternatives for when the statement is reviewed in 2003. I have concentrated on just two themes for further discussion here, both based on my experience of teaching ethnoarchaeology at the University of Wales, Lampeter, this summer.

Firstly, there should be a broadening of the debate about university accountability itself – the question of how universities are accountable, and to whom, is more complex than can be covered in government audit. Without this there is the possibility that balancing accounts in one area, through the QAA alone, will come into conflict with university responsibilities towards students as individuals, towards university teaching as a profession involving high levels of creativity, and towards the local communities in which universities are situated. Universities can be accountable in many ways and at many levels, not just in what is taught i.e. the graduates that are produced, the end product, but also in the quality of the process by which this takes place (Fewster 1996).

Secondly, as part of the wider pedagogical philosophy explored in this paper, there should be a consideration of the possibility of incorporating the non-quantifiable values that a degree in archaeology embodies at all levels of teaching and learning. This would have implications for not only the way that university students are assessed, but also the way that university teachers are assessed. The wider debate on pedagogical philosophy suggests that substantivist strategies of teaching are dominant to the detriment of imaginationist teaching strategies and such pedagogical practice is intimately bound with the dissemination of power and the role of government in social control through education. From within such an educational philosophy it is small wonder that QAA-induced directives such as the subject benchmarking statements have not seemed incongruous and have received little resistance from academics, despite the extra time, work and money that TQA demands of academic departments.

Had the pedagogical setting into which the QAA was placed been a more liberal one, committed to imaginationist practice, the reaction might have been different.

References

Agar, M.H. 1980. *The Professional Stranger: An Informal Introduction to Ethnography.* London: Academic Press.

Clifford, J. and Marcus, G. (eds). 1986. *Writing Culture: The Poetics and Politics of Ethnography.* Berkeley: University of California Press.

Coleman, S. and Simpson, B. 1999. Unintended consequences? Anthropology, pedagogy and personhood. *Anthropology Today* 15(6): 3-6.

Ellen, R. F. (ed.) 1984. *Ethnographic Research: A Guide to General Conduct.* London: Academic Press.

Fewster, K. J. 1996. EWP schools and the early Brigades: a case study in education and development from Botswana. *Education with Production* 11(2): 45-74.

Freire, P. and Faundez, A. 1989. *Learning to Question: A Pedagogy of Liberation.* Geneva: World Council of Churches.

Gazin-Schwartz, A. and Holtorf, C. J. (eds) 1999. *Archaeology and Folklore*. London: Routledge.

Giroux, H. A. and McLaren, P. 1994. *Between Borders: Pedagogy and the Politics of Cultural Studies*. London: Routledge.

James, A., Hockey, J. and Dawson, A. 1997. *After Writing Culture: Epistemology and Praxis in Contemporary Anthropology*. London: Routledge.

Mascarenhas-Keyes, S. and Wright, S. 1995. Report on Teaching and Learning Social Anthropology in the United Kingdom. *Social Anthropology Teaching and Learning Network*.

Naroll, R and Cohen, R. (eds) 1973. *A Handbook of Method in Cultural Anthropology*. New York: Columbia University Press.

Russell, B. 1932. *Education and the Social Order*. London: George Allen and Unwin.

Shore, C. and Wright, S. 1999. Audit culture and anthropology: Neo-Liberalism in British higher education. *Journal of the Royal Anthropological Institute (N.S.)* 5: 557-75.

Tonkin, E. 1992. *Narrating Our Pasts: The Social Construction of Oral History*. Cambridge: Cambridge University Press.

3.5

Changing career paths and archaeology in the new millennium: the Society for American Archaeology teaching archaeology in the Twenty-first century initiative

George S. Smith

Introduction

Stewardship, diverse pasts, social relevance, ethics and values, written and oral communication, basic archaeological skills, and real world problem solving – these principles are at the very core of archaeology as the evolving, dynamic discipline that it is, and must be, in order to understand, interpret, manage, and protect the past. The profession and the people who practice it, in all its diverse applications, are and have been influenced by shifting paradigms and changing levels of understanding. Each day we use terms and technology that did not exist a few short years ago. The discipline is changing. In addition to research, archaeology is now being called upon to provide data to manage, in the public interest, the non-renewable resource we call our national heritage. This brings with it additional responsibilities which require new and/or modified skills, knowledge, and abilities to meet these challenges.

The discipline of archaeology in the United States is continually assessing itself in terms of education and training. For example, in 1974 the Society for American Archaeology (SAA) prepared the *Airlie House Report – The Management of Archeological Resources* (McGimsey and Davis 1977) to deal with the growth of archaeology due to various pieces of legislation and the need to identify individuals and institutions who could assist in meeting these new legal responsibilities.

In 1989, and again in 1994, the SAA convened 'Save the Past for the Future' working conferences to examine various issues facing the profession (SAA 1990; 1995). In 1995 the SAA forum on 'Restructuring American Archaeology' and the resulting conference 'Renewing our National Archaeological Program' examined increasing professional knowledge and expertise at all levels of archaeological resource management (Lipe and Redman 1996). At the 1989 Chacmool Conference in Alberta, Canada a session was held on dealing with our professional responsibility to the public (Bender 1995). In 1997 a conference sponsored by the Professional Archaeologists of New York City examined changing career paths in archaeology and the training needed to meet these new career opportunities (Schuldenrein 1998a; 1998b). These are some of the recent benchmarks in our effort to re-examine our profession, and be assured there were others that took place at regional and departmental levels, not only in the United States but in other countries around the world.

If one thing can be drawn from these efforts it is that archaeology has changed considerably in the latter part of the Twentieth century. As a result many students and practicing professionals are not receiving the education and training needed, either through formal education or continuing education, in order to successfully perform the majority of jobs currently available to archaeologists today.

The Wakulla Springs workshop

Reflecting on archaeology as we enter the new millenium was the focus of the SAA's 1998 Wakulla Springs workshop on Teaching Archaeology in the Twenty-first century. The twenty-four archaeologists that attended were very aware that this was an evolving issue which was being discussed in various venues. This was verified by the fact that when contacted by the SAA, and asked if they were interested in supporting this effort, the Society for Historical Archaeology, Canadian Archaeological Association, American Anthropological Association, Archaeological Institute of America, and the National Association of State Archaeologists whole-heartily endorsed the workshop and programme. These organizations in some form or another were grappling with the same issues.

What has changed in archaeology is that research, teaching, and publishing are only part of the duties archaeologists perform today, regardless of where they practice. In the past two decades, archaeological practice has been transformed by forces both internal and external to the profession. These transformations include:

- a growth in the antiquities market accompanied by unprecedented site destruction
- destruction of our archaeological heritage by construction and development activities
- implementation of cultural resource legislation and the subsequent growth of the cultural resource management profession
- passage of legislation regulating access to human burials and artifact collections, and
- a heightened popular interest in archaeology, including the growing interest of descendant communities in their archaeological pasts.

These forces have required archaeologists to develop new skills and ethical principles for professional practice (Bender and Smith 1998).

While the social, political, and employment contexts of practicing archaeology have changed over the past twenty or so years, curriculum structure and content and postgraduate opportunities have been relatively unaltered. One reason for this can be found in the development of archaeology in the United States. For over 100 years archaeology has been a formal academic discipline taught as one of the four classic sub-disciplines of anthropology with the traditional outlet for most archaeologists being the academy (Michaels 1996:192). However, given how archaeology is currently practiced it has, by necessity, expanded beyond the academy. In fact, the majority of archaeologists in the United States are employed in governmental and private sector settings (Smith et al.1995; Zeder 1997).

This brings us to the question of what skills are needed to accommodate these changes in the profession and how they can be incorporated at the undergraduate, graduate and postgraduate levels. We need look no further than recommendations from the conferences and workshops previously mentioned. All recommend improved education and training and report that students are not prepared for most of the jobs currently available and continuing educational opportunities for practicing professionals are limited. They report that students and many practicing archaeologists are not prepared for jobs that require:

- understanding and application of historic preservation laws
- ethics
- cultural resource management strategies
- resource evaluation
- National Register evaluations
- proposal writing
- personnel management, and
- business practices (Blanton 1995).

They stress the need for instruction in:

- public relations
- writing for the public
- working with land owners, developers, governmental officials, teachers and students in grades K-12
- promoting cultural diversity
- understanding current education methods and trends
- protecting archaeological resources
- site stabilization, and
- working with descendant communities and avocational archaeological groups (Fagan 1994; Lynott 1997; Lynott and Wylie 1995; McManamon 1991; SAA 1995; Smith et al. 1995; White and Weisman 1995; and others).

Planning for the SAA's Teaching Archaeology in the Twenty-first century workshop began with the selection of a group of archaeologists who would be representative of the diverse stakeholders in such a curricular change – the teachers and future employers of our students. Conference participants were thus drawn from the ranks of diverse faculty at community colleges, four-year liberal arts colleges, and university departments of anthropology (private and public). Similarly, potential employers were represented by professionals practicing archaeology in federal, state, and local agencies, as well as consulting firms – either for profit or affiliated with a university department. Moreover, representatives from the American Anthropological Association, Society for Historical Archaeology, Archaeological Institute of America, the National Association of State Archaeologists, and the American Cultural Resources Association were invited to encourage dialogue beyond the boundaries of the SAA membership. Input from current students was solicited through the SAA's Student Affairs Committee as well as a student representative at the workshop. It was recognized that meaningful reform could proceed only from a dialogue in which the wide variety of practicing archaeologists could see their concerns represented.

Prior to the workshop participants drafted position papers responding to issues dealing with curricular reform. These papers indicated that the first task would be to reach agreement on the core principles for curricular reform, in light of a widespread sense that in general, current curricula do not contain many of the important issues affecting archaeological practice today. Moreover, the papers revealed that the task must be accomplished in a format that responded to the needs and constraints of a diverse profession without privileging or stereotyping any one sector. The second pre-workshop initiative was a survey of departments of anthropology, in the United States and Canada, in order to assess levels of interest in and impediments to the type of curricular reform contemplated. Perhaps the most important result of this survey was it provided a sense that a majority of the responding departments were interested in integrating 'applied archaeology' into their curricula if they did not already do so.

I use the term applied archaeology to mean the application of archaeological method, theory, and knowledge to meet local or national needs. It includes advice, administration, or instruction relating to the understanding, interpretation, protection, and management of cultural resources. As such, it includes cultural resource management, heritage resource management, cultural property management, public archaeology, and contract archaeology. In the United States we are struggling with these terms. Their use varies from being interchangeable to having very different meanings depending on the author. It would be very beneficial to define and use a common terminology not just in the United States but internationally.

When departments were asked to identify obstacles to teaching applied archaeology, the most common response, at both the graduate and undergraduate levels was 'other courses take priority.' This was clarified in a number of cases to reflect departments and/or programmes with only a few faculty that spent the majority of their time covering general anthropology courses. At both the graduate and undergraduate levels, departments reported 'lack of faculty interest' as the most frequent reason for not teaching applied courses followed by 'lack of faculty training', 'lack of student interest', and 'inappropriate in their academic setting.' (Krass 1998).

The results of the SAA's student survey, taken through the Student Affairs Committee, indicates that almost two thirds of the students responding were preparing for jobs as university professors while a third were working towards employment in the governmental or private sectors. A few were hedging their bets and preparing for both. It is not surprising that the majority of those seeking positions in the academy were those enrolled in PhD programs while the majority of non-academic job seekers were MA degree candidates. Given that the majority of the respondents were preparing for academic positions, it is interesting to note that two thirds of them saw the need for incorporating applied archaeology into the curriculum. PhD and MA degree seeking students agreed that the vast majority of them would not find employment as university professors and that they would, at least during some part of their careers, find employment in the applied field, in private and/or governmental sectors, and needed the skills to compete for and be successful at those jobs.

Principles for curricular reform

Workshop discussion began by defining principles for curricular reform. It was felt that these provided the most succinct and encompassing statement of the context to which archaeological practice must respond in the Twenty-first century. In addition, workshop participants recognized a number of skills that should be fostered through curricular reform were clearly imbedded in the traditions of a liberal education and were thus seen as a powerful rationale for curricular reform.

Having agreed on the principles, participants were divided into work groups, each charged with envisioning how the principles might be suffused throughout the curriculum to create a new learning environment for students and practicing professionals. Three work groups were convened – undergraduate education, graduate education, and postgraduate education/professional development. The latter group was formed because it was recognized that at least two sectors of the profession would need to be served as a result of the reform being contemplated – the faculty who will teach the new curricular elements and professionals who may not have had the opportunity to keep abreast of the field's rapidly changing sociopolitical and technological contexts.

The principles identified for curricular reform and their application are as follows:

- *Stewardship.* It must be made clear that archaeological resources are nonrenewable and finite and must have complete and substantial documentation.
- *Diverse Pasts.* It must be made clear that archaeologists do not have exclusive rights to the interpretation of archaeological resources, but that various publics have a stake in the past. Diverse groups such as descendant communities; state, local, and federal agencies; and others compete for, and have a vested interest in, the non-renewable resources of the past.
- *Social Relevance.* If archaeology is to be justified as a discipline, in terms of both public support and interest, it must be made clear that understanding the past has direct application to the present and future.
- *Ethics and Values.* The articulation of ethics and values is seen as a sign of growth and maturation in the profession. The seven principles discussed here are fundamental to archaeologists' conduct with regard to archaeological resources, data, colleagues, and the public.
- *Written and Oral Communication.* Archaeology depends on the understanding and support of the public. Therefore, archaeologists must be able to communicate their goals, results, recommendations and enthusiasm for the past to a diverse audience. We must be able to think logically, write effectively, and speak clearly.
- *Fundamental Archaeological Skills.* Archaeologists must master a set of basic cognitive and methodological skills that will enable them to operate effectively in field and laboratory contexts. These skills must include project management, excavation, analysis, report writing, and long-term curation.
- *Real World Problem Solving.* Archaeology can be significantly enhanced by asking questions that engage problem solving work. Archaeologists must learn to apply knowledge and skills in the solution of fully contextualized archaeological problems.

The application of these principles within the context of undergraduate and graduate programs with continuation after graduation (in the form of continuing education), will provide a firm basis for those who practice archaeology in all its diverse applications.

Based on this work the SAA established the Task Force on Curriculum. The Task Force has been charged with identifying the intellectual and ethical principles and technical skills required to practice archaeology in all its diverse applications in order to help students and practicing archaeologists meet the challenges of the Twenty-first century. Recently, the SAA Board of Directors voted to expand the charge of the Task Force to involve the international community.

Task Force on Curriculum accomplishments

Accomplishments of the SAA Task Force on Curriculum include organizing a workshop in 1998 that identified, addressed, and assessed the issues, resulting in seven working principles that form the basis for undergraduate, graduate, and post graduate education. Based on the results of the workshop four articles were prepared for the *SAA Bulletin* (Bender and Smith 1998; Davis et al. 1999; Lynott et al. 1999; and Messenger et al. 1999). In addition, an electronic bulletin board (www.saa.org) designed to foster a national, and now international dialogue, on the teaching of archaeology was established, and a report entitled *Teaching Archaeology in the 21st Century* (Bender and Smith 2000) was prepared. The report was distributed to some 6,500 SAA members as well as to departments of anthropology in the United States and Canada, through a grant from the Getty Grant Program. An article was also published in *Antiquity* (Smith and Bender 2000). Based on responses from the electronic bulletin board, an email list has been established for individuals who want to be kept informed about Task Force activities. Presentations were also made at two international conferences in Wales and Portugal.

The SAA is also working on a programme to help redesign introductory level courses, using modern teaching techniques to develop student's analytical skills, while incorporating the profession's newly articulated ethical principles. The proposal calls for archaeologists at several institutions to help design these courses. Faculty members would work together with pedagogical experts to learn about outcome-based course construction, alternative ways of organizing learning, and advances in teaching technologies. Professional evaluators will help them build evaluation into their plans. Through a series of workshops, courses would then be developed, taught, and evaluated. Course descriptions, syllabi, and resource materials would be made available in printed and electronic form.

Planning is underway for a proposal dealing with graduate education and another for professional development as well as sessions and workshops at upcoming professional meetings in the United States and abroad. This is truly a global issue, the solution of which lies in international cooperation and sharing of ideas.

Conclusion

Based on the various efforts to examine archaeology and prepare ourselves and our students for the Twenty-first century, we are at a point where we must collectively decide where the profession is heading and chart that course into the new millennium and beyond. What has been discussed may sound like an issue for only those practicing archaeology in the governmental and private sectors. Nothing could be farther from the truth. The very nature of the public financing of all but a very minute segment of archaeology, and our responsibilities to the archaeological resource base and the public requires the dedication and participation of those preparing for careers in archaeology as well as its practitioners.

Acknowledgements

I would like to thank the individuals who participated in the Wakulla Springs workshop and the members of the Society for American Archaeology Task Force on Curriculum for their vision and direction. In addition I would like to thank the sponsors and supporters of this initiative – the Society for American Archaeology, Society for Historical Archaeology, American Anthropological Association, Canadian Archaeological Association, Archaeological Institute of America, National Association of State Archaeologists, National Park Service, Bureau of Reclamation, and the Getty Grant program for their support.

References

Bender, S. J. 1995. Professional choice, public responsibility: The SAA Public Education Committee. Symposium presented at the 28th Annual Chacmool Conference, Calgary, Alberta, Canada.

Bender, S. J. and Smith, G. S. 1998. SAA's Workshop on Teaching Archaeology in the 21st Century: promoting a national dialogue on curricula reform. *SAA Bulletin* 16(5): 11-3.

Bender, S. J. and Smith, G. S. 2000. *Teaching Archaeology in the 21st Century*. Washington, D.C.: Society for American Archaeology.

Blanton, D. B 1995. The case for CRM training in academic institutions. *SAA Bulletin* 13(3): 40-41.

Davis, H, Altschul, J. H., Bense, J., Brumfiel, E. M., Lerner, S., Miller, J. J., Steponaitis, V. P. and Watkins, J. 1999. Teaching Archaeology in the 21st Century: thoughts on undergraduate education. *SAA Bulletin* 17(1): 18-20.

Fagan, B. M. 1994. Perhaps we hear voices. In *Save the Past for the Future II, Report of the Working Conference*, Special Report. Washington D.C.: Society for American Archaeology, pp. 25-30.

Krass, D. S. 1998. SAA survey of departments regarding CRM/public archaeology teaching. Paper prepared for the SAA workshop on 'Teaching Archaeology in the 21st Century', Wakulla Springs, Florida, February 5-8.

Lipe, B and Redman, C. 1996. Conference on 'Renewing Our National Archaeological Program.' *SAA Bulletin* 14(4): 14-7.

Lynott, M. J., Anderson, D. G., Doran, G. H., Elia, R. J., Franklin, M., Pyburn, K. A., Schuldenrein, J. and Snow, D R. 1999. Teaching Archaeology in the 21st Century: thoughts on graduate education. *SAA Bulletin* 17(1): 21-2.

Lynott, M. J. 1997. Ethical principles and archaeological practice: development of an ethics policy. *American Antiquity* 62(4): 589-99.

Lynott, M. J. and Wylie, A. (eds) 1995. *Ethics in American Archaeology: Challenges for the 1990s*. Special Report. Washington, D.C.: Society for American Archaeology.

McGimsey, C. R., III and Davis, H. A. 1977. *The Management of Archeological Resources: the Airlie House Report*. Special Publication. Washington D.C.: Society for American Archaeology.

McManamon, F. P. 1991. The many publics for archaeology. *American Antiquity* 56: 121-30.

Messenger, P. E., Blanton, D. B., Brimsek, T., Broadbent, N., Cressey, P., DeGrummond, N., Ehrenhard, J. E., Krass, D. S., McGimsey, C. R. and White N. M. 1999. Teaching Archaeology in the 21st Century: thoughts on postgraduate education/professional development. *SAA Bulletin* 17(2): 13-4.

Michaels, G. 1996. Education in archaeology: professional training and popular education. In *The Oxford Companion to Archaeology* (ed. B. M. Fagan). New York: Oxford University Press pp. 192-3.

Schuldenrein, J. 1998a. Changing career paths and the training of professional archaeologists: observations from the Barnard College Forum, Part I. *SAA Bulletin* 16(1): 31-3.

Schuldenrein, J. 1998b. Changing career paths and the training of professional archaeologists: observations from the Barnard College Forum, Part II. *SAA Bulletin* 16(3): 26-9.

Smith, G. S., and Bender, S. J. 2000. The Society for American Archaeology teaching archaeology in the 21st Century initiative. *Antiquity* 74: 186-9.

Smith, G. S., Bender, S. J. and Keel B. C. 1995. Legislation and college curriculum. *Archaeology and Public Education Newsletter* 5(4): 5.

Society for American Archaeology 1990. *Actions for the 90s, Save the Past for the Future*. Final Report, Taos Working Conference on Preventing Archaeological Looting and Vandalism. Fort Burgwin Research Center, Taos, New Mexico.

Society for American Archaeology 1995. *Save the Past for the Future II: Report of the Working Conference*. Breckenridge, Colorado. Special Report. Washington D.C.: Society for American Archaeology.

White, N. M. and Weisman, B. R. 1995. Graduate education in public archaeology at the University of South Florida, Tampa. Paper presented at the 28th Annual Chacmool Conference, Calgary, Alberta, Canada.

Zeder, M. A. 1997. *The American Archaeologist: a Profile*. Walnut Creek: AltaMira Press.

PART IV

INTERROGATING PEDAGOGIES – REFLECTIONS

4.1

Audit or educate. Archaeological reflections on a world gone mad

Paul Halstead

Aroused from my daydream, I find the landscape is white. Perhaps winter has started early. Maybe global warming was a myth and the next ice age is upon us. Then I see familiar faces and the nightmare is back.   It's a departmental staff meeting and my colleagues are filling their 'Aspect Boxes' for TQA. Someone announces that 'Teaching Quality Audit' has now been renamed - presumably because it was not really concerned with either Teaching or Quality. Now it's called 'subject review', even though the Quality Assurance Agency handbook being passed along the table seems to be a generic blueprint for everything from Engineering to English Literature.

One colleague, normally imperturbable, is sobbing in the corner. Even Parker Pearson has lost that silly grin: this is no laughing matter. Paper everywhere. A student rep. (with dreads - must be a Landscape MA) is berating us for laying waste the rainforests. Someone has calculated that this exercise will cost the department three man years (mostly, in practice, woman years). A bit hard to grasp, so I try to put this figure in context. Assuming a 50-hour working week, and fifty working weeks to the year, that adds up to 7500 man-hours. Of course, most of my colleagues are working round the clock, whereas all that feasting debris suggests our Neolithic ancestors took a more rational approach to the Protestant work ethic. Still, it suggests we have collectively blown the equivalent of a Neolithic long barrow on the conspicuous consumption of labour that is TQA (cf. Renfrew 1973: 547). On that basis, academics alone at the University of Sheffield must have sacrificed something like half a million man hours – enough to build several causewayed enclosures. Add in the administrators and we might just manage a small henge monument. Taking the UK university sector as a whole, we could easily manage Silbury Hill or even the final phase of Stonehenge.

Of course, these figures may overestimate the extra hours worked in academia. A student tries to get me to leave the meeting to keep a tutorial appointment. She looks suicidal. Too bad - I've got to finish my policy document on pastoral care. Anyway, there must be significant savings in labour through cancelled classes and reduced preparation time. And of course, we must not forget how impoverished the British Neolithic would be without all those henge and cursus monuments. They may be rather pointless gestures by our own standards, but the past is a foreign country and should not be judged in terms of modern economic rationality. For one thing, the Neolithic population of southern England may not have had any pressing alternative focus for its human labour-force. The Department of Education, however, has no such excuse. One of the beauties of money as a universal medium of exchange is to make it abundantly clear that the £100 million plus squandered on TQA over the last ten years (*THES* 30.3.01) could instead have been spent on buying sorely needed library books or computer terminals.

But am I being hypocritical? Only last week, I complained in a tutorial (one not axed to prepare for TQA) that our understanding of Mycenaean society would be so much better if more of their documents had survived. Just imagine if they had had a Xerox machine capable of duplicating clay tablets. Even with the fragmentary record that has survived, however, it's clear that administration of the kingdom of Pylos was highly centralized, perhaps fatally so, in the weeks leading up to its collapse and the conflagration that preserved all those clay tablets for posterity. Perhaps that's what the university TQA advisor meant last week. Her claim, that we'd see the benefits once we had been through it, was a coded reference to Binford's 'Pompeii premise'. The sudden catastrophe, when normal life is instantaneously frozen and sealed under a mud slide or fall of volcanic ash. Just imagine every archaeology department in the country, suddenly smothered in paper. 'It's the *Motel of the Mysteries* come true', mutters Parker Pearson in my ear – I must have been thinking aloud. Ideal material for a reflexive discipline committed to inspecting its own entrails – if anyone survives the catastrophe. But the back cover of *Motel of the Mysteries* implies that the author was trying to be funny.

'Why?', I ask plaintively. I still cannot kick that old processual habit – wanting to explain rather than describe. Barrett says something profound about 'practice' (or was it 'practise') and Edmonds encourages me to 'engage' with something. I must have been thinking aloud all along. They're telling me why Stonehenge. I try again: 'Not Stonehenge, TQA'. Silence. Perhaps this is a good testing ground for competing paradigms. As a processualist, I recognize higher education today as an example of the old phenomenon of 'systems collapse'. But labeling the problem doesn't make it feel any better (it never did, come to think of it). Zvelebil mentions ecology. Perhaps he too is talking about Stonehenge, because he doesn't shed any light on why TQA. Surely, if the energy consumed outweighs the energy captured, the strategy is unstable. Perhaps going back to Darwinian basics will help: survival of the fittest.   The Head of Department says several colleagues are under more or less severe medication and we cannot expect to complete TQA without taking casualties. Not sure how a leaner, fitter and smaller staff will help teaching quality, but looking at the state of some of my colleagues should help our more vulnerable students put their emotional and psychological problems in perspective. And we do need to lose one lecturer so that we can designate his/her office as TQA base room.

Someone puts up an overhead from a theory lecture on the history of archaeological thought. Thomsen's Four Age System, culminating in the 'Age of Paper'. Come to think of it, the 'Audit Culture' sounds like something out of the charts in the back of Childe's *Dawn of European Civilisation*, its type fossils doubtless the box file and the shredder. Barrett's now talking about 'agency'. Not sure if he means the audit Quango or the need for us to control our own destiny. Must be the former, because the latter is no longer credible.

Another day over. My aspect box is fuller and I haven't seen a student, so the cause of teaching quality must have advanced. Wonder how late the bus will be. Funny thing, but I haven't seen a ticket inspector for weeks. And what's more, everyone throws their ticket away when they get off. What kind of quality control is that? If the driver issued tickets in duplicate and kept his copies for a run of five years, the bus would be so full that no passenger could get on. Then he might run to time, providing a prompt and fully accountable service to no-one.

I think back over the day. In fairness, universities provide a public service and must be accountable. But surely the key to accountability is auditing procedures which are not so heavy-handed as to undermine the quality of education. It all seems so obvious that I am genuinely curious to know why it is not equally apparent to the Whitehall mandarins who dreamt up the dead hand of TQA. Even if TQA has nothing to offer archaeology, could the reverse be possible? Perhaps, as some prehistorians have argued for conspicuous mobilization projects like Silbury Hill and Stonehenge, the QAA subject us to this corvée labour simply to underline the fact that they can. In other words TQA is an end in itself. A senior colleague joins me at the bus stop. With his usual cynicism, he grumbles that the paper chase is meant to cover up underfunding. Perhaps he's right. It will be hard to complain about resources when we have all assured our QAA inspectors that our departments are awash with facilities, library books and optimistic teachers.

On balance, though, I suspect the QAA is not a clever and considered strategy for controlling academics or covering up underfunding, but just another example of the asphyxiating tendency for bureaucracies to extend their control for its own sake. Ironically, we probably could (and would) just about deliver a decent education to the hugely increased numbers of students passing through our universities, if only we were allowed to focus on teaching instead of auditing.

Postscript

These despairing reflections were written in November 2000, five desperate, paper-ridden months before our QAA visit. Now the visit is behind us. The panel members were pleasant and courteous, and we were graded 'Excellent', so perhaps we should feel it was worthwhile. The reality is that, thanks to the QAA brief to which the panel must work, we learnt nothing about how well or badly we teach (as opposed to how exhaustively we create an audit trail). Among my colleagues at Sheffield there is disagreement about the legitimacy and value of cost/benefit analysis in the investigation of past human societies, but I suspect we are unanimous in concluding that the costs of TQA (both the direct costs of the visit and, especially, the time diverted from the preparation and delivery of teaching) have been enormous and its benefits negligible (the repainting of the department's entrance hall!). Of course, just because we can look at Silbury Hill and Stonehenge with wonder and pleasure, we should not assume that all those who laboured on these monuments with Neolithic technology did so with a willing heart. But they may have shown their handiwork to their grandchildren with pride. No-one in their right mind will be admiring my Aspect Box in years to come. Nor, I wager, will the QAA website be visited in the future as a source of enlightenment – unless perhaps as prescribed reading for undergraduates studying the early 21st century AD collapse of British higher education.

Reference

Renfrew, C., 1973. Monuments, mobilization and social organization in neolithic Wessex. In *The Explanation of Culture Change* (ed. C. Renfrew). London: Duckworth, pp. 539-58.

4.2

Archaeological education as potential liberation

Sophy Thomas-Goodburn

I graduated from Lampeter in July 2000, having studied archaeology and anthropology BA (SH), so my time as an undergraduate student was still relatively fresh in my mind when I was invited to help with the registration at the workshop 'Interrogating Pedagogies' and subsequently to attend it. I had an interest in the topics that the workshop was going to address for two reasons in particular. Firstly, my dissertation had been about the ideology and material culture of an international college in South Wales, where I had been before university. The study raised many questions in my mind about the purposes of education, especially regarding its relationship to the transmission of ideologies and their reception. The workshop's programme seemed to include items that could have a strong bearing on those kind of questions. Secondly, higher education and the issues within and surrounding it are highly relevant to understanding my work within the Students' Union as the Welfare Officer.

At first, attending Interrogating Pedagogies felt like eavesdropping on a discussion, the workshop was made up of a mixture of people brought together by their interest in archaeology and higher education, but who were either out of the 'education system' or were employees of it, rather than students within it. During the last three years I had been in an educational environment where the majority had always been students, now they were not there. The diversity of the participants was novel, these were not just people from academia but those from 'professional' archaeology; those that some frequently refer to as from the 'real world' and for me it was a new experience to see these two groups talking about education together. Recently graduated and the students' Welfare Officer I was the closest it got to student participation.

What should people who are studying archaeology be learning? This seemed to be a key question throughout the workshop and one that many were eager to discuss. However, what archaeology is and why certain definitions of it should be studied were not always explored to as great a depth as it could have been. What the term archaeology can mean certainly has an essential bearing on what is believed should be taught and learnt. The function and meaning of education, in a broad sense, was looked at explicitly by some, however there were certainly undertones of disparate, and sometimes voiced differences over the ideas of what its functions and meanings should be. These, unfortunately, were on occasions not taken to what might have been their very interesting conclusions. In this paper I wish to comment on how education, with specific reference to archaeological education, could be a self-empowering and liberating experience for all involved. The concepts I hope to shed some light upon could be applicable to education of any kind. My experience of studying archaeology and anthropology at Lampeter was one where self-reflexivity and contexualisation, particularly in relation to socio-political and economic factors, was the primary basis for study. For any student of archaeology and anthropology, at Lampeter at least, it would have been hard to escape thinking about ones own situation, as a student, in a similar vein to other foci of study. I would suggest that potentially this could become a more explicit aspect of the educational process.

Few, if any would deny that archaeological activity operates within political and ideological systems, it is itself a political process and act (e.g. Shanks and Tilley 1987), whether conscious to its agents or not, so too is education. 'Finch (1984)...argues that the process of educational policy-making may best be seen as a battle between...those who see education as being primarily concerned with individual self-development and the fulfilment of potential and those who see it more as serving the needs of the economy and industry by preparing pupils for future positions in the occupational structure.' (Pollard et al. 1988: 4). Education in its broadest sense, and only when it is at its best, is about the empowering of people, through the proffering of skills and information that allow people to make critically informed decisions and take action, or provides them with the skills needed to analytically seek out the information necessary to make informed decisions. Most importantly education should be about providing people with the skills to learn. This will not only be a political process because of the broad societal context, but also because of the particular politics of those teaching and learning. Education is selective, certain perspectives may be proffered over others, it is not an objective activity.

Education leading to employment was a concept introduced early in the workshop. The term production was frequently used in relation to educational processes, implying that graduates could be products ready for the labour market. Observations made by the workshop on the history of archaeological higher education raised interesting points. For example, now that a degree in archaeology can lead to a vocation in any area, direct employability is no longer anticipated for the majority of graduates. The notion of education as providing 'a gateway' to employment, of whatever kind, was condoned by the workshop. This concept, among others, had enabled the discipline to survive and expand, which is a valid enough argument to ensure funding. However, is the purpose of education to provide those studying with a ticket to get a job? Certainly the potential employability of graduates would be of concern to the government bodies that provide funding to higher education. Many students too, are concerned with this side of their future and of course people need to work in order to have the means to reproduce themselves, within this society. However, education like archaeology can play a role that can be 'emancipatory or dominating' (Hodder 1999: 208), it can either free people to think about the society in which they live and are part of from a critical perspective, or it can uncritically and unconsciously transmit society's dominant ideology.

The fact that the discipline of archaeology has expanded into a highly diverse one was explored, activities are not restricted to the practical realm of, for example, excavation or curation but can be theoretical analyses. The field of archaeological activity could be living groups of people, perhaps their conceptions of the past: in a local community, a classroom, or the media. Many attending the workshop appear not to have been too willing to accept someone's activity of analysing power relations in the photography of ancient monuments, for example, as an archaeological one. For these participants the fundamentals of the discipline lie in the practical not the political or theoretical, and in my mind a false dichotomy is made. From much of what was stated, by those that saw the basics of archaeology as the 'practical' aspects it seems that they did not acknowledge that these were themselves political and theoretical.

I agree that it is essential that the 'practical' side of archaeology is taken into account and that those studying the subject are made aware of a range of aspects, from law to trowels. Students should gain an understanding of a variety of practical issues and at the very least it is important that they are aware of their existence. The significance of this knowledge lies in being able to base deeper and substantiated argument about the past, in relation to other realms, whatever these might be and inevitably having a bearing on the present. I would never argue that practical dimensions be ignored or that work that does not substantiate itself not be criticised. To talk about material remains of the past in a decontextualised ill-informed and detached (from concepts and knowledge that archaeology may have produced pertaining to the practical) manner achieves very little and can easily be dismissed. This is the reason why an understanding of the 'practical' dimensions of archaeology can be important, rather than the 'practical' being the innate basis.

By some, the public's fascination with the practical dimensions of archaeology was proffered as a reason to emphasise their significance above the theoretical. The argument for this seemed to be based on a supply and demand theory. My main objection to this is, not that it dismissed critical analysis as essential, but that it does not explicitly state its fundamental basis; there is a market for practical archaeology and like a business higher education could meet it. The unconscious, or at least unstated, economic dimension and compliance with situations as they stand stifles innovation and the potential for the public's access to other archaeological realms. To take an

example from elsewhere, huge numbers of people find pop music wonderful, they purchase recordings and show us that there is a vast 'market' for that kind of music, however this does not necessarily mean that every musician decides to produce popular music, nor does it mean that it is automatically and universally accepted as a 'good thing' due to the number of consumers it has. People who wish to study should be given access to assessing their own position in the socio-economic context. Thus informed, they may decide to abide by and believe in the status quo, but to some extent they will do so knowingly. Perhaps others might seek to change their own and others' situations and perspectives through pursuing archaeological activity as political action.

I would agree with many of the points raised by members of the workshop, regarding their concern with the lack of awareness of certain aspects of archaeological practice shown by recent graduates. Aspects of some archaeological practice, such as the laws that surround and in many cases determine and restrict it, should be understood by graduates (and hopefully even those who went to lectures but never got a degree). However, this should not be for the future employability of the person or even for the continuation of what 'British archaeology' is today, but for the potential understanding of the socio-political and economic issues that archaeological practice in whatever shape or form is integrally tied to. The emphases should be on the possibility of these being challenged and altered. Surely education, especially one in a discipline which can have strong ideas on self-reflexivity, should integrate a call to analyse 'the powers that be' and peoples' situations and perspectives within society, inspiring possible alternatives to arise, rather than merely accepting the employers' (be them governmental or private based) requirements as the unchangeable status quo.

References

Hodder, I. 1999. *The Archaeological Process: An Introduction*. Oxford: Blackwell.

Pollard, A. Purvis, J. and Walford, G. 1988. Ethnography, policy and the emergence of the new vocationalism. In *Education, Training and the New Vocationalism* (ed. A. Pollard, J. Purvis and G. Walford). Milton Keynes: Open University Press, pp. 3-14.

Shanks, M. and Tilley, C. 1987. *Social Theory and Archaeology*. Cambridge: Polity Press.

4.3

Retrospect and prospect

Paul Rainbird

As a co-convenor of the Lampeter Workshop I offer here some brief comments based in part on my experience of the workshop and the editing of this volume. My comments should also be understood as being derived from six years experience as a lecturer in higher education with equal time spent employed in universities in Australia and Wales.

The mix of academics and 'employers/professionals /practitioners' at the meeting proved extremely fruitful and although illustrating the diversity of practice within archaeology, and reminding us of past attempts to draw this broad constituency together, it did provide common ground in identifying consensus in regard to all participants' commitment to the subject and interest in its future. In terms of provision of archaeology in higher education as Don Henson (this volume) reveals there are 28 full departments of archaeology in Britain, but almost three times that number teach archaeology in one form or other. This rather brought into question how SCUPHA (the Standing Committee of University Professors and Heads in Archaeology) can be regarded as fully representative of academic archaeology.

The benchmarking document produced by members of SCUPHA for the QAA provided the focus of much discussion. It was noted that the SCUPHA members, in preparing this document, appeared to be restricting the teaching of archaeology to departments from which their members are drawn. Many of the non-archaeology departments and non-traditional methods of higher education provision (e.g., distance learning) may fall outside of the broad, although apparently not ultimately prescriptive, requirements of the benchmarks. Vehement concerns were raised that although not prescriptive at present, the documentation and tabulation of expected 'standards' could easily, and perhaps ultimately, turn into a checklist of absolute minimum requirements assessed by the QAA (subsequent meetings ahead of the next round of Teaching Quality Assessment and commentary published in the *Times Higher Education Supplement* and *Guardian Education* indicate that such prescription is rapidly becoming reality). It was also noted that some departments had immediately put into effect changes to their curricula to meet the perceived needs of the document. The participants of the workshop were in general agreement that the benchmarking document requires far greater circulation, and basic debate, prior to its expected revision in 2003.

The bureaucratization of archaeology teaching in higher education has already had an effect on the current delivery of undergraduate courses and must lead to different expectations of graduate students and employers. A number of contributions raised concerns that processes such as these threatened to homogenise the provision of archaeology in higher education and, in so doing, reduce the diversity that makes archaeology such a vibrant subject for study. This bureaucratization is not limited to the benchmarking and QAA reviews, and workshop participants from outside the academe reminded us that they too were subject to paperwork pressures in relation to such issues as 'best practice' for example.

Continuing professional development was considered a necessary component for all undergraduates choosing to pursue a career in archaeology. The participants from outside academe requested more vocational training in the undergraduate degree, but the question had to be asked 'what would then be left out?' An outcome of these discussions was that undergraduates needed to be made aware at an early stage in their courses what skills and experience they would need to demonstrate if they wished to go straight into the 'profession'. The IFA is unwilling to make taught Masters degrees a requisite to entering the 'profession' as it would imply extra cost to the student as, in most cases, they would need to self-finance the degree. Although sympathetic to student financial difficulties, it was pointed out that taught postgraduate degrees had become increasingly popular (with figures continuing to rise) and that, due to successive legislative changes, the burden of debt was already present within the undergraduate degree structure. Further issues related to career development and regarding the specifics of teaching archaeology in higher education were also presented to the meeting and included a consideration of 'applied' postgraduate research degrees (see the papers by Collis and Smith).

Archaeology is not alone in having to face a future where the only certainties are that there will be changes and these might be dramatic. It is clear that the role of university education as a means to providing experience and opportunity, based on the development of educated critical awareness is being eroded rapidly by a global system related to 'costs' and 'outcomes'. The experience of the workshop and subsequent process of publication has illustrated that the removal of the wide provision of archaeology in higher education would be a rapid outcome of a homogenised vocation-led teaching strategy. Archaeology in higher education has only in the last 20 years or so been able to take its place alongside the other humanities and social sciences as a mature discipline that can bear, not only internal debate, but also contribute to wider debates in such areas as cultural politics. The current moves to further bureaucratization in higher education has the potential to return archaeology in British universities to the situation prior to the 1960s when it was regarded as a degree only available to those of independent means.

As I write this I am acutely aware that I will need to justify my time in an appropriate category for a 'Transparency Review' required by the funding councils. In this particular case more form filling diverts time from the core activities of teaching and scholarship. My colleagues and I are left wondering how to account for conversations in the corridor with staff or students, and whether the work we all do in the evenings and at weekends ought to be included, especially if it might be concluded that we are doing too much research. As the paper trail lengthens and more space is swallowed up for storing the output, more meetings are arranged to fulfil the form filling tasks, the risk is (and anecdotal evidence from colleagues all around the UK supports this; see also Harrison *et al.* 2001) that 'accountability' will reduce the time for teaching, research and, equally importantly, pastoral care for students (and staff) to the lowest common dominator that reduces the university experience for all members of the academic community to a level of mechanical reproduction.

Clearly these are important issues and the Lampeter Workshop, it is hoped, has ignited discussion and debate that will continue in further meetings to be arranged through a new Steering Committee for Archaeology in Higher Education. The necessary further discussion and debate is also enhanced by the Academic Archaeology listserver at <www.arch.ac.uk>. In taking our lead from the Society of American Archaeology's decision to make available to a wide readership the results of their workshop it is hoped that, unlike the meetings on similar topics that have occurred in the UK over the past 30 years, this publication will stand as a major contribution to further discussion and debate as to the role of archaeology in higher education.

References

Harrison, M., Lockwood, B., Miller, M., Oswald, A., Stewart, M. and Walker, I. 2001. Trial by ordeal. *Guardian Education*, January 30th: 12-3.

Notes on contributors

David Austin is Professor of Archaeology at the University of Wales, Lampeter. His research focus is in medieval communities and their landscapes, theory of medieval archaeology, and medieval castles. His major excavation programmes in the north-east and south-west of England have concentrated on medieval upland landscapes, lowland villages and castles. Contact: Department of Archaeology, University of Wales, Lampeter, SA48 7ED, Wales, austin@lamp.ac.uk.

Graeme Barker taught prehistoric archaeology at Sheffield, and was then Director of the British School at Rome before moving to Leicester as Professor of Archaeology and Head of the School in 1988. In 2000 he was appointed Dean of the University's Graduate School, but remains a research-active Professor in Archaeological Studies. His research interests have focused principally on relations between landscape and people, in Europe and the Mediterranean, in arid zones (Libya, Jordan) and now in tropical environments (Sarawak). Beyond Leicester, he is actively involved in promoting archaeology in higher education, is Chair of the SCUPHA. He was elected a Fellow of the British Academy in 1999. Contact: School of Archaeology & Ancient History, University of Leicester, University Road, Leicester , LE1 7RH, United Kingdom, gba@le.ac.uk.

Beverley Ballin Smith is a graduate of Warwick University and the Institute of Archaeology, University of London. She worked for many years as a freelance archaeologist in the Northern Isles, where she specialised in complex Orcadian multi-period sites. She continued her Iron Age interests in Scandinavia, working in Sweden and southern Norway. Since 1997 she has been employed as a project manager within the Department of Archaeology, University of Glasgow. Here she is responsible for prehistoric sites and recent structures. She also teaches and has been able to marry her archaeological interests with exploring innovations in the teaching of archaeology in higher education. Contact: GUARD, Department of Archaeology, University of Glasgow, Glasgow G12 8QQ, Scotland, bbs@arts.gla.ac.uk.

Mike Bishop has been County Archaeologist of Nottinghamshire since 1974. He has served for two terms on the Council of the Institute of Field Archaeologists and is currently Chairman of IFA's Professional Training Committee. Contact: mike.bishop@nottscc.gov.uk.

John Collis is Professor in the Department of Prehistory and Archaeology in the University of Sheffield. He has for several years been on the Professional Training Committee of the IFA (formerly the Career Development and Training Committee), including a period as Chairperson. He is now Chairperson of the IFA's recently formed Higher Education sub-Committee, and is also a member of the Archaeology Training Committee, representing the Standing Conference of University Professors and Heads of Archaeology. He recently presented the IFA's and ATF's thinking on training and education in an article in *Antiquity*. He acts as convenor for the Round Tables on Training and Education at the annual meetings of the European Association of Archaeologists. Contact: Department of Archaeology and Prehistory, University of Sheffield, Northgate House, West Street, Sheffield, S1 4ET, j.r.collis@sheffield.ac.uk.

Kathryn Fewster took her first degree in archaeology and prehistory at the University of Sheffield. She has Masters degrees in social anthropology (University of Cambridge) and development studies (University of Manchester) and completed

her PhD on ethnoarchaeology at the University of Sheffield. She is Lecturer in Archaeology at the University of Wales, Lampeter and has previously taught at the University of Duham. Contact: Department of Archaeology, University of Wales, Lampeter, SA48 7ED, Wales, k.fewster@lamp.ac.uk.

Annie Grant read archaeology and anthropology at Cambridge, where she also took her PhD. After research posts at Oxford and Reading, she moved to Leicester in 1991, and is now Director of the University's Educational Development and Support Centre. The EDSC offers a range of central support services to students and also includes the University's Teaching and Learning Unit, which provides support to staff wishing to develop their teaching. She has written and presented on various aspects of teaching archaeology in HE, including fieldwork. She maintains her research and teaching interests as an Honorary Reader in the School of Archaeological Studies. Contact: Subject Centre for Classics, History & Archaeology, College House, University of Leicester, Leicester LE1 7RH, ag2@leicester.ac.uk.

Paul Halstead is a senior lecturer in archaeology at the University of Sheffield. He is an experienced archaeozoologist, as well as having research interests in subsistence economics and the prehistory of south-east Europe. Projects in the field have included excavation and ethnoarchaeology in Greece. Contact: Department of Archaeology and Prehistory, University of Sheffield, Northgate House, West Street, Sheffield, S1 4ET, p.halstead@sheffield.ac.uk.

Yannis Hamilakis (PhD, Sheffield University, 1995) is Lecturer of Archaeology at the University of Southampton (where he is also Departmental Teaching and Learning Co-ordinator) and has taught at the University of Wales, Lampeter (1996-2000). His research interests are the archaeology of embodiment and of food consumption, prehistoric Greece, the politics of archaeology and the past, and archaeology and education. Contact: Department of Archaeology, University of Southampton, Southampton, SO17 1BJ, y.hamilakis@soton.ac.uk.

Don Henson (BA [Hons], MPhil, MIFA) is currently Education Officer for the Council for British Archaeology. He previously spent six years as a museum education officer and has been an adult education lecturer since 1979. His archaeological career began at Sheffield University and there he spent several years researching Neolithic and Early Bronze Age flint tools before seeing the light and moving into archaeological education. Contact: Council for British Archaeology, Bowes Morrell House, 111 Walmgate, York YO1 9WA, DonHenson@britarch.ac.uk.

Richard Hingley is a lecturer in Roman archaeology at the University of Durham. He has specialist interests that include Roman imperialism, material culture and historiography. Past employment involved periods working for central government (Historic Scotland), local government and the commercial archaeological sector where he developed and interests in historic landscape characterisation, community involvement, valuation and education. Contact: Department of Archaeology, University of Durham, South Road, Durham DH1 4RJ, Richard.Hingley@durham.ac.uk.

Cornelius Holtorf is currently teaching archaeology in the Department of Archaeology, University of Cambridge. His main professional interests are in the meanings of both archaeology and the distant past in the present, archaeological theory, and the life-histories of prehistoric monuments. He has recently published a substantial e-monograph entitled 'Monumental Past' (http://citd.scar.utoronto.ca/CITDPress/Holtorf/). Contact: Department of Archaeology, University of Cambridge, Downing Street, Cambridge CB2 3DZ, ch264@cam.ac.uk.

Matthew Johnson has taught at Cambridge, Sheffield and Lampeter and is currently a Professor of Archaeology at the University of Durham. His research interests include domestic architecture and landscape history in Britain AD1200-1800, and archaeological theory. Matthew has published three books: *Housing Culture: Traditional Architecture in an English Landscape* (UCL Press and Smithsonian, 1993), *An Archaeology of Capitalism* (Blackwell, 1996) and *Archaeological Theory: An Introduction* (Blackwell, 1999). He is publishing a book on late medieval castles with Routledge in 2002. Contact: Department of Archaeology, University of Durham, South Road, Durham DH1 4RJ, m.h.johnson@durham.ac.uk.

Mark Pluciennik is a lecturer in the Department of Archaeology at the University of Wales, Lampeter. His doctoral thesis (University of Sheffield, UK, 1994) was on the mesolithic-neolithic transition in southern Italy, and he is currently engaged in a survey project in central Sicily in collaboration with Enrico Giannitrapani. Publications and research interests include European politics and archaeology (Archaeology, archaeologists and 'Europe', 1998, *Antiquity* 72: 816-824); narratives and their analysis (Archaeological narratives and other ways of telling, 1999, *Current Anthropology* 40: 653-678), and the politics and ethics of fieldwork and representation (with Quentin Drew: 'Only connect': global and local networks, contexts and fieldwork, 2000, *Ecumene* 7(1): 67-104). Contact: Department of Archaeology, University of Wales, Lampeter, SA48 7ED, Wales, m.pluciennik@lamp.ac.uk.

Paul Rainbird is Lecturer in Archaeology at the University of Wales, Lampeter. He was educated at the University of Sheffield (BA, 1991), and the University of Sydney (PhD, 1996) and has previously taught at the University of Sydney, Charles Sturt University, James Cook University and the Gotland Institute of Higher Education. His research interests include the archaeology and anthropology of island societies, the politics of heritage representation, and the archaeology of colonial encounters in Oceania. Contact: Department of Archaeology, University of Wales, Lampeter, SA48 7ED, Wales, rainbird@lamp.ac.uk.

Michael Reynier studied archaeology at the University of Nottingham, taking his BA in 1990. He worked at the British Museum in the Department of Prehistoric and Romano-British Antiquities while undertaking his PhD, on Early Mesolithic Britain, at the University of Nottingham. He joined the University of Leicester as lecturer in 1998 and has since worked in the Educational Development and Support Centre. In 2000 he became the Archaeology Co-ordinator for the LTSN Subject Centre for History, Classics and Archaeology. He is an honorary lecturer in the School for Archaeological Studies and sits on the CBA Education Committee and the IFA Higher Education Committee. Contact: Subject Centre for Classics, History & Archaeology, College House, University of Leicester, Leicester LE1 7RH, michael.reynier@leicester.ac.uk.

Kathryn Roberts is an Assistant Inspector of Ancient Monuments with Cadw: Welsh Historic Monuments with particular responsibility for the selection of ancient monuments for scheduling. A graduate of Cardiff University archaeology department she subsequently obtained a doctorate from Cambridge University through her research on the archaeological applications of geophysical survey techniques. Prior to joining Cadw she worked as a lecturer in the Archaeology Department of Trinity College, Carmarthen and in the aerial photographic unit of the Royal Commission on Historic Monuments of England. Contact: Cadw: Welsh Historic Monuments, Crown Building, Cathays Park, Cardiff CF10 3NQ, Wales, UK, Kathryn.Roberts@Wales.GSI.Gov.UK.

Anthony Sinclair is Lecturer in Archaeology at the University of Liverpool, where he teaches a range of subject from introductory social anthropology, archaeological theory, ethical issues in archaeology and some Palaeolithic archaeology. His research interests lie in Palaeolithic archaeology, and the archaeology of 18th century polite society in Britain. He currently runs excavations in the UK and in South Africa. Contact: Department of Archaeology, School of Archaeology, Classics, and Oriental Studies, University of Liverpool, P.O. Box 147, Liverpool L69 3BX, A.G.M.Sinclair@liverpool.ac.uk.

George S. Smith holds a Doctorate Degree (honorary) from the University of South Florida (2000), a Master's Degree in Anthropology from the University of Alaska-Fairbanks (1978), and a Bachelor's Degree in Anthropology from the University of South Florida (1971). He is currently the Associate Director at the Southeast Archeological Center in Tallahassee, Florida, USA. He holds a faculty appointment in the Department of Anthropology at Florida State University where he teaches Public Archaeology. He has served on various Society for American Archaeology committees as well as on the Board of Directors, and currently co-chairs the Task Force on Curriculum, which has recently received a National Science Foundation grant to enhance the undergraduate curriculum in archaeology. In addition to numerous journal articles and reports he co-edited the books *Protecting the Past* and *Teaching Archaeology in the 21st Century*. Contact: Southeast Archaeological Center, National Park Service, 2035 East Paul Dirac Dr., Box 7, Johnson Building, Suite 120, Tallahassee, FL 32310, USA, George_S_Smith@nps.gov.

Sophy Thomas-Goodburn read Single Honours Archaeology and Anthropology at the University of Wales, Lampeter graduating in 2000. Following this she took up the elected sabbatical post of Deputy President/Welfare Officer in Lampeter's Students' Union. She intends to continue her studies in higher education.

www.ingramcontent.com/pod-product-compliance
Lightning Source LLC
Chambersburg PA
CBHW061003030426

42334CB00033B/3350